Stony Ridge Branch Library
5805 Fremont Pike
Box 250
Stony Ridge, OH 43643

Alliance Lake
Be Still...

Timothy Jay

© 2018 by Timothy Jay. All rights reserved.

Published by Redemption Press in 2017, PO Box 427, Enumclaw, WA 98022 Toll Free (844) 2REDEEM (273-3336)

Redemption Press is honored to present this title in partnership with the author. The views expressed or implied in this work are those of the author. Redemption Press provides our imprint seal representing design excellence, creative content and high quality production.

No part of this publication may be reproduced, stored in a retrieval system, or transmitted in any way by any means—electronic, mechanical, photocopy, recording, or otherwise—without the prior permission of the copyright holder, except as provided by USA copyright law.

Unless otherwise noted, all Scriptures are taken from the Holy Bible, New International Version®, NIV®. Copyright © 1973, 1978, 1984, 2011 by Biblica, Inc.™ Used by permission of Zondervan. All rights reserved worldwide. www.zondervan.com

ISBN (paperback): 978-1-68314-603-2
ISBN (epub): 978-1-68314-604-9
ISBN (mobi): 978-1-68314-605-6

Library of Congress Catalog Card Number: 2018930319

Dedicated to those who leaned on their
own understanding early in their life's
journey and were tired of the results—crooked paths.

Psalm 3:5-6

Acknowledgements

MY FIRST NOVEL IS all about life's journey. I can definitely affirm that writing is an extreme journey that has been incredibly fulfilling. I would like to thank several people for their love, support, and contributions.

To my wife, Sue, and daughters, Lydia and Leah, thank you for your love and encouragement as I was achieving my chapter goals. Also, it was great motivation to celebrate with a quarter-pound hamburger when I was a quarter complete and then with a half-pound hamburger when I was halfway done with the book. I am so glad I decided to switch incentives so I could keep control of my waistline.

Thank you to my mom and dad, along with my brother and sister, Troy Tressel and Carla Ford, for being four early readers and very important people with whom I started my journey. Also, I cannot thank my other early readers enough: Diane Sturdavant, Kathy Baugher, Tracy Hartlage, and Gary Smith. A very special thanks to Suzie Pinkelman who helped read and edit my "final" manuscript. I also need to thank Barrie Rhodes, Kathy Baugher, Joe Sturdavant, Don Waters (my car guy), and Troy Tressel, who opened up their lives to be interviewed for fictional purposes, of course.

Thank you to those who are on my team at Redemption Press, including Niki Manbeck and Hannah McKenzie, Chris Holtz, and also the outstanding editing polish of Paul Miller. Next for the help in bringing my book cover to reality, I thank Chelsea Schroeder, Colten Schroeder, Christine Schaller, and then Jamie Koluch, who shot the pictures and worked her magic. At the last moments before publishing, I received great advice to rework the wording on the back cover from Linda Frederick, Sarah Beard, and Amanda Weber (who also did my headshots and set up my social media platforms) - Thank you very much!

The Lord led me to some very wonderful professional writers and experts along the way. First, author and director of Taylor University's Department of Professional Writing, Dr. Dennis Hensley; also Rene Gutteridge, Jen L. Stephens Riffle, and writer and filmmaker Rik Swartzwelder. A special thanks to Alan Gutchess for his passion and expertise on the stories of early America. Lastly, I am thankful for the experience I had at the Breathe Christian Writers Conference in Grand Rapids, Michigan.

Please visit my social media for more of the backstory of this book and its characters. Enjoy the novel.

Email: Tim@TimothyJayAuthor.com

Website: www.TimothyJayAuthor.com

Facebook: facebook.com/AuthorTimothyJay

Instagram: instagram/TimothyJayAuthor

To the Reader

WHAT YOU ARE about to read is a work of fiction. The settings take place in many familiar places around the state of Ohio. There are many themes to discover, but one of them has to do with highlighting and reliving some of the nostalgic things that have all but disappeared over the last thirty to forty years.

Scott, one of the characters in the story, is also the narrator, and is thinking back on earlier years. He only inserts himself as this present-day narrator during the first half of the Prologue and all of chapter one.

Please enjoy this "coming of age" story learning about a group of six ordinary and ornery kids individually and together, forever bonded by a tragic event.

The characters and time periods have been notated at the beginning of each chapter for helpful reference.

Contents

Prologue	15
Chapter 1: Innocence Lost	21
Chapter 2: Daddy's Little Star	33
Chapter 3: Coach E.'s Secret to Success	45
Chapter 4: The Happiest Place on Earth?	57
Chapter 5: Reality Check	75
Chapter 6: Giving PKs a Bad Name	83
Chapter 7: Muscle Cars and Making Out	99
Chapter 8: The Plan	111
Chapter 9: The Prank	121

Chapter 10: Epic Christmas Prank	135
Chapter 11: Building on What Lasts	141
Chapter 12: Summer 1987 (Real World: Real Shock)	153
Chapter 13: Anchors Aweigh	169
Chapter 14: Best Friends, but Big Changes!	187
Chapter 15: It's Just a Phase	199
Chapter 16: Two Big Boys	211
Chapter 17: Once a Prankster Always a Prankster	227
Chapter 18: Real Pressure	241
Chapter 19: The Heart of the Matter	251
Chapter 20: I'll Just Crash Here	261
Chapter 21: Life Just Got Bigger	269
Chapter 22: Falling in Love Twice	281
Chapter 23: Let's Go	295
Epilogue	301

Prologue

(Scott's narration—present day and story in the future)

COMFORT CAN TAKE many forms and is very individual and unique. Soaking in a warm bath for you would be a wet coffin for me. Give this country boy a walk around a pond or small lake and my spirit is renewed. I can always find my center, my inner voice, that place that gives me peace. Whether I was walking the banks forty years ago with a pole in my hand, dropping a line and moving around to the next hopeful spot, or taking time to find those perfect stones to skip across the water to get the most out of defying gravity, I never minded going in circles. I always knew where I was heading—right back where I started. When I got back to the start, my time was up and the session was over. I had my inner conversation and worked it all out. My journey was complete, at least for that round.

Anyway, back then it was time to race home and find out if I was going to drink down, in a never-ending gulp, a gallon of the Country Time Lemonade or Tang from the full pitcher that Mom always kept in the refrigerator.

Alliance Lake ~ Be Still

(Excuse me, but please indulge my rant. Whatever happened to Tang? Whatever happened to one of NASA's greatest contributions to all of mankind? Sure, all the GPS technologies, cordless tools, microwave ovens, and even memory foam are useful and very much still with us today, but the decade and a half of gluttonous Tang consumption by the generation that grew up on Schoolhouse Rock and Tuff Skins had to dry out and come down from the orange crystal-powder sugar high we were all on. Did I miss the episode of Miami Vice where Crockett and Tubbs seized control of the Tang crystal production in the U.S., and in one epic slow-motion automatic-gun death-spray battle ended the addiction to Tang for the kids of the 70s and 80s, replaced later by another addiction when we discovered Starbucks' Caramel Macchiato?

But seriously, what happened to us? We were too young in the 70s to understand the climate of the culture, and then again too young in the 90s for anyone to pay attention to us, when the subtle destruction was already happening. The 80s — this was the decade that changed my life and the lives of those I knew. I sadly reflect now about those who didn't realize how it came about, especially after seeing the Huxtables settle all their life's issues in a neat and tidy way until the next Thursday's must-see TV on NBC at 8:00 p.m., when they did it again.)

Okay, after getting that off my chest, let me get back to the story of Alliance Lake. Even though it hosted many of my fondest memories, there were also many secrets and tears that poured into those serene waters over time.

Dotted across our landscape are little oases of magnificent beauty and wonder. It is this very place where animals would go if they could take a vacation. They would come here to my favorite lake—Alliance Lake. It was the type of lake that was just big enough to allow you to get lost in its various coves. It was that picturesque lake that was set way back in the woods. You could drive to it, but you had better slow down the last couple of miles to avoid a trip to the local mechanic for a new exhaust system or front-end alignment. Nature created the initial lake when it was carved out from the rushing water run-off that ran through the limestone rock. Then civil engineers decided to use more of the small valley floor for flood control, and a beautiful idyllic lake—Alliance Lake—was made.

Alliance Lake was a hidden jewel to most. I would guess nine out of ten people are oblivious to treasures like this around them. Why don't more people like to hunt for treasures? Why don't more people like to surround themselves with the strings of the many pearls found everywhere? Even today, kids enjoy a themed birthday party or the excitement of a pirate movie, but I don't think they really like treasure hunting. They might if given the chance, but the "captains" of their ship would not put the time into planning, training, and executing the hunt. So the "shipmates" don't have the patience when plans B, C, and D turn into a "Now what, Honey?" situation.

I guess "captains" in these modern days are not as inspired to find real treasures when virtual ones will do. Also, is mutiny on the Dodge Grand Caravan really worth it when there is only a three-and-a-half hour window before it's time for little Charlie to run down the soccer ball once again? Where is our sense of adventure and purpose to experience "the hunt"? Ah, well, it's exhausting trying to be captain of your own ship or SUV, whichever the case may be.

Well, if anyone did want to explore and uncover the jewel known as Alliance Lake, it would be totally worth it. But then you would have to be patient before you could tell anyone about it because of the isolated dilemma of not having any cell-phone signal or service out there. That's right—even today if you go to my favorite "X marks the spot" place, you had better be fine with talking to yourself, or better yet, talking face-to-face with others. I know it sounds daunting, but believe me, there are other ways to stay connected than with batteries and signal strength bars.

Now, when I think about Alliance Lake, the memory that comes rushing back to me first is one that was told to me (that's right—I did not even personally witness this one). How strange! It was one of those times in life when someone tells you about something that happened, and because you spent so much time in that very location, you can imagine exactly what he or she is describing. You can vividly see it in your mind's eye. The sights, the sounds, and even the smells are as real as if you were there in person.

But please remember, I wasn't there. Maybe that is why what happened will never leave me—not even for a moment. As I have gotten older, life and all its circumstances have finally slowed down, which has allowed those characters known as perspective and wisdom to have their chance.

There wasn't anything special about that late summer day at Alliance Lake. It was the time of day when late afternoon passes into early evening, and when the light and colors are so vivid and perfect that artists and photographers only dream of capturing this fleeting image. Gentle breezes allowed every weeping willow tree to bend down and take their final drink for the day. Swallows were in their flying formations, swooping over the water to get their last meal for their families back at the nest. For the water bugs that escaped this siege, there was always a chance to hear a splash from a fish that ended his day with a lucky strike that did not include any hooks, lines, or sinkers.

Prologue

Several brigades of ducklings followed their marching orders from their mothers-in-charge as they waddled into the water to be given their bedtime baths. Then, as the shadows lengthen, some of nature's four-legged regulars would show up at the water's edge. Families of raccoon, fox, and deer would begin to explore for their evening menu, stopping by for a cool drink before the main entrée; all the while, bullfrogs were warming up their deep voices for their night's performance. It was quite a fantastic showcase of sights and sounds that nature never requires you to applaud, but to simply be still and appreciate.

As the light began to dim, the shadows expanded into dusk. Even the air was heavier, as the wind was lying down for the upcoming nighttime. In the distance, mist began to slowly roll out her blanket and cover the valley. There are those who find this mist a cover of comfort, while others look at it as a restrictive hindrance to movement. As the mist turned to fog and was about to fully settle, all of a sudden, at the far end of the lake in one of those secluded coves, the suspended fog frantically stirred in all directions, and all creatures in the air and on land made a panicked dash to seek a safe haven elsewhere. The only thing that was visible by this time was a set of automobile headlights that were being muted by the fog.

It was too hard to take in any real detail concerning the vehicle at this point, let alone about those who were making the mysterious journey. Did someone take a wrong turn and not realize there was no way to drive back to a populated road? If it were kids looking to party, there would surely be a bonfire that would begin to flame. However, as the minutes went by, the scene only grew darker and darker. Who was out there? What purpose could anyone have at this lake during nightfall?

The next thing that could be heard was screams and gasps of breath from many different people. It was easy to let your imagination run wild with what could be happening down in that cove as the screams and gasps turned to silence. About the time when you thought the worst, the clouds parted briefly to let the moonlight reveal something more. Again, the silence was broken with a ferocious amount of splashing, water bubbling, and churning everywhere. Arms and legs were flailing about in never-ending attempts to find refuge on something stable. Just as the light from the silvery moon began to shine the brightest, the clouds closed in to act like an eighteenth-century candle snuffer.

    The light disappeared, but the sounds of gasping for air would not stop. The sounds could be heard over and over until the silence returned and nature's cadence resumed. Someone had to be responsible for what just happened, but who? The vehicle's lights could be seen again, but now only the two red rear lights were visible, leaving like a snake slithering off with his beady eyes fixed.

Chapter 1:

INNOCENCE LOST

(Scott's narration—present day)

IT WAS 1975, AND America had lost her innocence; but I was still in the middle of mine. I was six years old. The worst thing I did was fight with my brothers. Generally, these fights consisted of everything from hiding G.I. Joe army men to stealing the prize out of the Honeycomb cereal box. But there was one fight with my brothers that forever changed me and made me understand my place in the family. It was a battle we had many times before, but this particular time was a Sunday morning when we were once again piling into the family wood-sided station wagon to go to church. There we were—the three of us—me and my brothers, the twins, Ryan and Shon. It was the battle for the rear-facing third seat in the back. The prized seat of honor in that giant boat of a car that popped up from below at most could only fit two small bodies. Once again, the fight was underway. We only had limited time to maneuver our strategic headlocks and noogies before Dad got in the car to back it out of the garage. We had better have our armistice terms worked out and accepted by then, or Dad would pull off his belt and settle the dispute for us. We all knew we had to work fast with precision or it would be bad—very bad.

For some reason, my brothers did not come at me with force this time, and that may be why I gave up without retaliation and headed for the middle seat to be by myself. What they did to me that day was worse than giving me a black eye; they used words to cut through me to the heart. It was a missile that hit its target.

They told me that I was adopted, which I already knew, but they said it in such a mean way. They told me that I was lucky to even be a part of their family and not rotting in some deep dark dungeon. I ultimately knew that they were right and it was true. Well, at least everything except the rotting in some deep dark dungeon part; I was hoping that wasn't true. Kids can be cruel, and after all, this was for supremacy of the rear-facing seat in the woody station wagon, and they pulled out all the stops.

So there I was in the middle, no one paying attention to me. Mom and Dad were in the front seat facing forward, driving to our destination, and my brothers were laughing and looking out the back window at where we had been. And where we had been, as a family, was really confusing, but let me try and sort it out quickly.

My brothers and I were the same age. As I said, they're twins. Beginning when I was quite young, Mom explained our family to others in the following way: I was the gift of theirs that required a "God-awful" amount of paperwork, while the twins were a surprise "gift from God."

After hearing it over and over, I didn't see the humor that my mom was trying to convey. She and Dad were struggling to start a family; I get that. She went to many doctors and had many procedures, but still with no luck. By 1968, their hope turned to despair when a last-ditch experimental effort did not produce a pregnancy, so they agreed to start the adoption process. When they received word late that same year that a baby boy,

Chapter 1: Innocence Lost

me—Scott— would be available to them by early in the new year, they were happy. I figured it was only a few nights after receiving this news that they in fact became pregnant. Maybe the pressure was finally off them, and well, *surprise*! Yes, the twins were born later that same year in 1969, and the Huff family totaled five.

As I realized much later in life, the one thing I really wanted was unconditional love and acceptance. I wished my adopted family would have treated me like that of an Indian-captive English boy during the French and Indian War. Being a student of American history, I've always been drawn to the many true accounts of Indian tribes taking young boys captive after killing their families during frontier raids. The boys then became the sole replacement for a child they had lost due to disease or warfare. There was a very common adoption ceremony that was performed: a young captive was taken into a stream up to his waist, and then the young squaws would begin to wash him down.

The purpose of this ritual was to show that every drop of white blood had been washed out of him, and he was officially a member of the Indian family, with all rights, privileges, and responsibilities as the person he replaced. From that day forward, they were literally treated as though they had been born into the tribe; nothing short of a prisoner swap would get them out of this culture, but even then, there was often great reluctance from the captive to return to "civilization."

I learned early on that the pecking order was the twins, Ryan and Shon, first, followed by me. And after that last car-seat battle, I resigned myself to the fact that they had indeed won the war, and my place in the family was to be there, but not too much there. I could come along, but my best role was to be the family historian. I was not to be a reporter, mind you, for reporters asked questions and were curious. I knew my place. I was a historian, only there to observe what had already taken place; and believe me, there was a lot more history to share. Ironically, it started later that very same morning in church.

Arriving at church always felt a little like the first day of school, with the anticipation of whether or not it would be just like it was when we were there last, with all the same familiar kids. I would soon find out, but first we had to stop off at the coatrack area to watch Mom and Dad pull themselves together and sneak a peek to see if "Dad's seats" were still available in the back row. If we did not get those seats, Dad would grumble the rest of the day that people should just know that those seats were for him and his family. Mom and Dad expected us to sit together as a family every time we were there.

I can remember like it was yesterday following my parents into the sanctuary behind Mrs. Jennings. Mrs. Jennings was a fancy lady who always tried to lead the way when it came to fashion trends, even though she was old—much older than my mom. She was also very plump, and let me tell you, fashion styles of the mid-70s did not flatter anyone, let alone someone who looked like the housekeeper Alice from *The Brady Bunch*, but was the size of Aunt Bee from *The Andy Griffith Show*.

You would hear Mrs. Jennings before you would see her. This was not because she talked loudly or talked a lot, but because you would hear the sound of an overly tight polyester skirt rubbing against her nylon pantyhose at the legs. I was always concerned that with all those different synthetic garments and the friction taking place as she walked, we were looking at a very real public-safety fire-hazard threat. I have seen Boy Scouts start fires with much less.

I'm sorry, but I told you my role was a historian, and seeing Mrs. Jennings every Sunday only proved to me that the fashion police had clocked out and had been at the donut shop for the past decade. Who could possibly think that a loose-fitting, long macramé vest over a tight long-sleeved cowl-neck collar shirt with a multi-shade-of-throw-up brown plaid skirt was a good idea? Anyone? I didn't think so.

Chapter 1: Innocence Lost

I guess I could also mention her hairdo while I'm at it. It was not just Mrs. Jennings, but most ladies at that church had hairdos that were huge. I thought hair for a woman was supposed to adorn them and complement them. Well to me as a child, the older ladies at my church all looked like they were trying to create shade for those sitting around them. Their hair was either very high, very wide, or both. And to achieve these sculpted masterpieces of girth, they spent all day at the "beauty" salon undergoing various follicle torture treatments and devices.

The results were hairdos in the styles of the Beehive, the Flip, and the Bouffant, or combinations thereof. Picture Dolly Parton in the mid-70s from the hair up. Believe me—the hair was the only comparison to Dolly. They sure didn't look or sing like Miss Dolly (sigh).

Anyway, even in a stiff breeze, the individual hairs could only manage to move in unison due to the amount of aerosol-released hairspray, or better yet, glue on their head. Now I really know who created the ozone problem and ushered in the greenhouse gas effect that we have been dealing with. It was not big industrial factories spewing carbon monoxide smog, but those vain women of the 60s and 70s!

Once we got our seat, the thing I would notice most was the smell. Maybe church seats are called pews because you are sitting close to other people and you can smell everything about them. For instance, there was the Conrad family. They lived on a farm, and I knew exactly who fed the animals that very morning. I don't think they realized that wiping their shoes off in the grass a few times does not qualify for clean Sunday shoes.

Then there was the Stevens family. They had a never-ending row of kids. It seemed like every other week they had another kid in tow. Besides the number of bodies in that family, I think they must have been one of the final holdouts to use cloth diapers over disposable. Their infants and toddlers would never be changed until they all had to be changed. I'm certain the older kids just let them sit in yesterday's supper until it was time to take them to the nursery, after we had sung exactly five songs. Believe me, I perfected singing and breathing out of my mouth at the same time.

Besides the smells of the very young, I never liked the smell of the elderly. There was something different about it. My first thought was it must be a touch of death beginning to take hold of them, but when Mr. Moorehead, the organ player, continued to show up each and every Sunday for years, I chalked up his smell to him not getting his Saturday night bath like I had to have. Also, maybe his "smell test" was not as strict as my mom's.

Then there were old ladies like Mrs. Frazer who poured on the perfume to mask their "old person" smell. I really think the concoction of old person smell and "Eau de Avon Lady" began the chemical reaction of the embalming process for undertakers. In the meantime, though, it was very toxic for the rest of us.

All the usual kids were sitting with their parents singing the last of what seemed to be the twenty-seventh stanza of "Amazing Grace," the fifth song, when I heard those sweet words from the song leader: "The children are dismissed to go to children's church." Like a mad dash for freedom, the children raced out, leaving the parents to pick up the crayons and other debris left in our wake.

We were heading up to the best part of church. All the kids knew the routine, and Mr. Ross made it fun—very fun. There were three round tables in our room for the six-year-olds to gather around. Only six little bodies could sit at each table, and as if an unspoken rule was already known by those three little ladies and three ornery gentlemen, the six most popular kids who sat together every class were Ryan, Shon, Joel, Beth, Mandy, and Colleen.

Chapter 1: Innocence Lost

I would consider myself friends with those six popular kids, but I was never popular. I guess I was too quiet to be popular, so I took my place right next to their table and listened to every word they said and every laugh they uttered. In fact, everyone else from the other tables was focused on their table, too. It just felt more interesting, more relevant, and more fun. Occasionally, they would get me involved with their table, but I still had to remember that I belonged at the other table.

I don't know what it was about this certain Sunday at children's church that I remember it so well, but Mr. Ross came in after we had settled into our usual seats at our usual tables and started class off by asking us if we were happy today. The kids at the popular table screamed and carried on like they were beyond happy, maybe even a little more wild and crazy because they were glad to be away from their parents for an hour. So Mr. Ross, with a very serious tone started the lesson by saying, "If you're happy and you know it, clap your hands."

Immediately, everyone knew that his tone was a trick, but it worked. We clapped our hands, but the kids at the popular table showed the most animation. We clapped when we were supposed to, but their entire bodies were noisemakers. As we went through the song and got to the final line, "If you're happy and you know it, then your face will surely show it. If you're happy and you know it, clap your hands." *Clap, clap.*

Then the next verse came up and Mr. Ross looked at Shon and sang, "If you're happy and you know it," and then paused so Shon could say something. Shon thought for a second and then blurted out, "Stomp your feet!" At the beginning of the next verse, Mr. Ross looked at Ryan, who immediately chimed in with "Spin in a circle!" Next, he looked at Colleen, who said, "Fly like a bird!" By this time, those at the popular table made it their right to continue the pattern. Mandy went next and screamed, "Jump real high!" Joel was next, and he wanted us to "Shake someone's hand!" To finish the song, Mr. Ross gently instructed Beth to "Say amen" to signal the end.

After we sang the rest of the songs, it was time to start the lesson. Mr. Ross pulled out a flannel board, the church's 1970s version of a video. Everyone fought to help the teacher reenact the Bible story and lesson. The lesson that is so vivid in my head was the lesson on Moses and the burning bush. As Mr. Ross opened the flannel board, the kids from the popular table lunged at him and began to fight over the flannel pieces.

When the scrum was over, Ryan, Mandy, and Joel had all the pieces between them. They began to help show Moses heading cautiously toward a flaming bush that wasn't being consumed. Then God spoke to him, telling Moses to remove his sandals because he was standing on holy ground. The kids switched the standing Moses to the kneeling Moses, but without his sandals, as Mr. Ross continued to tell the story. Something about the flannel-board stories usually made us settle down.

Just as I now remember that image of the burning bush and those popular kids around the Sunday school table, it wasn't hard for me to remember each of them twelve years later during a late summer party for the graduating seniors. It was a way for everyone to say goodbye before some went off to college, and before we all headed out for the next phase of our lives. We met up at the usual teen party spot, Alliance Lake. A fire was always burning, providing the only peer-approved light and heat for miles.

I can't forget to describe the music that we had playing. Someone would bring his latest boom box with an endless supply of cassette tapes and D-cell batteries. For an end-of-the-summer party such as this, you bet there was plenty of drinking, smoking, and experimenting of all kinds. Some might wonder how we could get cigarettes and alcohol. Well, it was the mid-80s,

Chapter 1: Innocence Lost

and cigarettes came out of a vending machine at every sit-down restaurant. And besides, the Marlboro man was the role model of the "Kool." As far as alcohol, let's just say that storekeepers weren't worried about looking at IDs too closely. If the money was green and you picked up the lightweight stuff, then who could get hurt, right?

There was a lot more scary stuff being introduced to our young teenage minds about sex than about alcohol and smoking combined. We were at the age when hormones and morals are at constant war with each other. Images were not stagnant on the page any longer or being made up in our heads; we could now scream in unison, "I want my MTV!" If seeing a video from Van Halen, Madonna, or Bon Jovi couldn't get you thinking about the opposite sex in a way that would change your body temperature, then there was no hope for you.

Yes, it did look like hormones would win the struggle everywhere, but then an A-bomb was dropped into our laps that made many of us think twice. The A-bomb was AIDS. Everyone at that time was trying to get answers and hoped to find a way to contain it as one of those annoying STDs to put up with. And with all that to process, I thought it best to say, "Pass me another beer," while I hoped that she would let me get on base—any base!

It was well after eleven o'clock and the music was fading. People were either ready to mellow out, or we ran out of batteries. Many of the cars had started to head back to town. As I walked up to the fire to get warm, I saw those same six kids from a decade ago around this fire that was quickly being consumed. Ryan had no problem yelling at me to get more wood. As I quietly bowed out of the group to find more wood, I noticed each of their faces were in a trance, staring at the hypnotic glow of the embers. Just like those flames intertwining, those kids had no idea how critical and intertwined their lives would be with each other.

My eyes, however, were fixed on Mandy as I backed away. What was she thinking? Well, if she was like me, she was replaying the last decade in her head. And to be honest, each of us have not always been ready to sing the "Happy and You Know It" song.

Part One:

THE EARLY YEARS

Chapter 2:

DADDY'S LITTLE STAR

(Mandy—early years: 1978-1982)

THE FINAL WHISTLE BLEW on that cold and rainy Saturday in October 1978. The soccer game was finally over. Mandy McConnell once again scored all the goals, eight this time. Mr. and Mrs. McConnell were soaked to the bone. Mr. McConnell said to his wife, "I'll take Grant and go and warm up the car. You get Mandy." Mr. McConnell folded up the chairs and blankets and headed to the parking lot. Grant was a muddy mess, as he had been playing with the other preschoolers at the park's playground during the soccer game. As father and son hustled to the car, a man from the opposite side of the field headed toward them. The rain was still pelting Mr. McConnell's face and running down his glasses, when he realized that he was probably in for a conversation that he wasn't in the mood for.

"Excuse me," said the stranger. "I'm Ken Colson, the coach for the Akron Arsenal. Do you know about our team?"

Mr. McConnell took off his wet and fogged-up glasses, pulled up his rain poncho, gave his glasses a few swipes from a dry spot on his shirt, and pushed his specs back on. He replied, "Yeah, I sure have heard of you guys. You're the best girls' soccer team in our area."

"Well, you're very kind to say that," Mr. Colson replied. "We've had a lot of great girls play with us over the years who then went on to play for championship high school and college programs." Mr. McConnell was no longer bothered in the slightest by the rain running down his face. He hung on every word that Mr. Colson said. By this time, Mandy and her mom were there.

Mr. McConnell introduced Mr. Colson to his wife and daughter. "Nice game, young lady," Mr. Colson said to Mandy. "I was just telling your dad that we have room for a player like you on our team. You're definitely ready to play with us."

Mr. McConnell then paused and said to Mr. Colson, "I thought the girls on your team were all twelve or thirteen years old. Mandy's only ten."

Mr. Colson replied, "Well, officially, you are correct, but if I see someone younger who can play at our level, then we can make an exception and permit her to be a part of our team and league."

Mr. and Mrs. McConnell's jaws dropped, as they could not believe what they were hearing, even as they were becoming more and more waterlogged. Mr. Colson said, "I know this is sudden and something for you to talk about as a family, and . . . " Before he could finish his thought, Mandy, with her wide hazel eyes and soggy limp ponytail, looked at her parents for their approval as smiles overtook them.

They both shouted, "Oh, yes!"

Practice twice a week turned into practice or a game every weeknight, and a road trip for a tournament most every weekend. Mr. and Mrs. McConnell gave up trying to participate in any school activities or neighborhood socializing. They purposely made a point of saying no to anything and anyone not related

Chapter 2: Daddy's Little Star

to Mandy's soccer. The McConnell family was all in on soccer, and Mandy was their little star.

Every time Easter and Christmas would come along, Mrs. McConnell would lament and say to her husband, "We need to take the kids to church." His response was always the same. "Dear, we haven't been to church in months. I don't feel comfortable showing up there anymore."

Mrs. McConnell would reply, "It was something we enjoyed doing as a family. We had a lot of great friends there."

To that he always said, "Yes, but now we enjoy doing Mandy's soccer weekends and having those friends. Anyway, our kids already know about Jesus and things that the church teaches."

Mandy played three years with the Akron Arsenal, and she grew into a star with that team like no other. She was the leading scorer in the region, and the team remained undefeated since she had started with them.

The daily practice routine involved Mrs. McConnell dropping Mandy off at the park and Mr. McConnell picking her up on his way home from work. One day as Mr. McConnell pulled into the park, he noticed Mr. Colson and Mandy speaking to someone else. He quickly parked the car and headed toward the conversation.

"Daddy!" screamed Mandy. "You won't believe it!"

"I won't believe what?" he answered.

Mr. Colson soon spoke up and said, "Mr. McConnell, this is Mr. Anthony." They quickly shook hands. Then he continued, "Mr. Anthony is a scout for the state of Ohio's new junior team."

Surprised, Mr. McConnell looked at his little girl; immediately grins broke out on both their faces. He quickly refocused to hear Mr. Anthony say that he wanted Mandy to be part of the new state team that would fly to other states once a month for huge tournaments, and of course, they would practice every weekend in Columbus.

Blown away, Mr. McConnell said that he couldn't believe that this whole thing with Mandy could have gotten any better, but it just did. He again shook hands with the two men, though this time for much longer; then he turned to Mandy and gave her a big hug. "Come on. Let's go home and tell your mother the great news."

All of Mandy's friends at school and her Arsenal teammates were thrilled to hear about Mandy's new opportunity. It was a two-hour ride down to Columbus to drop Mandy off every Friday for her soccer life. She would stay with a local family there and participate in the weekend workouts and training. On Sunday, Mandy would be picked up at 4:00 p.m. for the two-hour ride back to her school and family life. There were only two months of weekends for the coach to decide who his starters would be.

It just so happened that the Ohio girls' junior coach was renowned player Cliff Epolaski from the area, who had played for the University of Akron and as a professional for a handful of years. He had decided to put his playing days behind him and start working on his advanced degree at The Ohio State University.

His new passion was the emerging field of exercise science. When the opportunity came up to be the girls' junior team head coach, it was the perfect timing to give back to a sport that gave him so much, plus it was a nice supplemental income.

The kids called him Coach E. He liked that, because he never liked his real name. Coach E. called the girls over to the bench as the final Sunday practice was over. He also motioned for the gathering parents to come closer. Coach E. said, "Okay, ladies, everyone has worked extremely hard and our improvement has been remarkable."

He then looked at the parents and said, "Parents, you should be very proud of your daughters. They have reached levels in their play and determination that I didn't think they would achieve for a very long time."

He turned back to the girls and said, "I'm going to take this coming week to finalize the starting roster. I want everyone to enjoy their week. On Friday, we will meet at the Columbus airport at 7:00 p.m. to fly to Dallas for the Texas Soccer Tournament. There will be eight states represented. This is where we get to show our stuff. Are you ready?"

The girls answered, "Yes!"

Coach E. yelled, "I can't hear you!"

Then the girls let out the kind of ear-splitting scream that only excited girl teenagers can do: "YEEESSS!"

After several restless nights of sleep, Mandy was ready for her first trip away from her family. At the airport, she hugged her mom and dad, and she even hugged Grant, who quickly ran out of her hold. The Ohio team was up, up, and away!

The Texas tournament didn't go so well for the Ohio team, and unfortunately, it did not start off very well for Mandy, either. She was not chosen to start. It was a double-elimination tournament. The winners would stay in the winner's bracket, and the losers would have to play until that second loss. Mandy stayed on the sidelines trying to cheer her team on, but after two quick goals by Virginia, she was tormented. She had never been on the sidelines except for when the coach had taken her out of the game when they were ahead by a lot. She did not know what to do with herself. She felt herself getting more and more frustrated, to the point where she had to get a towel and bury her head and let the tears flow. As she was in the middle of this personal struggle, she sensed a voice telling her not to be so selfish.

Mandy hesitated for a second, very confused under her towel, but then she peeked at the field to see the Virginia team score another goal. She closed the towel and began to sulk some more.

Mandy's behavior did not go unnoticed by Coach E., although he did not let on. Virginia ended up winning 5-1, and Ohio moved into the loser's bracket.

There they regrouped and won impressively against Nevada and Oregon. The difference this time was that Coach E. let all the girls play, and Mandy got in to score two goals in each of the contests. Her mood was definitely better, and Team Ohio moved on to the last game of the afternoon, which was against Louisiana.

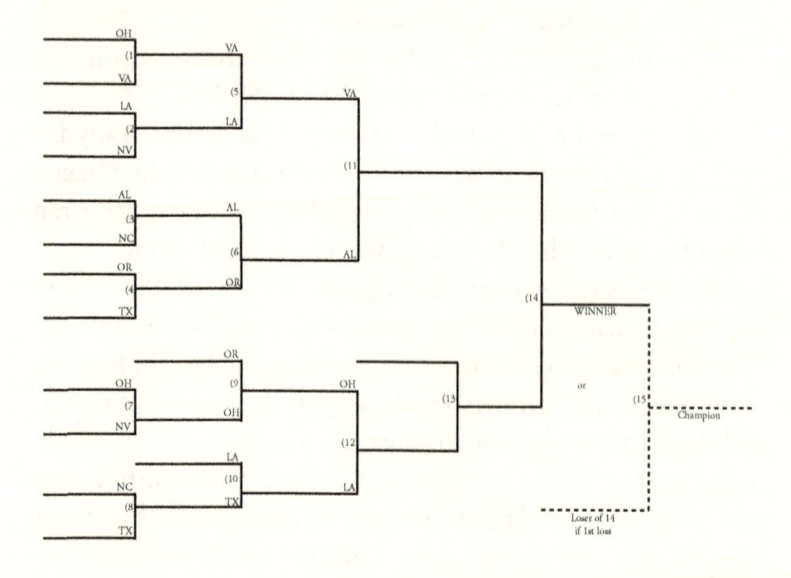

Each team had one loss, but the winner could look forward to making the final four and playing Sunday. The whistle blew and the game started with Mandy in the game. The ball stayed in the middle of the field. Each team made a good defensive play before it could get too close to the goal. The game was back and forth, with no one wanting to make a mistake. Coach E. knew the half was almost over, so he called for the girls to run the play that they had practiced over and over again in Columbus. He signaled it by putting his fist in the air.

Chapter 2: Daddy's Little Star

The play was to have Steph throw the ball in to Mandy, who was to immediately kick it to the opposite side of the field. Lori would then work it up the sideline before kicking the ball to the middle of the field, where Mandy would be sprinting hard toward the goal.

As Mandy was getting in place for the pass, she noticed that her opponents were not guarding her closely. She took the pass, but instead of following the coach's plan, she began to take the ball down the field herself. Coach E. wasn't happy about Mandy not giving the plan a try, but he was more upset that she wasn't passing the ball. He yelled, "Pass it ahead!" Mandy, however, focused on what she did best, and that was dribbling the ball and scoring.

She got to midfield and saw a crease in Louisiana's defense. As Mandy made a break for it, out of nowhere one of the opposing players stripped the ball from her. Quick as a flash, the ball was being passed back toward Ohio's goal and in no time struck the back of the net right before the official blew the whistle signaling halftime. The score was 1-0, with Louisiana ahead.

The other girls on the Ohio team looked at Mandy with wrinkled faces in disbelief. Coach E. was unusually upset, but the other coaches soon calmed him down. Mandy noticed the other girls upset with her, but she brushed it off and walked toward the bench.

Coach E. calmly said, "Well, that didn't go as planned. Take a few minutes to catch your breath, and then we'll talk about the second half." He walked away to gather his thoughts and develop the second-half lineup. He returned as the official blew the whistle to have the players step onto the field. He named the girls who would start the second half, and Mandy's name was not called. He talked to the girls quickly and with purpose. Mandy stepped out of the circle before Coach E. was finished with his instructions. She was halfway to the bench when the other girls all let out a cheer to start the second half. Coach E.

did not miss what just happened with Mandy, and he felt more confident than ever that she needed to be taught a lesson—a life lesson.

Everything was much different the second half. The ball was down at Louisiana's end the whole time. The Ohio girls just kept passing the ball back and forth until they had a scoring opportunity. They ended up scoring three times, and Louisiana never got any more than the one goal from the first half. The girls rushed off the field hugging each other and falling down. Even the girls from the sidelines, including Mandy, met the girls on the field to enjoy the winning fun.

Coach E. looked at his coaches and said, "Now that's how you play together and win."

Walking back to the rental van, they made a stop at the tournament headquarters to see who they would be playing in the morning. To everyone's surprise, Virginia had lost their final game of the afternoon and would play Ohio again! The girls were very excited about the rematch, but were too tired to show it.

The coaches took the girls back to the hotel, where they enjoyed a big pizza party. They relaxed and called home to give their nervously awaiting parents the play-by-play details from the day's matches. By this time, Mandy had cooled down, and because the phone was in the common hospitality room, she didn't mention anything to her parents about the frustration from some of the earlier games. She was just glad to hear their voices and their enthusiasm about getting to the final four.

After a couple hours, Coach E. said, "Everybody back to your rooms. Decide if you want showers now, in the morning, or both. Believe me—some of you need it."

The girls laughed, and Crystal yelled back, "So do you, Coach E." She held her nose, and the laughter continued as the girls headed to their assigned rooms.

Chapter 2: Daddy's Little Star

The next morning, the girls were all in good moods and ready for the rematch. They got to the soccer complex and started to warm up. Coach E. watched very intently as the girls warmed up. He wanted to see who was focused. As the start time was getting close, Coach E. walked around to each girl and talked to them about whether they were starting this game or not. Coach E. approached Mandy and said, "Mandy, you are not ready to start this game. Your focus is all over the place." Mandy knew he was right, but she just stared at the ground until he left.

The game started, but this time Ohio did not allow Virginia to be the only aggressive team. When Virginia had the ball, Ohio rushed to defend. They did not let Virginia move the ball as easily as last time. It was only about five minutes into the contest when Ohio got an easy score. The Virginia goalkeeper misplayed a ball that was kicked toward the goal. She thought her player would get to it, but realized at the last second that she wouldn't. The goalkeeper sprinted toward the ball, but Steph was already at full speed and was able to make a quick shifty move and kick it in for a score. The Ohio side went crazy. Coach E. took a quick glance at Mandy and saw that she was at the far end of the bench, not even excited about the first goal of the game. That concerned him greatly.

After the first easy goal by Ohio, Virginia could do no wrong. They quickly tied it up, and then scored twice more before the end of the half. Minutes before halftime, Mandy again became frustrated and yelled into a towel. Amid all the chaos in her head, she heard a calming voice asking, "Is this really who you want to be?"

The question startled her to the point that she froze, and instantly the memories of when she was younger and going to Sunday school and VBS came flooding into her mind. Right then and there, she was aware of how selfish she was being. Her tears of frustration and selfishness instantly turned into tears of sorrow. She threw the towel down and ran quickly toward Coach E. Out of the corner of his eye, he saw Mandy running directly toward him, but something was different. She stopped right under his 6'5" gaze and said, "Coach, I'm sorry for my selfish behavior. I don't deserve to be on this team."

Coach E. bent over, put his lanky arms around her for a quick hug, and said, "I agree that your old self doesn't belong as part of this team, but I love your new self."

Mandy looked up into his eyes and said, "My new self is ready to be part of this team, big time!" And with that, the whistle blew for halftime. Mandy sprinted out to the field to meet the girls, encouraging them to be positive and to get settled for some water and rest.

Coach E. looked at the other coaches, and they quickly exchanged an unspoken moment of pleasure about their team. Even with this great breakthrough from Mandy, Coach E. wanted to see her on the sidelines in the second half. She did not disappoint him. She ran up and down that sideline, yelling out her best cheers and advice. Even on timeouts, she was the first to get the water bottles and towels for the players. However, when the game was over, Virginia had won again, this time 5-2. Ohio was out of the tournament.

The girls watched the other games, but mostly had fun together goofing around, getting candy at the concession stand, and being teenagers. They also made every effort to look around for cute "cowboys" to be pen pals with.

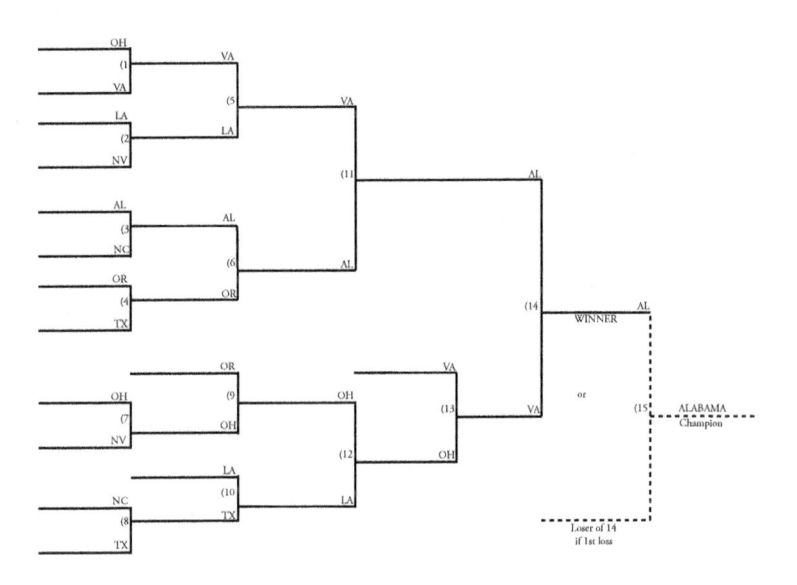

OH							
(1)	VA						
VA	(5)	VA					
LA	LA						
(2)							
NV		(11)		AL			
AL	AL						
(3)	(6)	AL					
NC							
OR	OR		(14)	WINNER	AL		
(4)						(15)	ALABAMA Champion
TX				or			
	OR	VA					
OH	(9)	OH	(13)	VA			
(7)	OH						
NV		(12)	OH				
	LA						
NC	(10)	LA					
(8)	TX				Loser of 14 if 1st loss		
TX							

Chapter 3:
COACH E.'S SECRET TO SUCCESS

(Mandy—early years, 1982 continued)

ONCE MANDY WAS HOME, she felt like a new girl. She was full of energy once again, and she couldn't wait until the school week was over and she could get down to Columbus and practice with the team. During the week, Coach E. knew exactly what his team needed, and they weren't going to be happy; but it was essential if they wanted to become a much better team.

On Friday, the girls were being dropped off at the indoor Ohio State athletic complex. The coach walked over to the girls and asked, "Are you all warmed up and ready?"

Julie asked, "Ready for what?"

Coach said, "Ready to get better!"

All the girls answered in the positive, but what they were really saying is "Duh, of course!"

"Good. I'm glad to hear that," he said as he smirked.

Then he heard someone ask, "Where are the soccer balls, Coach?" The rest of the girls were soon echoing the same question.

Coach E. smirked again and said, "This weekend will be a little different." The girls looked at each other with wide eyes. "This weekend will be all about running. Line up!" The girls didn't ask questions. They got to the line and the running began: long distances, short distances, and everything in between. Even after Friday was over and they were worn out, they had to continue running on Saturday morning. After lunch, Coach E. gathered the girls up and sat down with them to tell them how proud he was of this weekend's practice. Deep down they knew they were going to be better for it, but right now they were exhausted.

Then Coach E. said, "Before we start back into practice, I was wondering if anyone would be disappointed if we took a break right now to go to the mall for food and a movie." As the words were coming out of Coach E.'s mouth, the girls could not believe what they were hearing. Again, they were teenage girls who would rather be at the mall shopping, or whatever they do at the mall around the clock if they could. And again, they let out such a high-pitch scream that Coach E. thought security guards would soon be there.

Coach said, "What are you waiting for? Your rides are waiting outside to take you home and get you cleaned up."

The girls started to rush off, but Mandy stopped them and whispered something to them. All of a sudden, fifteen girls were headed toward Coach E. for a quick hug. He said to the other coaches nearby, "Wow! That worked better than an *After School Special.*"

Everyone enjoyed the afternoon full of window shopping and boy watching, or in some cases, boy chasing. Everyone was told to meet at Chi-Chi's Mexican Restaurant by the movie theater at 6:00 p.m. There they would eat and decide what movie to go see. As they waited for their food orders to come out, everyone munched on chips and salsa. Coach E. let the girls decide

Chapter 3: Coach E.'s Secret to Success

between watching either *E.T.* or *Tootsie*. After the movie, it was time to go home for the night. The girls chattered in their cars all the way to their hosts' homes.

Everyone showed up for Sunday's practice with a new sparkle in their eyes. The sparkle remained until Coach E. said, "Time to run. Follow me!" Coach took off and jogged through the doors of the indoor complex and right out onto the Ohio State campus. They ran past the Horseshoe, onto Woody Hayes Drive, and then over the Olentangy River to the recreation center for a quick break.

During the break, one of the coaches said, "Girls, let's hear it for Coach E. and the best weekend practice ever!"

Again, the girls did not hold back, but they screamed like crazy. When their voices began to quiet down, Coach spoke up and said, "Thank you, but do you know what I think is pretty cool?"

"What? What? What?" the girls asked like a steel ball bouncing in a pinball game.

"This is a soccer team, and we haven't used a ball this whole weekend," Coach answered. "All we did was run. Do you know what they call a practice when you run all the time?"

Again came a chorus of "What? What? What?"

Coach E. got his famous smirk on his face and said, "Duh, cross-country!"

The girls and the coaches groaned and rushed at him and tackled him on the grass right in front of the union student center. He was on the very bottom of the mass of all the arms and legs, and everyone was laughing. Finally seeing a little light, Coach E., still on the ground, yelled out, "Last one back to the soccer complex is a rotten egg!" All the girls took off running.

The other two coaches just looked at Coach E. and said, "Really? Cross-country? You are a nut."

He threw up his hands and asked, "What? What?"

The other coaches left Coach E. on the ground, but as they jogged off together they heard him ask, "Well, isn't it?"

They looked back and said, "We know who the rotten egg will be." Then they kicked in the jets and started to leave Coach E. far behind. Eventually Coach E. made up some ground, but he was last and got razzed some more by everyone.

He gathered the girls and told them that he was extremely proud of all of them this weekend. Everyone had worked extremely hard. He began to pass out a paper that said, "Running Schedule." He then spoke up and said, "Ladies, we need to keep our running going, both sprinting and endurance. That is the way we will begin to win our tournaments. I want you to commit to two running workouts Monday-Wednesday. You can choose when, but I want your Thursday to be a rest day. Then when we get together we can really work on our ball skills and plays. Our weekends will have a lot of running, also. Do I have your word on this? If you don't want to commit, then you can tell me privately. You can just stay home next weekend and go about other things in life you want to do." They all nodded their heads in agreement. It was the end of practice, so Coach E. went over to all the parents to tell them about this new commitment and to get their support.

The next two weekends went great. Coach E. could tell that the girls were sticking with their commitment. He saw their speed improve, and their endurance was off the charts. He began to implement special plays for each girl, which made them feel special. They also practiced and practiced many different plays until everyone learned to execute them flawlessly.

At the end of the final practice before the next big tournament, Coach E. sat the girls down and said, "I'm very proud of your commitment and your trust with each other. Next weekend is the Midwest Soccer Tournament. Again, there will be eight

Chapter 3: Coach E.'s Secret to Success

teams, all from the cornfield states." The girls laughed. He continued, "I'm passing out another paper to give to your parents about the game in Indianapolis. This is the game that your parents must get you to, so should anyone come to Columbus after school on Friday?"

"No," all the girls answered.

"Great," Coach said. Then he added, "Don't forget to run at home this week."

Without being too thrilled, they answered, "Yes, Coach." He could almost feel their eyes rolling as they answered, but he knew his team, and he loved everything about them.

The weekend arrived, and the coaches checked in to the Indianapolis tournament and were handed the brackets.

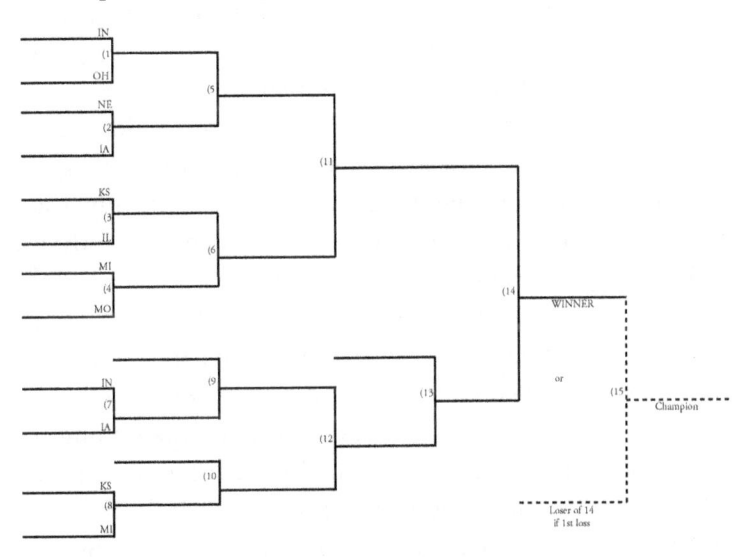

All the girls were gathered and ready to go. Ohio had an incredible cheering section. They played the home team, Indiana, right away. As the girls were finishing their warm-ups, Coach E. went around to each girl and told them whether or not they were going to start. As he approached Mandy, she got a very tense feeling throughout her body. She thought she was prepared to handle whatever Coach E. was about to tell her. When he motioned for her, she stepped out of the warm-up line and approached him. Coach E. gave his trademark smirk and said, "It's time to play."

She wanted to give him a hug, but she only said in return, "You know it."

Coach E. then gathered the girls in a circle for his final group pep talk. He looked each of them in the eye and noticed how tense they all looked. He said, "Our cornfield is better than theirs. Let's go!" They all laughed and rolled their eyes.

Ohio controlled the ball and also the pace of the whole game. They did not get worn out, and they won 4-0. Mandy scored two goals. Their next game was against Nebraska, and they played even better. They won 6-0, and Mandy scored three goals.

The last game of the day was against Missouri. Both teams had been in the winner's bracket the whole time. This game was going to be extremely tough. Coach E. made only a few adjustments of positions and players, but once again Mandy was playing. The game got underway, and for the entire first half the ball did not penetrate very deep into either defense. Despite the many promising plays that Ohio ran, the Missouri defense was up to the challenge. Halftime came and went, and as the second half was nearly over, Mandy received a pass along the far sideline. She maneuvered the ball from her foot to her knee and then to her head as she bumped the ball over the defender. The Ohio crowd cheered uncontrollably. Mandy used a burst of speed to get around the defender and race toward the goalkeeper. She sized it up, gave a fake to the right, moved the ball to her left foot and kicked the ball hard to the top left of the net. The Ohio crowd went crazy giving each other hugs.

Chapter 3: Coach E.'s Secret to Success

As Mandy sprinted back to her position, she locked eyes with Coach E., and they flashed satisfying smirks to each other. As the ball was placed in the middle of the field for Missouri's kick-off, the official blew the whistle. The game was over! What a day for the Ohio team! They had won all three games on Saturday, and on Sunday were to play the winner of the losers' bracket.

The whole team had a great time celebrating with their families. Supper at the Sizzler was a blast. Everyone carried on for hours. Finally, Coach E. got up and said, "Families, let me start off by again thanking you for your commitment to this team. Also, thank you for giving me and the other coaches your trust with your daughters. I am seeing great things happening, and tomorrow we are going to finish it off with a win. Everybody get a good night's sleep. I'm heading back to the hotel. Good night."

Of course, there was a cheer from everyone nearby. Then the girls said in unison, "Nighty-night, Coach. Sweet dreams."

The team met for a quick breakfast at the local pancake house next to the hotel. They did not have to be back at the tournament site until 10:00 a.m. The finals of the losers' bracket, involving Missouri vs. Illinois, was the first game of the day. Coach E. made sure all the girls were loose and having a good time with each other. The parents were also having a great time bonding this weekend. As Coach E. announced that it was time to leave for the soccer fields, Mandy's dad stood up and said, "Coach E., would you please come over here?"

Coach E. started to shuffle toward the door in the opposite direction. The girls all sprung out of their chairs and piled out of the booths to stop him. They led him back to Mandy's dad. Mandy's dad said, "On behalf of all the parents and girls, we want to give you a gift to show our appreciation."

Everyone clapped as Mandy's dad handed him a photo album that read on the front cover, "Your 1982 Ohio Girls' Soccer

Team." He was very touched by the gesture and had to bow his head to control his emotion. He opened the album to the first page and saw several team Polaroids that one of the parents took during this great fun weekend. As he flipped to the next page, he saw that each girl was given a page of the photo album to decorate and to express herself to Coach E. There were beautiful drawings of nature scenes, some poems, and even a little needlepoint of a soccer ball with "Ohio Girls' Soccer 1982" in the middle.

Coach E. was very touched by this very personal gift. He took a deep breath, swallowed, and said, "Let's not finish this great weekend with anything other than a win!" And with that, everyone headed to their cars and off to the soccer fields.

The first thing everyone wanted to find out when they got there was who they would be playing. They quickly saw that Missouri was going to be the winner of the current game. They were ahead 3-0, and time was running out. The score was still 3-0 when the final whistle blew.

"Okay, ladies, let's take the field and start our warm-ups," Coach said. The excitement was already starting for the parents as they found their seats. The other coaches began to set up the drills and warm-ups, while Coach E. turned his attention to studying the girls and how sharp each one looked. By the end of the allotted warm-up time, Coach E. knew who would be starting.

He went around to each girl and told them whether or not they would be starting. Once again, Mandy would be in the starting lineup. The girls knew they were in for a tough game, because Missouri would be fighting to stay in the tournament. Ohio was able to kick off to begin. They worked the ball down to the corner. One of Missouri's players pushed Kimmie down to steal the ball. The official blew the whistle for a penalty. Ohio had a free kick outside the box near the corner. Missouri set up their defense. As the ball was kicked, it lofted higher and longer

Chapter 3: Coach E.'s Secret to Success

than any of Missouri's players expected. Debby broke back from the pack and headed the ball into the net for the first score of the game. Then just before halftime, Missouri intercepted a pass, made a great quick pass, and tied up the score.

At halftime, Coach E. knew that the girls were feeling uptight about having such a close game, so he told them that if they would win this game and not have to play the next one with Missouri again, he would take them out for a dessert lunch.

Barbie asked, "What is that?"

Coach E. answered, "I'll take you to Baskin Robbins for any dessert you want, and that will be your lunch." The girls couldn't believe their ears. Their eyes lit up. Coach E. knew he said the right thing at the right time, and he would somehow talk the parents into allowing it.

The second half began with close back-and-forth play, but Ohio did not seem to be tired at all. Coach E. noticed some of the Missouri girls getting tired, so he knew it was time to run more plays that would require Ohio's offense to attack Missouri's defense. Once again, Mandy was the one who would get the job done.

She continued to give all her effort to try to get to the ball before the defense did. She finally did and she did not waste her opportunity. Mandy dribbled the ball past the defense and toward the goalie. With all the strength in her left leg, she struck the ball and she scored. The Ohio girls gathered around her and patted her on the back, as they all ran back to await the kickoff from Missouri.

Time was short, so the coaches made their final substitutions. Mandy was taken out, and she was not happy about it. She went to the bench breathing hard. She threw open the lid to her water bottle and once again realized that she was feeling cold and angry. She immediately jumped off the bench and walked over to the coach and began to cheer for her replacement and the other girls. The Missouri team worked hard, but the Ohio defense met every challenge. They cleared the ball every time. Before long, the whistle blew. Ohio had won the game 2-1 and were the Midwest Tournament champions! The girls all piled onto the field hugging each other. The coaches all hugged, as well. The parents, too, were doing their share of hugging.

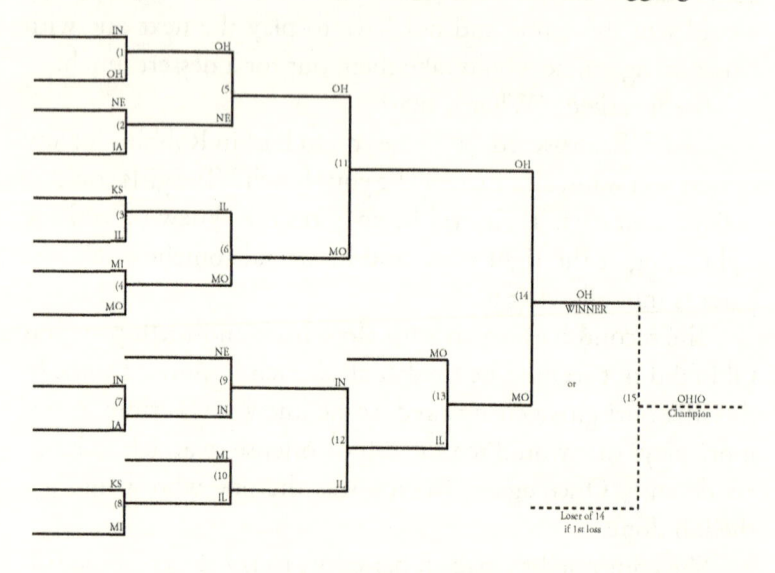

The two teams gathered on the field in front of the stands. All the coaches and players shook hands. Missouri received their second-place ribbons and trophy. Then it was Ohio's turn. The trophy brought out was the largest one that anyone had ever seen. There was a gasp in the crowd. The girls just giggled, enjoying the moment. As Coach E. accepted it, the wind caught the top of the trophy and almost pulled it down. The girls giggled some more. Coach E. set the trophy down so the team could gather around it for pictures. All the parents took turns photographing the winning accomplishment.

When the pictures were over, Coach E. addressed the parents and said, "Um, I made a promise to the girls that, um, if they win the game this morning, um, I would take them out for an,

Chapter 3: Coach E.'s Secret to Success

um, dessert lunch. I know it isn't my place to spoil them and their lunch, but, um, is it okay?" The parents all looked at each other and began to laugh.

One of them said, "If they can win tournaments like this, we will start a tradition of dessert lunches every time!" Everyone agreed, cheered, and headed off to claim the sweet spoils of victory — ice cream!

After everyone had their fill of ice-cream treats, Coach E. got up and said, "Alright. We have another few weekends of practice before our next soccer tournament. It's time for our trip to Orlando, Florida, for the Disney Soccer Challenge!" With that announcement, the girls began to scream out of control, probably due to the sugar from the ice cream that made everyone more hyper. This would be the last soccer tournament before the holiday break.

Chapter 4:
THE HAPPIEST PLACE ON EARTH?

(Mandy—early years 1982 continued)

AS TOUGH AS THE next few weekend practices were, the girls met every challenge Coach E. threw at them, and he knew they were ready. While some of the families were joining the team on the trip, Mandy's family decided that with Christmas right around the corner, they couldn't afford it right then. When the day of the flight to Orlando came, Mandy's dad saw his daughter and her teammates off safely.

As he headed back home from the Columbus airport, he couldn't shake the feeling that he really should have gone on the trip. He saw a phone booth and pulled over. He called home collect and spoke to his wife about his turmoil. She decided to look and see if there was a flight to Orlando from the Akron-Canton regional airport that night. Mandy's dad immediately came to life, excited for the possible opportunity to see Mandy play some more amazing soccer. He told his wife that he would drive a little farther, find another pay phone, and call her to see how she made out.

The road sign announced an L&K restaurant eighteen miles ahead, and he knew that they would have a pay phone. It would be the perfect amount of time for his wife to make the call to the airport. He pulled off at the exit, parked the car, and went into the restaurant. The hostess immediately asked if he wanted a table or booth. He said, "Well, I actually only want a phone, but I'll take a piece of pumpkin pie to go." They both laughed as she took him around the corner to use the phone.

He was nervous about this plan, but it would be a wonderful surprise for Mandy. He dialed "0" to get the operator, who then dialed his home number to first talk to his wife to see if she wanted to accept the call from him and the charges. Mrs. McConnell answered the phone and agreed to accept the charges for the phone call. When she was connected to her husband, her first words brought him joy. "Yes! There is an evening flight that leaves at 7:50 p.m."

Mr. McConnell quickly replied, "Gather up a weekend bag and meet me at the airport. I will be cutting it close." She understood the plan and hung up.

The hostess met him at her welcoming station with a piece of pumpkin pie. He handed her a five-dollar bill and said, "Keep the change." He jumped in the car and headed back north, but now he was driving a little faster than before. He glanced at the dashboard clock as he got off the interstate. The clock glowed 7:30. Driving up to the short-term parking booth, he was a bundle of nerves.

The attendant asked, "How long will you need to park your car here?"

"Through Sunday," Mr. McConnell answered.

The attendant handed him a ticket for his windshield, and Mr. McConnell quickly found a parking space. He made sure he had everything out of the car that he needed, and he raced to the airport ticket counter. He hoped it wouldn't be busy so he would be able to make the flight. The automatic door slid

Chapter 4: The Happiest Place on Earth?

open to reveal his wife and son there with a big smile. He smiled back, gave his wife a hug, and whispered, "Honey, thank you. Please let this be my only Christmas gift."

She handed him a small bag, and as he rushed off to the front of the line, she called out to him, "Well then, I guess I need to take a few things back to the store this weekend while you're away." He rolled his eyes and shook his head.

When the ticket agent finished processing his ticket, she handed him the boarding pass and told him, "Go quickly. I will call the gate and have them hold the plane for you." And just like O. J. Simpson running through an airport turning, twisting, and jumping over luggage, Mr. McConnell got to the gate in no time. The lady grabbed his boarding pass and escorted him through the mobile tunnel and onto the plane.

The door of the airplane shut immediately. The pilot poked his head out of the cockpit and said, "Let's get this bird in the air."

Before Mr. McConnell even had his seatbelt buckled, the plane had moved backwards, made a turn, and began to taxi to the main runway.

The engines revved up, and this massive metal tube rolled along picking up speed until the cadence of the tires moving across the runway cracks went away. The lights from the highway quickly appeared to get smaller and smaller, and the city lights soon seemed to decrease in size, too. Mandy's Dad sat back and began to plan his surprise.

Meanwhile, the team had arrived at the hotel and had settled in. The coaches from all the teams met together to draw to see who they would play. Many of the same teams they had played at the other two tournaments were at the Disney Challenge. There were a total of sixteen teams, but unlike the other tournaments, this tournament was single elimination. Lose and go home.

Each coach took turns going up to the bowl with Mickey Mouse's picture on it. Inside were sixteen pieces of folded papers. Coach E. pulled out the number thirteen. He couldn't help but

Alliance Lake ~ Be Still

think of that unlucky number as he walked up to a big board where he showed the tournament coordinator, who wrote every team's number in the official bracket.

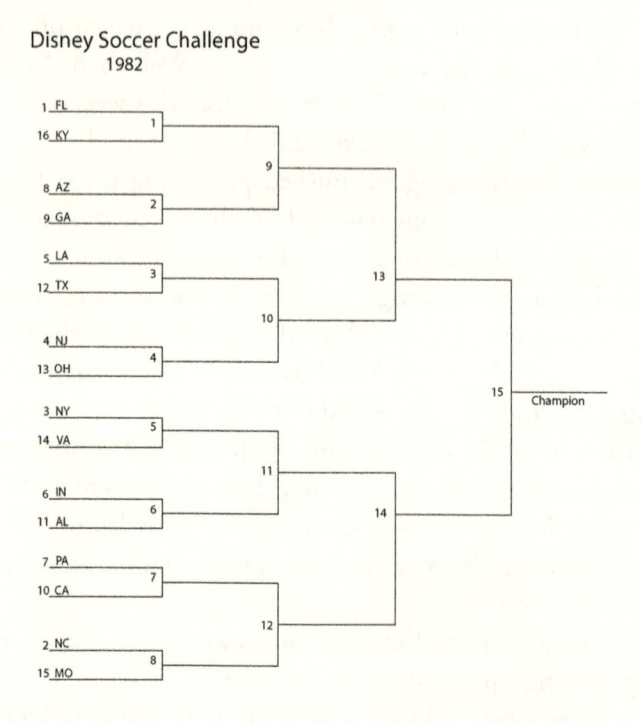

```
Disney Soccer Challenge
        1982
```

Seed	Team		
1	FL		
16	KY	1	
			9
8	AZ	2	
9	GA		
5	LA	3	
12	TX		13
		10	
4	NJ	4	
13	OH		
			15 → Champion
3	NY	5	
14	VA		
		11	
6	IN	6	14
11	AL		
7	PA	7	
10	CA		12
2	NC	8	
15	MO		

Coach E. was very pleased that Missouri was on the other side of the bracket, along with Alabama, which had won the Texas tournament. He also knew that there were many teams equally as good on Ohio's side of the bracket. When the process was over, Coach E. headed back to tell the girls who they would be playing. Everyone had gathered in the hospitality room right next to Coach E.'s room. Coach opened his tournament folder that he had received. He pulled out the paper that revealed the brackets. Ohio would be playing New Jersey first. The girls were all fighting to see who was playing whom. Coach said, "Listen—the winner of this tournament has to win four games in a row. Why shouldn't it be us?"

Chapter 4: The Happiest Place on Earth?

The girls and the coaches all cheered.

Coach continued, "Everyone's first game is at 9:30, so we have to get up early and get down for breakfast in the room reserved for the soccer players and coaches. The shuttle buses will take everyone over to the Disney soccer fields at 8:30. So let's plan to head down to breakfast together at 7:45. Set those alarms, because the coaches will be knocking on doors at 7:00 to make sure everyone is up and about. Remember, ladies, this Mickey Mouse soccer tournament is a big deal." He was interrupted by their laughing. He continued and said, "Seriously, let's get our sleep tonight and do what we came here to do."

Mandy yelled out, "Win!" The girls all came together in the middle of the room and put their hands on top of each other. Mandy volunteered the cheer, "Mickey Mouse on three: one, two, three! *Mickey Mouse!*" The night was extremely short for everyone, including the coaches. There had been a lot of tossing and turning during the night. In the morning, it was time to let adrenaline help make up for the lack of sleep.

Everyone went downstairs and met up with all the teams eating breakfast at roughly the same time. The Ohio team was unusually quiet, or maybe they were tired. Coach E. knew coffee would help him get going, but the kids would have to put some extra maple syrup on their waffles. After breakfast, everyone loaded onto the shuttle buses and went to the soccer fields. Coach got off the shuttle first, and there waiting before him were the parents who had come down to watch.

There was also another familiar face, that of Mr. McConnell. He had the widest smile the coach had ever seen. Coach E. just began shaking his head. Then Mandy saw him and froze. He held out his arms and she bolted at him, jumping up into his arms like she was five again.

She said, "But Daddy, how…"

He stopped her and said, "This was too important for me to miss. Besides, Mom said it was okay."

They hugged some more, when Coach E. said, "Come on. Let's warm up! We have a tournament to win."

Coach E. watched the warm-ups, talked to each girl, and set the starting lineup. Mandy was very pleased that she would start. The whistle blew to start the game. Ohio took control with a quick goal. Later, right before halftime, Mandy snuck the ball through the goalkeeper's hands to add to their lead. Even though Mandy's shot was just off to the goalie's left side, the ball had been kicked too powerfully for New Jersey's goalie.

After halftime, Mandy got a breakaway, made such a great fake that the goalkeeper lost her footing and fell, and Mandy booted the ball into the net. Up 3-0, Coach E. took some of the girls out of the game—including Mandy. Coach knew it could be a long day, and he wanted to rest some of the starters when he could.

As if someone hit the momentum switch on the New Jersey team, New Jersey scored a goal. Mandy and the other girls were still catching their breaths, when they quickly stood up and rushed over to the sidelines. Coach E. said, "Go sit back down. I'll let you know who I need and when."

The New Jersey team began to play much more physically. Coach E. could not believe that the referees did not see his girls getting knocked down with obvious trips and shoves. He kept his cool, though. Minutes later, after another shove, a New Jersey girl scored to make it 3-2.

As Mandy and the other girls went back in the game, Coach E. warned them, "The refs are letting things get rough out there. Be tough, but more than anything, you need to be quick. Use your quickness and speed and let's keep the ball away from them and score again."

When the subs were allowed in, that is exactly what Mandy and the Ohio girls did. Anytime a New Jersey player was ready to run into the Ohio player who had the ball, she would make a quick move and pass the ball to an open Ohio girl.

Chapter 4: The Happiest Place on Earth?

This continued to happen until Mandy saw the opening that allowed her to race toward the goal. Using her powerful left leg, she scored her third goal of the game. With time running out, New Jersey tried everything they could. Even when they made a shot on goal, Ohio's goalkeeper handled the ball well. The whistle blew and the game was over. Ohio moved on to the next round, where they would play either Louisiana or Texas. Coach E. was ready to find out which team they would play.

Their next game was on Field C, where the teams were currently playing. The Ohio team rounded the corner and saw the scoreboard. It said Louisiana 5, Texas 1. Everyone knew who they would be playing next. The Ohio team was enjoying the extra rest and time to visit with their families.

The referee blew the whistle, and Louisiana was moving on to round two. There was a mandatory twenty-minute break after the last team of the previous round finished before a ten-minute warm up could begin. Coach E. loved that his girls had a little more rest.

After each team finished their warm-ups, it was time to start the game. Coach E. decided to start the game with the same girls who started the last game. Right away, Coach E. could tell that Louisiana was being way more aggressive than last time. He could also see that his girls were matching their intensity.

Mandy received a long pass, made a quick move around the defense, and scored. Mandy soon received another long pass, but this time she made a move to the outside, while Steph raced with her toward the goal. At the last minute, Mandy faked a kick at the goal and passed the ball to Steph, who kicked the ball in for a goal. Ohio celebrated with a 2-0 lead.

After halftime, Ohio poured in two more goals, from who else but Mandy. When the score got to 4-0, Coach E. could see the Louisiana players start to jog to the ball instead of race. He noticed that they gave up mentally as well as physically.

Alliance Lake ~ Be Still

The Louisiana coach called a timeout to try and turn around what was happening. At that time, Coach E. was confident that he could take out some of his key players to give them some needed rest, sure that the subs would hold the lead. After the timeout, the Ohio players remained focused and were the more aggressive and faster team. Louisiana just couldn't break through the defense, so once again they started to jog.

Even though Ohio did not score any more goals, they finished with a strong performance from the subs. The whistle blew, and Ohio was on to the semi-finals, round three. Once again, Coach E. told the other Ohio coaches to take care of the girls; he was going to headquarters to get an update on who they would play next.

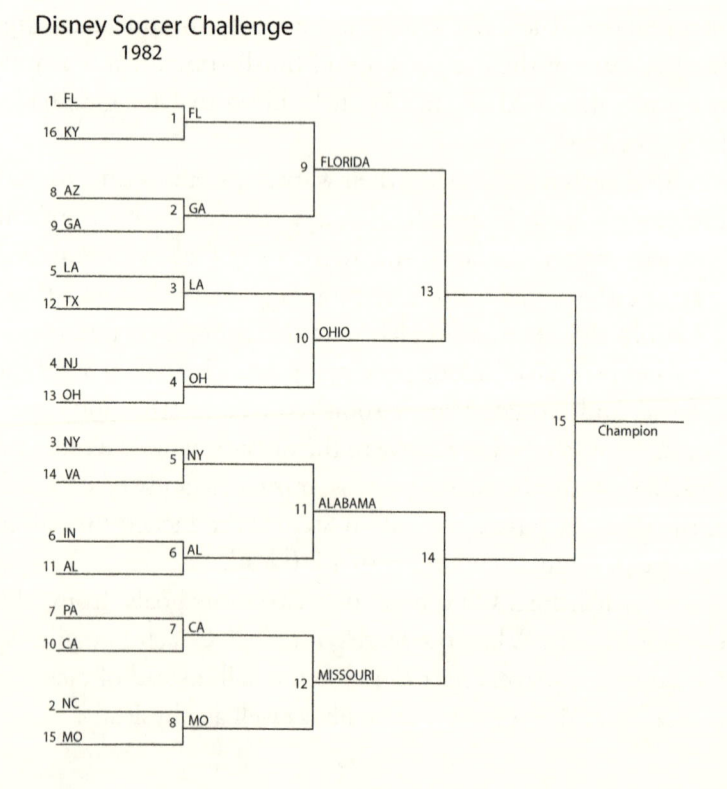

Disney Soccer Challenge
1982

Seed	Team	R1	R2	R3	Final
1	FL				
16	KY	1 FL			
			9 FLORIDA		
8	AZ				
9	GA	2 GA			
5	LA				
12	TX	3 LA		13	
			10 OHIO		
4	NJ				
13	OH	4 OH			15 Champion
3	NY				
14	VA	5 NY			
			11 ALABAMA		
6	IN			14	
11	AL	6 AL			
7	PA				
10	CA	7 CA			
			12 MISSOURI		
2	NC				
15	MO	8 MO			

Chapter 4: The Happiest Place on Earth?

Next up for Ohio was the Florida team. During warm-ups, Coach E. couldn't help but notice the stands filling up like he had never seen before for this level of game. He thought that Ohio was at a definite cheering disadvantage. Coach talked to each girl individually and thanked her for what she brought to the team. Like he always did, he also told them whether or not they would be starting the next game. With only minutes before the start of the game, he gathered his team together and said, "Look over at the stands. Do you see our fans?"

The girls said, "Yes, of course, Coach. We know where they are."

Coach said, "Okay, but can you hear them?"

The girls replied, "No way. There are too many Florida fans."

Then Coach said, "Exactly. If you want to hear our fans, you better play fast, play hard, and play to score so you can hear only our fans. I guarantee you that if Florida scores, you will hear it loudly from every dad, mom, brother, sister, aunt, uncle, grandma, grandpa, and cousin. Am I clear?"

"Yes, Coach!"

"Ohio. On three!"

"Ohio!"

The girls took the field and the other Ohio coaches came over to Coach E. and said, "That was quite a good little speech."

He looked at them with his trademark smirk and said, "I hate away games."

The whistle blew to start the game. Right away, Mandy took control of everything. She passed the ball to the correct open person, and then used her speed to get back open. Having the extra rest was paying off. Mandy knew that what the coach said was important, and she wanted to make sure Ohio scored the first goal. Just then, her hard work and speed allowed her to catch up to a ball passed to her, and with a few quick moves, she kicked it into the back of the net for the game's first goal. The small group from Ohio in the upper corner of the stands let out a loud cheer, as did the Ohio girls on the sidelines.

Mandy hugged her teammates on the field and said to them, "I like the sound of that. Let's do it again."

The other girls answered, "Yes—and again and again and again." And they all laughed; but that is exactly what happened. Mandy scored three more times before the game was over. The final score was Ohio 4, Florida 0.

On the other side of the bracket, Alabama ended up winning a hard-fought game 3-2 over Missouri. Before the finals, there was a mandatory one-hour rest at the end of the last game. During this time, the teams could get some additional rest and relax and have a light snack or meal. As the team was enjoying their rest, the coaches were in the corner of the pavilion chatting about Alabama. Coach E. said, "Well, we know how good Alabama is. They won the Texas tournament."

"Yeah," Coach Keys said. "Mandy is our special player, but Alabama has one of its own, Mia, who scores goals in bunches."

Coach E. said, "Perfect. It's Mandy versus Mia. I would pay money to see that, but lucky for us, we'll have a front row seat." They all laughed.

It was time to head back to the field and begin warming up. As the teams were doing their drills, Coach E. was talking with the girls when he noticed a bunch of Disney characters in the stands having fun with the spectators. There was Goofy wrapping his big floppy ears around a little girl, and Bashful was being all bashful when he would approach any of the young ladies. Also, Donald Duck was storming up and down the bleachers acting all upset about something.

The whistle blew, and a voice was heard through the loudspeaker: "Ladies and gentlemen, today's 1982 Disney Championship game features Alabama versus Ohio." The crowd clapped politely. The teams lined up, and as each girl's name was announced, she stepped forward and waved to the cheering crowd. After the coaches were introduced, the voice from the loudspeaker boomed out, "Would Mandy McConnell from

Chapter 4: The Happiest Place on Earth?

Ohio and Mia Hamm from Alabama please step to the middle of the field for the coin toss?"

This surprised both coaches, but they knew their players would handle everything just fine. Mandy and Mia met at the center of the field and shook hands. The voice over the loudspeaker said, "Ladies and gentlemen, at the middle of the field for the coin toss are the tournament's two top-scoring players. Both have scored ten goals. This game could very well settle who the scoring champion for our tournament is. We will have Mia Hamm call the coin flip in the air. The coin has good ol' Mickey Mouse's head on one side and the Disney castle on the tail's side."

Mia looked at the referee and called out, "Heads!" The coin finished its flips and hit the soft grass with the castle side showing. Mandy and the rest of the Ohio team cheered at winning the coin toss, but they really hoped they would eventually be able to win the game.

The whistle blew to begin the game, and Mandy flip-kicked the ball over and ahead to Kimmie. She then sent it back to Mandy, who quickly kicked it ahead to Debbie, who was sprinting down the sidelines. Debbie controlled the ball down the field on the out-of-bounds line. Right before she got to the corner, she booted a beautiful entry pass in front of the net. Players from both sides were converging on the ball to attempt to head or chest-bump it in the goal or to try to keep it out, when the Alabama goalkeeper suddenly jumped high in the air with her arms outstretched and caught the ball.

The Alabama fans let out a big sigh of relief that they did not get a quick goal scored against them. Coach E. liked the start his girls were getting on this very aggressive team. The goalie kicked the ball past midfield. Alabama began to pass the ball. The entire Alabama offense was clearly centered around Mia Hamm. The other Alabama girls did everything they could to get the ball to her. Luckily for Ohio, they had a pretty good player shadowing her! Wherever Mia went, Mandy was right there. Mandy never played against someone her equal, and she wondered if Mia felt the same way. She actually enjoyed the challenge, and she hoped Mia did, too.

Each team had its chances to score, but the ball literally bounced Alabama's way on a very unfortunate play for Ohio. Sara, the Ohio goalie, made an easy save that was kicked right to her. She tried to make a quick throw, but the ball hit the back of an Alabama player and ricocheted right over to Mia, who blasted it in for the first goal of the game. The Alabama fans in the stands went crazy. Everyone knew this was going to be a low-scoring game, and Alabama definitely had the advantage at this point.

The score was still 1-0 when the whistle blew for halftime. Players went to their benches to get some rest and instructions from their coaches. The Ohio girls, especially Sara, were looking down. Then Coach E. said in his best Donald Duck voice, "What's the matter here? WHAWHAWHAWHA!!!!" Everyone cracked up. Even the Alabama players were caught off guard and gave the Ohio bench dirty looks.

Coach E. then said in his regular voice, "Are you kidding? This is the championship game. This game is supposed to be tough. I need to see your fight. You girls are running with them and defending with them, but I need to see you a half step quicker on everything in the second half. You have to all be faster—not just a few of you. Play faster than you're used to. It probably won't feel right, but that's where I want you to play. Do you understand?"

All the girls said, "Yes, Coach."

Mandy said, "'Ohio fast' on three." They all put their hands into the middle, yelled, "Ohio fast," and headed out to their positions. On the way out to start the second half, Mandy noticed Mia walking closer and closer to her. Mia, passing her, said quietly, "I hope we can be teammates one day." Mandy smiled and nodded.

Chapter 4: The Happiest Place on Earth?

As Alabama started the game, it was clear that they wanted to play defensively by keeping the ball away from Ohio and slowing everything way down. Ohio tried its best to be fast and steal the ball, but Alabama would pass it too quickly. After several minutes, Coach E. called for a timeout.

Coach E. said, "Okay, we are playing fast enough, but we have to begin to play a much tighter defense. I know it is riskier, but we are fast enough to recover if something gets by. Everyone got it?" The girls all nodded.

As play began again, Ohio was no longer playing back waiting for Alabama so they could attack the pass, but they were using great defense to attack the players. No one could get open during the passes. Mandy was guarding Mia extremely closely. A few elbows were naturally exchanged to get a better position advantage.

All of a sudden, Ohio's Kimmie stole the ball and was racing down the middle left side of the field, with Mandy catching up fast. Mia was also on the chase. As Kimmie got into range of kicking the ball toward the goal, she lost her nerve and made the pass to Mandy, who knew Mia was closing in. Everyone knew Mandy's strongest leg was her left, so Mandy made a quick decision to switch the ball to her right foot.

Right at that point, Mandy planted her left foot to kick, when at that very moment Mia stepped on that left foot. With a desperate effort, her right-footed kick had just enough momentum to get by the diving goalie's attempt to stop the ball. Mandy scored, but during this kicking process, Mandy heard a horrible pop and felt excruciating pain course through her entire left side. She fell to the ground, with her teammates piling on her in celebration. She didn't, or couldn't, scream. She just lay on the ground in shock. When the girls finally got up, Mandy stayed down. Coach E. sprinted out to Mandy reaching her before the other coaches could. Mandy's dad and others who were cheering for Ohio turned their excitement to concern as they began to hold their breath and hope for the best.

Coach asked, "Are you hurt?"

Mandy calmly replied, "I'm not sure, Coach. I heard a pop and felt pain through my entire left side. I think it was something in my hip, but right now, I'm not in pain."

Coach said, "You're coming out for the rest of the game."

Mandy said, "No way!"

Coach looked at her very sternly and repeated, "You are coming out for the rest of the game!"

Mandy knew not to push it. She got up with the help of the other coaches and hobbled to the sidelines, fixing her eyes on her dad for some extra comfort. She noticed that he was visibly mad because she was being taken out, when to him it clearly looked like she was shaking it off. The game was tied 1-1 with only minutes left to play in regulation. The Ohio players knew they had to step up and come through for Mandy and Coach E.

Mia Hamm and the other Alabama players were really working hard to keep the ball, waiting for the perfect shot. Knowing time was now getting really short, Mia got around her defender. With two other Ohio players closing in on her, she passed the ball to a teammate who had a fairly open shot. Mia's teammate kicked the ball with all the force she had, but got too far under the ball, which sailed just over the crossbar. The whistle blew, and the second half ended tied: Ohio 1, Alabama 1.

Because this was a tournament, they would not play overtime. It was time for a shootout. In these overtime shootouts, the coaches selected five players to each take a penalty kick. The teams take turns until one team is mathematically eliminated. Coach E. quickly considered several scenarios and then gathered his team and said, "Ladies, I am very proud of all of you. The players I am going to select are those who will give us the best chance to win right now. If it is still tied after these five

Chapter 4: The Happiest Place on Earth?

have a chance, I have to select five different players for another shootout."

He went on and said, "This will also be the order in which I want the players to kick." He paused and said, "Kimmie, Steph, Karen, Kathy, and . . ." With each player named, Mandy's head sunk lower and lower. She wanted to finish this game off. Then Coach shocked everyone by saying, "Mandy." Everyone, even the other coaches, looked at him. Mandy's head snapped up and her face lit up. She said, "Yes!" Mandy's dad looked on and gave his approval to Mandy when their eyes met.

Coach E. turned to the goalie and the five penalty-kick players and said, "Let's stop their shots and let's drill our shots." Everyone hugged and headed to their spots. First up for Alabama was Mia. Sara was doing her best to try to read into which corner Mia was going to kick the ball. The referee put the ball on the mark and blew the whistle. Mia took a deep breath, briefly looked up, took a couple stuttered steps, and kicked the ball with unbelievable power. Even though Sara guessed correctly and dove to the left, the ball sailed past her without her getting even a finger on it. The Alabama players and fans went crazy. They knew how huge that shot was. Coach E. hoped it didn't shake Sara's confidence.

First up for Ohio was Kimmie. The referee blew the whistle, and Kimmie aimed for the top left corner. The ball got by the outstretched hand of Alabama's goalie, but hit the goalpost and bounced away. Once again, the Alabama players and crowd screamed their heads off.

The next three players from each team kicked on goal, but the goalies were up to the task and either caught the ball or blocked the shots. The shootout score remained 1-0 in favor of Alabama. The fifth and final Alabama kicker was very important at this point. If she scored, then Alabama would win. Ohio could not tie, and Mandy would not even have a chance to kick.

Ohio's goalie was taking a lot of deep breaths as she positioned herself in the goal. She was doing her best to block everything out of her mind except the next few moments. The whistle blew. The Alabama player didn't hesitate, and she strongly kicked the ball to the left. Sara reacted a little late, but took one quick step and leaped into the air. She got her fingertips on the ball, but the ball continued past her—but Sara had deflected the ball just enough so that it went just wide of the side post. The Ohio team cheered in relief and ran over to Sara to smother her with hugs.

A knot began to form in Mandy's stomach as she walked over to the ball. Everything seemed quiet to her. She saw a lot of commotion around her, but all she was aware of was her body. Her heart was beating faster, her eyes darting around trying to discover any last second tells the goalie was giving away, and then there was her left leg. It was throbbing, but she wasn't paying attention to that. The whistle sounded and brought her back to the job at hand. She made a start at the ball but shifted at the last moment and struck the ball with her left leg with all the force she had. When she saw the ball come off her foot, she collapsed, knowing it wasn't good enough. The Alabama goalie handled it with no problem. Mandy buried her head into the ground as the Alabama players swarmed the goalie and fell over each other in the goal.

Mandy's dad was crushed. He put his head in his hands as he realized that his daughter would not be the hero he thought she should have been. The coaches shook hands and the two teams moved to the center of the field for the award ceremony. The voice from the loudspeaker said, "Ladies and gentlemen, the second-place team which played wonderfully but came up just a little short—Ohio." Everyone in the stands began to applaud politely.

Then the announcer said, "At this time, I want to mention that the scoring champion and MVP for this tournament is

Chapter 4: The Happiest Place on Earth?

Mia Hamm." This time the crowd exploded in applause. The only one not applauding was Mr. McConnell. He just couldn't bring himself to congratulate someone who took the moment away from his daughter.

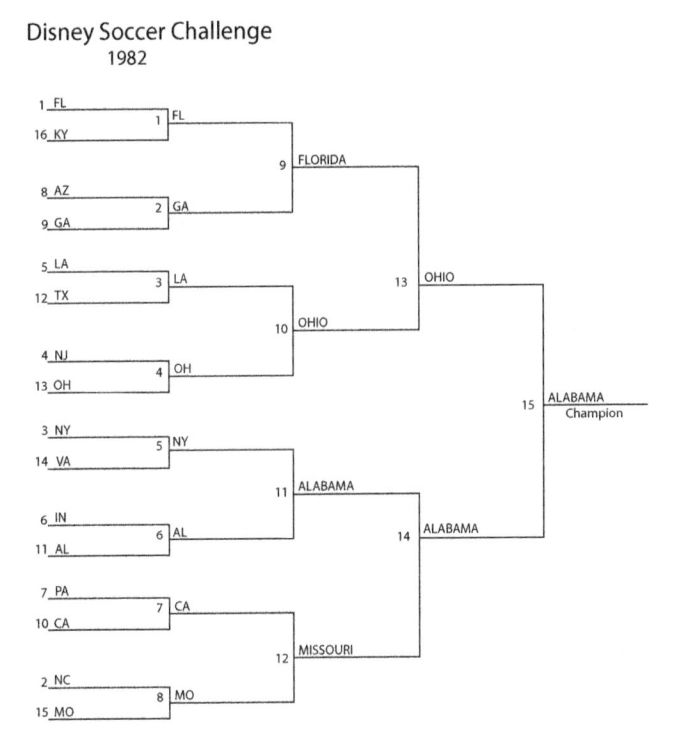

Disney Soccer Challenge 1982

```
 1 FL  ┐
       ├─1─ FL ┐
16 KY  ┘       │
               ├─9─ FLORIDA ┐
 8 AZ  ┐       │            │
       ├─2─ GA ┘            │
 9 GA  ┘                    │
                            ├─13─ OHIO ┐
 5 LA  ┐                    │          │
       ├─3─ LA ┐            │          │
12 TX  ┘       │            │          │
               ├─10─ OHIO ──┘          │
 4 NJ  ┐       │                       │
       ├─4─ OH ┘                       │
13 OH  ┘                               ├─15─ ALABAMA
                                       │     Champion
 3 NY  ┐                               │
       ├─5─ NY ┐                       │
14 VA  ┘       │                       │
               ├─11─ ALABAMA ┐         │
 6 IN  ┐       │             │         │
       ├─6─ AL ┘             │         │
11 AL  ┘                     ├─14─ ALABAMA
                             │
 7 PA  ┐                     │
       ├─7─ CA ┐             │
10 CA  ┘       │             │
               ├─12─ MISSOURI┘
 2 NC  ┐       │
       ├─8─ MO ┘
15 MO  ┘
```

The announcer, breaking in over the applause said, "Your 1982 Disney Soccer Champion is Team Alabama!"

As the cheering continued, Mia found Mandy. She said, "I am so sorry. I was going for the block off your left foot."

Mandy said "I know. I'm sure we'll play again."

Mia looked at her, and as she was backing away she said, "Yes, but I hope someday we can play together and not against each other."

Mandy just smiled and said, "You can count on it."

Chapter 5:

REALITY CHECK

(Mandy—early years: end of 1982-1985; then crosses paths with Beth, 1986)

THE TRIP BACK TO Ohio was difficult for the team. The coach told the girls to enjoy their extended holiday break, and that he would be contacting them about their next practice at the end of February. Mandy's family and the other girls' families were waiting for them at the Columbus airport. They all cheered for the girls and gave their own family member a big welcome-back hug. Mandy was favoring her left side quite a bit. As everyone began to walk away, Coach E. ran to Mr. McConnell and said, "Please have someone look at Mandy's leg. I'm worried about it."

Mr. McConnell just replied, "Oh, we'll give her a chance to have Christmas, and she'll be as good as new." Coach E's heart sank. He just stood there speechless in unbelief as Mandy and her dad turned away from him and walked away.

Christmas came and went. New Year's Day came and went. Mandy wasn't excited about anything during the entire school break. When school began again in January, her gym class played dodge ball. She loved dodge ball because she could inflict pain on the boys. The boys actually feared her, and she knew it. However, during the first game she found that she didn't have the same power to push off her left leg and get away from the onslaught of red rubber balls coming at her like heat-seeking missiles. She was immediately hit again and again and again.

Something was wrong, and everyone knew it. Mr. Elliott, the gym teacher, called Mandy over at the end of class and said, "You need to see a sports medicine doctor about your leg. I will give a doctor's contact information to the secretary. Have your mom or dad call the office and get the information from her."

Mandy knew she needed someone to look at her leg, but telling her dad was not going to be easy. At supper, she began to tell them how her leg still ached and that she didn't have any real strength in it like she used to have. Then she just started crying uncontrollably. Mr. McConnell said that he would get the name of the sports medicine doctor and make an appointment. That began to calm Mandy down. She excused herself, saying that she had a lot of homework.

Mr. McConnell got the name of the doctor, but couldn't bring himself to make the appointment. He kept putting off making the phone call. It was toward the end of February when Coach E. called one evening.

Mandy answered the phone, "Hello."

She heard a familiar quirky voice on the other end say, "Hi, Mandy. How are you doing?"

She quickly perked up and automatically said, "Good, Coach," and then caught herself and started to cry.

He immediately said, "Please tell me what's wrong."

Mandy settled down enough to say, "Coach, I'm still waiting to go see the doctor. I have noticed some things that aren't getting better. My dad hasn't told me when the appointment is." As soon as she got that last sentence out, she began to cry again.

Chapter 5: Reality Check

Coach then said very calmly, "Mandy, may I please speak to your father?"

She said, "He's down in the basement in his woodworking shop. I'll get him."

When Mr. McConnell got to the phone, he said, "Hi, Coach. When is the next practice?" There was silence. Mr. McConnell said, "Coach . . ."

Then Coach E. spoke up and said, "Mr. McConnell, I'm sorry, but Mandy cannot start practice until I see that she is cleared medically."

Again there was silence, but this time from Mr. McConnell. Then he said, "Okay, Coach. I understand. I will make sure to schedule her appointment soon and get back to you with the results."

"Great," said Coach E. "I look forward to hearing from you."

Mr. McConnell hung up the phone and said to Mandy, "Honey, I saw you doing better and better every week. Your limp is almost gone. I just thought you needed a break, and then you would be fine, which I still believe; but because the coach is insistent, I will make the appointment so you can get back with your Ohio team where you belong." Mandy cracked a smile and knew her dad would finally follow through.

It took another two weeks before Mandy could see Dr. Jensen. He was the best orthopedic doctor around. He specialized in athletic injuries and performed many surgeries on Cleveland's professional athletes. Mr. McConnell felt very confident that the doctor would look things over, give her a few exercises to do, and write the note allowing her to return to soccer.

After speaking to Mandy about her many soccer accomplishments, he gave her a very thorough examination that centered on her left hip. Dr. Jensen said to them both, "I need Mandy to get some x-rays done, and then I will have a complete idea of what's going on. The nurse out front will help you get that scheduled at the hospital. I'll then call you for a follow up."

Mr. McConnell looked at Mandy and then at Dr. Jensen, smiled, and said, "Sounds good. Then after all that we will get a signed note that says she can get back on the Ohio All-Star Team!" Mandy did not say a thing, and neither did Dr. Jensen. The doctor shook their hands and excused himself.

They were able to get to the hospital for x-rays on Friday of that same week. Then on Monday afternoon, Mr. McConnell received a call at work from a nurse at Dr. Jensen's office. The nurse asked him to bring Mandy and his wife the next day to speak with Dr. Jensen. Mr. McConnell thought that seemed a little odd, but thought that the doctor wanted to make sure everyone could see the exercises that Mandy would have to do to get back playing soccer. Mandy's parents took a half day off work so they could pick Mandy up from school and go to the doctor's office. Once there, they were escorted into a big conference room with a lot of different x-ray viewers. The three of them sat down in very comfortable leather swivel chairs and waited. About ten minutes later, Dr. Jensen entered the room and introduced himself to Mrs. McConnell and greeted Mandy and her dad.

The doctor pulled four films out of the big envelope he carried under his arm. He shoved them under the clip on the x-ray viewer and snapped the lights on to reveal different images of a hip bone and the pelvic area. Dr. Jensen got out his pointer and started talking about synovial ball structure, articular cartilage, acetabulum, and avascular necrosis. When he got to that last one, Mr. McConnell interrupted him and said, "Doctor, please just tell us in plain non-medical terms. What do you see on those x-rays?"

Dr. Jensen snapped off the x-ray lights on the viewers, sat down at the conference room table, and said, "Mandy has one of the worst hip injuries I have ever seen. The blood supply to

Chapter 5: Reality Check

the bone has been completely disrupted, and the ball of the hip is essentially dead. She is going to need a hip replacement, or she will begin walking with a cane."

At that moment, the room was silent. Mr. and Mrs. McConnell were in shock. Deep down in her heart of hearts, Mandy already knew it was bad.

Dr. Jensen spoke up and said, "You have a lot to process, but it is my recommendation that you get the surgery done sooner rather than later. It also will be a very lengthy recovery. Do you have any questions?"

Mr. McConnell cleared his throat and asked hesitantly, "Will she ever play soccer again?"

The doctor replied, "It won't ever be the level of soccer Mandy was used to. I'm sorry." He got up and walked over to Mandy and then said again, "I'm sorry," swung the door open and walked out, letting it shut with a heavy click of the latch.

Once again silence returned to the room. Instead of anyone offering Mandy a hug, they picked up their things and Mr. McConnell said, "Let's hurry home. The bus will be dropping your brother off. We can make it there before he has to go to the neighbor's house."

A few weeks later Mandy had the surgery, and it was successful. The recovery and rehabilitation were long, hard, and painful. Mr. McConnell always thought that Mandy could make it back to elite status if she worked hard enough, but he got more and more discouraged when her improvement was slow. As her recovery progressed, it became clear that Mandy's goals were no longer the same as her dad's goals for her. Their relationship became more and more contentious.

They ended many conversations by outright yelling and screaming at each other. One night Mr. McConnell yelled the thing that crushed her spirit more than her hip injury ever did. He said, "Well, if you are all done trying, then it's time to see if your brother can be the star that you failed to be." He turned and went down the stairs into his woodshop to leave her by herself, crying and hurting—hurting deeply.

Mr. McConnell begged and pleaded with his son to take soccer more seriously. He needed to practice every free chance he had in order to get noticed by the traveling teams, but all he wanted to do was hang out with his friends and explore nature. Mr. McConnell became more and more angry and verbally abusive to everyone in the family. He reached his breaking point when Mandy's brother told his dad that he was done with soccer. Mandy's dad packed up his things and moved out. The divorce was finalized some months later, leaving Mrs. McConnell to pick up the pieces of her broken family, including herself.

~ April 1986 ~

Back at school, Mandy got through her days, but it was hard not being the popular athlete. In fact, many of those whom she thought were her friends did not hang around her anymore. One day after entering the cafeteria to grab her grease-filled pizza, she headed for a table in the back where no one would bother her as she read a book. She saw Beth Russell there sitting by herself looking at a magazine. Beth was the daughter of the pastor whose church the McConnell's used to attend before Mandy did all the traveling soccer. Beth was getting a pretty racy reputation, but Mandy didn't care.

Mandy approached Beth and said, "Hi Beth. Can I sit with you?"

Beth looked up to display her dark eye shadow and even darker lips and said, "Sure, whatever."

"What magazine are you looking at?"

This time Beth didn't look up, and not a single hair on her teased-out jet-black punk-style hair moved when she said, "*Tattoo Arts.*"

Chapter 5: Reality Check

Mandy said, "Wow! I would love to get one of those!"

That response got Beth's attention. She looked up and asked, "You would really like to get a tattoo?"

"Yeah, for sure I would," Mandy replied.

"Well, then," Beth said, "You and me have somewhere to go Friday night." Beth flashed a devilish grin. Mandy took a bite of her greasy pizza and smiled back at Beth.

Chapter 6:
GIVING PKS A BAD NAME

(Beth—early years: 1979-1985; then crosses paths with Mandy, 1986)

AS PASTOR RUSSELL SAID goodbye to the last person in line, he was focusing on getting back to his office and checking anything that might have been left on his desk for his review. On his way to "his sanctuary," he had to go through the sanctuary. As he was almost through to the other side, he heard words that he wasn't expecting.

"Pastor, Pastor," Mrs. Tomblin, the choir director, shouted. "Could I have a quick word with you?"

Pastor Russell had gotten very good at deciphering the category of the issue based on the first few words and tone of the person. It was either one of three things:

1. Have a need or something to pray about

2. Have a compliment

3. Have a complaint

This one definitely fell in the category of complaint.

"Oh yes, of course," Pastor quickly said.

"Well," Mrs. Tomblin sighed, "that daughter of yours!" Pastor braced himself for what was going to be said next. "Did you notice how much of a distraction she was with those little pencils from the pews?"

Of course, he did not let on that he knew what she was talking about, because he had been a bit of a troublemaker in his youth, and he thought most things Beth did were cute and blown out of proportion by others.

Pastor Russell by all accounts was an excellent preacher. He told great stories and held the attention of the congregation as he spoke. He always made a mental note while he was preaching of how many sleepers he had during his sermons. He never counted anyone with white or blue hair. He figured they probably got up at 4:30 a.m. and were ready for a midday nap. There were never more than two sleepers in one service at a time. Of course, he did not count those who quickly nodded off, snapped their heads back up, and returned to consciousness.

Beth, though, being only nine, didn't appreciate the stories or a real-life challenging message. She got distracted very easily and would sit in the back of the sanctuary while her little friends would dare her to do things during the middle of the service. This time it was with the little pencils.

The floor of the sanctuary was sloped all the way down to the altar. Beth made it a personal challenge of hers on a dare to get a little pencil to roll all the way down front. If she could distract her dad during his preaching, she would get extra points. The first two attempts ended with the pencil turning to the left and hitting the side of the pew just a few rows down. But on the third attempt, the pencil got off to a straight start and picked up momentum, making a perfect path like a Boy Scout's whittled-out race car zooming down the track.

Chapter 6: Giving PKs a Bad Name

The pencil did catch the eye of the pastor, but he didn't even flinch as he continued to preach without pausing. Squeaky laughter briefly broke out. When people turned to look, the girls were already hiding behind the pews in front of them. Luckily for them, the pastor wrapped up the sermon and asked everyone to stand for the closing song.

Mrs. Tomblin continued, "Well, I saw little pencils rolling down the aisles. It was very distracting and rude to you."

Pastor replied, "I am very sorry for Beth's behavior, and I will have a talk with her. Thank you very much." He then continued to his office as he heard a huff behind him from Mrs. Tomblin.

Those cute and overblown behaviors became more and more worrisome. The pastor and his wife were more than once summoned to confront the aftermath of things that Beth took part in. Even in those early tween years when most girls were collecting 45-rpm records and Tiger Beat posters of their favorite heartthrobs, Beth found a way to skip that phase while always trying to look older.

Older brothers and sisters had a way of speeding up the adolescence process, or maybe it's because the parents were too old or too tired to care.

In Beth's case, she knew all the right things to say, and by the time she was twelve years old, her dad had to chase her down multiple times in the middle of the night for sneaking out to be with the older kids in the neighborhood. Word definitely got out about this family problem, but Beth would always act like an angel the next time she was in church or encountered adults. She was a brilliant actress.

It was just after she turned thirteen when things really changed for the Russell family. Beth's parents were at a conference together, and her older brother Drew was in charge. Friday night came and went, and all was well in the Russell household; but Saturday evening was very different. Beth said good night to everyone. She told them that she didn't feel good and wanted to go to bed early, while the rest of the household started watching a James Bond action movie. As the guns and bombs started going off during the opening battle scene, Beth was able to quietly open the window and slip out to a waiting car parked down the block. She made a clean getaway, like Agent 007 was very much used to.

This group of older friends had plans to make their mark and have Beth home before James Bond finished his mission. Off they drove with beer can tops already popping. Beth asked, "What's planned tonight?"

David, who was driving, said, "Oh, just have a beer and let me get us there." Just after that, a voice came into Beth's head that she had never heard before; but before she had a chance to react to it, the other girl in the car handed her a beer and told her to relax. The car continued, with the clock ticking and a secret mission of their own to accomplish.

They arrived at the Canal Fulton Village Park fifteen minutes down the state highway. Here they turned off the car's headlights and slowly rolled into a spot behind a big bush. David took the last sip of his beer and told everybody to finish up. He got out and opened the trunk. There Beth saw every color of spray can. David said, "Come on; it's time to make our mark." Everyone grabbed two cans and followed David to the back of the cinder block baseball dugouts.

David said, "Let's split up and get both of these done and then get out of here." As Beth was walking to her canvas, she heard the voice again, but the rattling of the ball in the spray paint cans drowned out what the voice was saying. She began shaking her can, and the voice went away. The paint marks of crazy pictures and even crazier sayings were being applied. As the last of the cans were spraying fumes, the kids ran back to the car.

When they were halfway to their car, another car pulled into the park and noticed the frantic activity happening across

Chapter 6: Giving PKs a Bad Name

the driveway and now heading to the big bush. All of a sudden, police sirens started blaring, with synchronized red and blue lights flashing. Everyone scattered, but Beth just ran to the car and waited for her fate.

The police gathered everyone up and called for another squad car. One of the officers then said, "Hope you didn't have any plans for the rest of the night."

David, irritated that he didn't get away with it, said, "Why, yes I do. I have to read my little sister a bedtime story."

The officer quickly and as matter of fact said, "Well, it would be better if your little sister read you that story, because you will be in jail for the night."

With attitude he replied, "What? You're kidding!"

The officer said, "No, I don't kid around about underage drinking and destruction of property."

Everyone was loaded up in the police cruisers and they were taken to the Canal Fulton police station. Each person was allowed to make one phone call. Beth figured that by this time her brother's James Bond movie was over and he would have opened the bedroom door to check on her and would be completely frantic. But right before that final climatic scene when the hero made the world right again, the phone rang and interrupted the movie.

Drew answered, "Hello."

Then Beth asked, "Drew, can you come to the Canal Fulton jail and make my world right again?"

It wasn't that easy though. When Drew got to the jail, he was obviously only Beth's brother, so they had to get in touch with her parents before he was able to take her home. Drew brought the phone number of the conference with him, which was being held at a hotel.

An officer made the phone call, reaching his parents and waking them up. "Pastor Russell," the voice said to him in his groggy state.

Alliance Lake ~ Be Still

"Yes, speaking."

"This is Officer Bratton of the village of Canal Fulton."

"Oh my; is Beth alright?" the pastor worriedly asked. The sound of Beth's mom's gasp was audible.

"Well, sir, she is physically fine, but she has been arrested for underage drinking and destruction of property."

With that, Pastor Russell didn't know what to do next. His emotions were all over the place, and it was probably for the best that he wasn't there, because the police might have needed to lock him up after he lost his temper with Beth.

Officer Bratton continued, "I am going to release her to your son, but you will need to come to the station Monday morning at 9:00 a.m. I have some paperwork for you to go over, and you will be having a hearing with the judge."

Pastor Russell agreed and hung up the phone. He looked at his wife and said, "It's time to get serious with Beth." Mrs. Russell put her face in her hands and began to sob.

The ride back home with Drew was brotherly verbal abuse like she had never heard. Beth just tuned it out and slumped over against the passenger door. When they got home, she ran into her bedroom and locked the door. Normally Pastor Russell would be preaching on Sunday, but he had made arrangements for an elder to give the message this week. Word travelled fast throughout the congregation about Beth's nighttime escapade. By the time the Russell's got back into town, it was 1:30 p.m. The church service had long been over, but a handful of cars were still parked there. He decided to swing in and find out why that was. When he walked in, he was met by the church deacons.

One of those deacons said, "Pastor, we have convened an emergency meeting to give you an ultimatum based on the church bylaws. It says that those in leadership must have control of their family life."

Pastor Russell knew right away that he did not, and tears began to form in his eyes. "Pastor," the deacon continued, "we

Chapter 6: Giving PKs a Bad Name

will give you six months to have it straightened out, or we will ask for your resignation."

Pastor Russell just shook his head in hopeless agreement and reached for a tissue to wipe his eyes. Another deacon spoke up and said, "Pastor, we highly recommend you consider Agape Children's Home."

Pastor Russell was aware of this resource and just couldn't believe how bad things had gotten with Beth. She definitely qualified to be in a home for troubled kids. At this time, Mrs. Russell came in to see her husband, as he was in the middle of wiping more tears.

She approached him and he said calmly, "Honey, I know what we have to do."

Walking in the house, the Russells dropped their things and headed straight to Beth's room. They knew Beth was in there because they heard her music blasting. They tapped on the door, but they got no response. They tapped a little harder, and ended up pounding on the door. At last, the music shut off and Beth opened the door.

Her dad said, "Can we come in?" Beth didn't say anything but just stepped aside.

"Honey," her mom said, "you have been acting in a way that we cannot accept. We are scared about the decisions you are making, and we know they are not godly."

Beth did not offer any response, so Pastor Russell continued. "Your mother and I stopped at the church right before coming here to have a meeting with the church leadership. There is a chance that I will lose my job if you don't straighten up. We are going to have a really hard day tomorrow with the judge at the hearing. I hope you understand that."

Again, no response from Beth. Pastor Russell then calmly turned and left. Beth's mom came to her and gave her a kiss on the head and then left. As soon as the door shut, the music resumed even louder.

The next morning, the three Russells found themselves at the Canal Fulton Justice Center with the other kids and their parents.

The judge addressed all the teens by saying, "You are all lucky you got caught. My punishment today will be welcomed by you if you just realize the danger you put yourselves in when you decided to drink and drive and be reckless."

As everyone stood in silence, the judge said, "I hereby sentence each juvenile to two weeks at the detention center." The parents all looked down and felt the weight of the decision. The teens, however, all looked at each other and their eyes seemed a little brighter than before.

Right before the gavel dropped, Pastor Russell spoke up and said, "Your Honor, may I approach the bench?"

The judge said, "Yes, you may."

Beth's dad said, "Thank you, Your Honor. I am Pastor Gene Russell and my daughter is Beth Russell. I would like to beg you to allow Beth to serve three months in the Agape House instead of two weeks in the juvenile detention center."

Beth finally shouted her first words: "Dad, no!"

The judge pounded the gavel a couple times and said, "Order! Well, Pastor, I make it a policy not to argue with better justice than I dole out." And with that he cracked the gavel down and said, "We're dismissed."

Beth's friends and their family members hurried out of the courtroom to get the instructions for the two-week sentence. Beth just folded her arms and stormed out saying, "This is crap. It is not fair, not fair, not fair!" Pastor Russell took his wife's hand, and they walked out last.

Plans were made quickly with the Agape House. Beth was dropped off that Friday. Mr. and Mrs. Robinson were the lead houseparents and showed the Russells around the complex.

Mrs. Robinson said, "Beth, you will be sharing a room with Joanne. She'll be back as soon as she and Claudia, one of the counselors, are finished getting groceries."

Chapter 6: Giving PKs a Bad Name

Mr. Robinson told them about the daily routine, which included school work, house chores, and quiet time. He described quiet time as sort of like study hall. He laughed and said, "A lot of times you might start off by doing your homework, reading your Bible, or even drawing, but you end up dozing off and taking a nap. And it is okay!" Everyone laughed except Beth. Beth was still acting cold toward her parents for making her do this, but she just wanted to do her time and get back to life with her friends. The Russells walked back to their car, hoping and praying that this would be what Beth needed to change her for the better.

It didn't take long for Beth to decide how to handle this detour at the Agape House. Right away, Beth and Joanne became fast friends. They followed all the rules of the house except one. Twice a week, they were able to help with grocery shopping or other errands. Beth and Joanne knew their biggest challenge and fun wouldn't come from sneaking out for all-nighters, but by sneaking boys in.

It started with the girls searching out the store aisles for guys to literally run into. They would be honest and tell them that they were currently living at the Agape House and would really like them to stop by. At first the girls would cover for each other and took turns meeting the boys in the backyard to exchange kisses and touches. Then the boys decided to park their car a little closer to the backyard and wait until dark. The girls took turns going outside to fool around with the boys in the backseat. Beth and Joanne had a challenge to keep it all straight; they met a lot of guys at the store.

Beth and Joanne never got caught. Beth managed to keep up with her school work and started to see the light at the end of the three-month tunnel. She was going to miss Joanne a lot. She wished that Joanne could actually come home and live with her, but Joanne had a family of her own that was waiting for her. Beth and Joanne had a tight bond. They would stay up all hours of the night talking about everything. They even planned the day after they graduated, when they would get tattoos and pick out an apartment to be roommates. There was no doubt that they would stay close.

Beth was going to be picked up on a Saturday afternoon. She knew that her dad only had three more months before he would get his answer from the church leadership about keeping his pastor position. She definitely didn't want him to lose his job; moving away would make it more difficult for her to see Joanne.

When they arrived, Beth acted much different. She went up to them with an engaging smile and threw her arms out to hug them. Pastor Russell asked Beth, "Are you ready to go home?"

Without hesitation, she answered, "Oh yes! I miss everyone." The happy mom and dad gathered her things, signed some papers, and headed down the road.

Her bed felt good to sleep in that night. The next morning, it was time for Sunday service, and the Russell family had a renewed joy with Beth in the pew with them. As she sat there listening to the message and catching glances of others staring at her from time to time, she thought to herself that she wasn't going to stop having fun, but she was going to be more careful, even if it meant one boy at a time.

The six-month meeting had arrived, and Pastor Russell was there promptly to hear his fate. The head deacon spoke up and said, "Pastor, we cannot fathom the turmoil and hurt your family has gone through, but because you have stayed faithful in finding a solution, we would like you to remain as our pastor."

Pastor Russell did not hesitate to respond, "It would be my pleasure to remain as this church's pastor. Thank you." He left the meeting and went right home to share the news with the family. Everyone was very happy they were staying. Beth was especially happy, for she knew that if she could be away for three months and end up meeting such a great friend and having so much fun, then she could certainly make it to the end of high school

Chapter 6: Giving PKs a Bad Name

when she would have to answer to no one and could have the time of her life. Beth also knew that Joanne would be ready to pick up where they left off with more adventures.

A couple of years passed without a hint of drama from Beth. One day at school during lunch, she was sitting all alone like she preferred, zoned out and flipping through a magazine, when she heard a voice asking, "Can I sit with you?"

Beth looked up, noticed it was Mandy, and said, "Sure, whatever."

"What magazine are you looking at?"

Without looking up, Beth answered, "*Tattoo Arts.*"

Mandy said, "Wow! I would love to get one of those!"

That response got Beth's attention. She looked up and said, "You would really like to get a tattoo?"

"Yeah, for sure I would," Mandy replied.

Beth knew she would still get a tattoo with Joanne, but couldn't help herself and said, "Well, then, you and me have somewhere to go Friday night," as she gave a grin over the top of the magazine.

That Friday evening, Mandy borrowed the car and drove over to Beth's house. Beth got in, closed the car door, and asked, "Are you ready for this?"

Mandy smiled at Beth and replied, "Tell me where to drive!"

They pulled out of the driveway just as the song "You Give Love a Bad Name" by Bon Jovi came on the radio.

Beth said, "Perfect," cranked it up as loud as it would go, and they began to sing their heads off.

Heading into town and driving to the main Friday night cruising area— "the Strip," as the teens liked to call it, Mandy and Beth passed a lot of people they knew and with whom they shared waves back and forth.

Mandy said, "Look. There goes Shon and Ryan in that great red car."

Beth replied, "Wow! That's definitely hot."

Mandy asked, "Shon, Ryan, or the car?"

They looked at each other and screamed, "All three!" and laughed some more. They couldn't stop laughing and talking about everything.

Cars were honking and people were screaming and whistling at each other trying to get noticed. They kept the radio blasting and the windows down. It had been a long time since they both felt this good, and the beginning of the friendship was off to a great start. They quickly realized they really, really needed each other to get through the rest of high school. As they continued to drive toward downtown, the bright lights on both sides of the Strip were beginning to fade. They saw the ominous glow of the city before them. Even though they were still on the same street, there was a different vibe, a dark one. Beth turned off the radio and asked, "Still okay with this?"

"Yes," Mandy said, "and I'll be the first to prove it. Just tell me where I'm going." That made Beth feel better.

They turned onto Cherry Avenue and then onto Fifth Street. The car ride was extremely quiet now, even to the point that both of them were sensing a voice that was telling them, "It's still not too late."

Mandy quickly said, "Tell me we're almost there."

Beth said, "Yeah. There is Orchard Avenue; turn."

Mandy turned and said with a laughing hush, "Don't think this place has any apple or peach trees." They both grunted out a laugh, but caught themselves and became serious again.

Beth pointed and said, "There it is." The flashing neon sign said, "Hidden Dagger Tattoos."

Mandy nervously giggled and pulled into a parking spot. They quickly ran to the front door, opened it, and closed it behind them. They were catching their breath when a voice from farther into the dimly lit shop belted out, "You two better be eighteen."

Chapter 6: Giving PKs a Bad Name

Beth spoke up and said, "Of course we are. Do you want to see our IDs?"

The gruff voice said, "Not really, but by law I have to." Beth and Mandy pulled out the best fake IDs money could buy, and they walked toward the voice in the back. They handed the IDs to a man who did not have many spots left on his arms to tattoo.

Trying to distract him a little, Mandy spoke up and said, "We're not looking for as many as you have." Beth and Mandy laughed, but the tattoo man didn't.

With a stone-like face, he looked up from inspecting the IDs and said with a grin that revealed some missing teeth and showed some dried tobacco juice in his wiry beard, "Boy, eighteen is looking younger and younger every day. Follow me." Mandy reached over and grabbed Beth's hand, and they headed farther back to where there were some padded tables and hair-salon chairs.

He said, "Who's first?"

Mandy slowly stepped forward. Still holding Beth's hand, she said, "Me, I guess."

The tattoo man said, "Great. Tell me what you want and where you want it."

Mandy replied, "I would like the tattoo on my left hip, and I want a falling star with words that say, 'Daddy's little star.'" The tattoo man never asked questions. He just told Mandy to remove one leg from her jeans, use the towels to cover up where she needed to, and lie down on the table. As Mandy did this, he was sketching some ideas on a note pad. She got on the table, still holding Beth's hand as he walked over to them. He showed Mandy the drawings, and she picked out the one she liked best.

She pointed between the two fresh scars that outlined her hip replacement surgery and said, "Between my scars, please." He used a marker to set up the star on her hip, along with a script that he stenciled underneath the star. All was ready and looked great to the girls.

The tattoo man said, "Okay, don't move. I'm going to start." Mandy squeezed Beth's hand even tighter as the noise and the pain began. When it was over, she got off the table and looked in the mirror to admire her body art. By this time, Beth had already taken off her pants and had jumped up on the table.

The tattoo man said, "Okay, you're not as shy. Where do you want your ink?"

Beth just pointed down to her inner thigh area and smiled. The tattoo man finally spilled out a raspy chuckle and said, "This ought to be good. What picture and what do you want it to say?"

Without hesitation, Beth said, "I want a petite rose with the words, 'What you see is what you get.'"

Mandy and the tattoo man looked at each other and began cracking up. Beth interrupted the laugh fest and said, "Would you please start sketching my rose and setting it up on me?"

The tattoo man cleared his throat and said, "Yes, madam."

Beth approved the design and wording, and then he gave the girls the warning to be still. He started the tattoo gun to finish the job. Beth couldn't wait to tell Joanne all about it. After the tattoo man was finished, he held a mirror for her to look it over. Beth gave him a satisfying smile. They received the final instructions on how to care for their new artwork, paid the tattoo man, and left for home.

So glad to be heading for the bright lights of the Strip now, Beth asked, "Do you want to track down a certain hot red car?"

Mandy answered, "I think I have had enough for one night."

"Just kidding," Beth quipped. "We need to let our tattoos heal." Mandy dropped Beth off and then pulled into her own driveway. She shut off the car and let out a big sigh.

Beth and Mandy continued to have lunch together every day and spending time cruising the Strip chasing down boys on the weekends. Beth was doing her best to be careful not to get into

Chapter 6: Giving PKs a Bad Name

trouble, knowing she only had a couple months to go before graduation. The plan after graduation was for Beth, Mandy, and Joanne to get jobs at the local cardboard box company. They would all be roommates and have a blast together. It was going to happen.

Chapter 7:

MUSCLE CARS AND MAKING OUT

(Ryan and Shon—early years: 1985)

FOR A BOY ABOUT to turn sixteen, there is nothing like the thought of getting a driver's license. It all has to do with freedom. Then reality hits, and you realize that you actually have to have something to drive. If you were lucky enough that your family had an extra car for the kids to drive, then you lived with whatever that vehicle was. But if you had to buy something, insure it, and put gas in it, then you'd better be making some good part-time money.

The twins not only insisted on the latter, but they wanted a muscle car—a 1968 Chevy Nova SS. They helped their dad fix and fiddle with cars ever since they could hand him tools. They liked the feeling of restoring something inside and out, of taking something that had been run down, beat up, and even left for the scrap heap, and making it new.

Ryan and Shon had very good part-time jobs across the road from their house, right on the outskirts of town. They were employed at Alliance's little country feed mill. The mill would take grain in from local farmers and process it for different livestock feed. They also had a little handy hardware and pet store for everybody close by. Many of the teenage boys could work there and earn extra money after school and on weekends.

Ryan and Shon thought it was great that they could work and also goof off at the mill with their best friend, Joel. They had a very colorful history of pulling pranks. By the time they were sixteen, Ryan and Shon had bought a little junker car, and then they began to save for the Nova. It was only six months later that a '68 Nova showed up in the local merchant paper. They were excited and didn't want to miss the opportunity. The price was a little more than they had, but they were hoping their dad or even their brother Scott, who was working at the feed mill, too, would contribute.

Around the supper table, the twins could not help themselves. They were talking a thousand miles a second and were drowning each other out by speaking at the same time. Mr. Huff could only pick up bits and pieces of their conversation and finally said, "Boys, one at a time."

Ryan quickly said, "There is a '68 Nova SS for sale, and Shon and I want to buy it. We need to call before someone else gets it."

Their dad took another scoop of mashed potatoes from the bowl, plopped it down on his plate, and said, "Well, let's hurry up and eat, guys!"

The twins started cheering and stuffing their faces. Mr. Huff looked at his wife, smiled, and said, "This will keep them out of trouble for a while."

Mrs. Huff replied, "Yes, until they get finished souping it up." Mr. Huff put a pat of butter on his bread and smiled at the boys as he spread it out.

Mr. Huff called the phone number from the ad. An older sounding man answered the phone and said, "Hello?"

Mr. Huff said, "Do you still have a 1968 Nova for sale?"

Chapter 7: Muscle Cars and Making Out

The voice answered him with a shocked, "Why, yes, I do. I really didn't expect someone would call me about it."

"Well, I have twin boys that would love to come out and see it. When can we come to check it out?"

"How about now?" the old gentleman insisted.

"Let me check with the twins." He took the phone away from his ear and asked Ryan and Shon, "Do you guys want to go right now?"

They didn't have to answer him. The chairs slid back as they ran out to put on their shoes.

Mr. Huff said, "Okay. Don't let anyone see it before us. We'll be there in half an hour. He then looked at Scott, who was still eating, and asked, "Do you want to go, too?"

"No," Scott said. "I got a lot of homework to do." Mr. Huff quickly ran out the door to catch up to the twins.

They pulled in the man's driveway. The garage door was open. Shon asked, "Where is the car?"

"Yeah," Ryan said. "He better not have sold it already."

Their dad simply replied, "Settle down. Let's get out and see what's up."

As they walked to the front door, the old man yelled out from the backyard, "Hey, back here!" The guys looked over a fence and saw the old man, but still no car.

The old man said, "Hi, guys. We have to go to the barn to see the car." When they reached the barn, they noticed a lot of missing boards. The three guests looked at each other and winced. The old man tried to open the door by himself, but it was too warped and it was stuck.

Mr. Huff stepped in and said, "Here, let me try."

With a big tug, the door let loose and flew open, leaving the sides of the barn vibrating. Inside, to their amazement, was the shape of a Nova with a cover on it. The boys thought that this could be a good thing. As the automotive treasure was unveiled, they quickly realized they had a big project to tackle. The car was dimpled with surface rust on the outside, and on the inside the dashboard and the seats had as many wrinkles as the old man standing with them.

As he popped the hood, the man asked, "Well, what do you think?" The guys peered under the hood and knew that the work under there was going to be significant. Mice had built nests throughout the compartment, but the engine was a 396 V8 big block and would eventually do a lot of damage on the Strip.

Mr. Huff asked the old man, "How much are you going to pay us to take this off your hands?"

"Well, now," he chuckled, "I don't think that's how it works. I know it's in rough shape, but I think $1,500 is a fair price." Mr. Huff knew all the work and expense the boys were going to encounter, but he also wanted them to have a project that they would learn a lot on.

The twins pulled their dad aside. Ryan said, "Dad, I know this is a lot of work, but we're up for it. They only made 234 of these 375-horsepower engines. This car will be amazing when we are through. It will be the best on the Strip. Please, Dad. Please!"

Shon piped up and said, "We'll get our school work and chores done, along with paying for all the parts we need for this baby."

Then Mr. Huff turned to the old man and said, "You got yourself a deal if you can haul this jalopy to our place on one of your trailers." They shook hands, and the car was theirs.

The following weekend the car was dropped off at their house and was pushed into the garage. Mr. Huff gave up his parking spot so the twins had a nice place to do their work. Shon and Ryan didn't waste any time; they knew what parts they needed to revive this classic beast.

For the next year, they gathered parts from junkyards and car-part swap meets, along with ordering some special custom

Chapter 7: Muscle Cars and Making Out

parts that would give their car some extra power. This car was completely taken apart. The twins eventually took over the entire garage, taking off every bolt and clip to handle each and every part with cleaning and polishing and upgrading if it would mean more power and speed. The twins knew they had the engine and the power, but wanted to make sure the car's rear axle could handle it, so they put in a beefy 4.10 twelve-bolt rear end gear with a posi-traction package.

The other thing that the twins insisted on was turning their automatic transmission into a manual four-speed. This proved to be the most work, as they swapped in new clutch linkage, a pedal, and a shifter. Next, they turned their attention to completely cleaning and checking every valve and gasket in the engine block, along with rewiring. Then they put some two-inch primary tube headers on to get the deep imposing growl they were looking for.

After putting in hundreds of hours of any free time that Ryan, Shon, or Mr. Huff had, nearly every inch of the '68 Nova's guts and drivetrain was restored or replaced. Now it was time to give this dull-red muscle beauty the paint job she deserved. The car was taken to Byer Body Shop, a local family business, where they were ready to provide their magic touch.

You would not have guessed that some of the best restorations came out of that little shop in Alliance, but when they were finished, the dream of the twins (and of Mr. Huff) was realized. The original factory color was called Matador Red. It was the perfect description, because this car could turn into a raging bull. The larger fifteen-inch jet-black racing tires were set off with a brilliant white Firestone embossed on each. Also, the five-slotted chrome wheels, along with the header pipes, reflected a gleam from underneath. The car was finished in the fall of their senior year, and it was ready to be turned loose. Mr. Huff insisted to be the first driver, even over the twins' protest.

The three of them went out to the old state highway. Mr. Huff stopped in the middle of the road and asked, "Are you guys ready to see what she's got?"

The twins were sitting in the back. Leaning forward, they yelled, "Floor it, Dad!"

With that, Mr. Huff stomped on the pedal, and the smoke and squealing were instantaneous. The car threw everyone back with a jolt, and with a hop the tires left some rubber behind. Mr. Huff eased up just a little to watch the tach and to go through the gears. It had to be only twelve or thirteen seconds before the car was registering over 100 mph. When Mr. Huff saw this, he let his foot completely off the pedal and waited for the car to coast to the next crossroad, where he pulled over. He looked at the twins in the backseat. They were speechless, but they had wide eyes and an even wider smile. "Boys, this car can fly! It's crazy how much power she has."

The twins started to scream, "My turn! My turn!" while Ryan pushed Shon back into the backseat.

Mr. Huff said, "Okay. Each of you can take a turn, but believe me, you guys have to promise me that you will behave and drive responsibly. This thing could get you killed. Do I make myself clear?"

"Yes, sir," the twins said in unison.

Mr. Huff got out and walked around to the passenger side as Ryan slid over. Before Ryan began to drive, Mr. Huff told them both that they can open up the car to go fast, but he did not want them to race it from a start like he did. They agreed, and Ryan drove off. Ryan got the needle to hit the 100 mph mark before he backed it down. He was very proud of this car and knew that it was everything he ever wanted. When Shon took his turn, he got the car up to 90 mph in a hurry and decided that was plenty for him.

Ryan said, "Why not take it to a hundred, bro?"

Mr. Huff quickly said, "Hey, he knows what she'll do."

Chapter 7: Muscle Cars and Making Out

Shon then replied, "Exactly. That's good enough for me right now. Let's practice a little more and be ready for the Strip."

Ryan punched him on the leg and with a dirty look said, "Shon! Why did you say . . . ?"

Their dad interrupted, and with his eyebrows to the top of his forehead he said "Boys, I get it. But you better be sure of what you do with this car. It can get you in trouble in a lot of different ways fast!"

The twins looked at their dad and chuckled. Ryan said, "Dad, we promise to be safe."

Shon then said, "For sure."

Their dad said, "Let me take over and drive home. It will be better that way with your mom." Everyone laughed as they made the final driver change and headed back to Alliance.

The twins were extremely proud of that car. Even though they didn't include Scott much with the restoration, Scott enjoyed seeing them have the best road machine around. The car did keep them out of trouble for a while, but now that it was souped up, it was time to worry about Mrs. Huff's half of the equation.

Cruising the Strip was always a good time. Occasionally, when the twins would let Scott go with them, he enjoyed the looks people gave on the sides of the road as they roared by. It did not matter what car would try and drag race them. Ryan was the best driver, and he never backed down. He knew the Strip and the timing of the lights better than anyone else. There were many other muscle cars that tried to beat him—a Road Runner, Barracuda, Cougar, Chevelle, and many others. Also, the newer cars, like a Firebird, Trans Am, and Camaro, tried to outrace him off the line, but could never keep up.

After a long winter that year, spring came in and warmed everything up quickly. It was a Friday night and all the kids knew where to be—on the Strip. Ryan and Shon were sitting in their usual parking spot at Burgertown enjoying the looks and the people stopping by to chat, when in from the Strip pulled a 1969 Boss 429 Mustang. Everyone immediately followed the car like zombies to the place it had parked.

Ryan and Shon stood there alone for a moment and then walked over to see the new arrival. The car's color was a deep-dark green that almost looked black until the light would hit it just right. An older guy wearing aviator sunglasses and having white hair and a chiseled chin rolled the window down and said, "Hi. My name is Paul; I hear someone around here has a pretty fast car."

Ryan quickly spoke up and said, "Yes. That would be us. The Nova over there. Where are you from?"

Paul answered, "Well, I'm originally from up the road in the Cleveland area, but now I live many places. I am back visiting my elderly parents, and wanted to get my baby out for a little workout." Then with a grin he asked, "Any chance you want to lose tonight?" That did it!

The teenagers' male hormones kicked in, and Ryan said, "Not a chance, old man. Let's go." And with that, the man rolled the window up. The twins knew that no one came to their Strip and showed them up.

They made a beeline for the '68 Nova SS and turned the key to awaken the beast. As they slowly rumbled and rolled out of the parking lot, people were jumping in their cars and getting down the road to the spots where they knew the drag race would be. There was a section of the Strip that had three stop lights, making a perfect raceway. The first light was for starting, the middle light was for getting up to quick speed, and then by the last light the driver should be slowing down before they went up the hill and were exposed to more attention from another area of businesses.

Shon rolled the window down and said to the man in the Mustang, "We start here on the next green and go for two more lights to see who wins." The mysterious man nodded his head

Chapter 7: Muscle Cars and Making Out

and revved his engine. The two muscle cars eked closer and closer to the crosswalk starting line. Ryan readied himself as he saw the light in the opposite direction turn yellow.

The light turned green, and Ryan stomped down on the gas pedal. Both cars squealed, smoked, and took off. Ryan knew right away he got the best of the Mustang at the start (a little home drag-strip advantage). He hit the red line on the tachometer and threw it into second gear. Moments later, as he approached the second light, he jammed it into third gear. The engine was revving and he was feeling good. Shon looked back and then ahead and yelled to Ryan, "You got him, you got him!"

Before Shon looked back to check again, the Mustang pulled beside him, hesitated, and then left him behind. By the third light, the Mustang was in front of the Nova, no problem. Instead of slowing down, the Mustang continued his top-end speed up the rolling hill.

Ryan said, "He better shut it down or else . . ."

Before Ryan finished his thought, he and Shon saw the red and blue flashing lights. Shon started laughing and said, "He might have won, but that ticket is going to cost him big bucks."

"Yes," Ryan agreed, as they continued to laugh. As they pulled up slowly past the police officer writing out a ticket, they were pointing and laughing. Paul had his sunglasses off by this time, and with one of his brilliant blue eyes, he winked and waved. The twins' jaws flew opened as they looked at each other and said in unison as only twins can, "That was Paul Newman!"

They quickly turned around, but by the time they looped around and began to head in the same direction, they saw the classic Ford Mustang taillights disappearing over the horizon. They were sad they lost, but it was to Paul Newman and his epic muscle car. They knew their place on the Strip was still secure. Ryan said, "Come on. Let's head back and see if there are any girls cruising tonight."

It didn't take long before that red-hot Nova was parked in its spot at Burgertown once again, and kids were gathered around to hear the story of the race. When they heard it was with Paul Newman, the twins became even more of a legend on the Strip. It was getting close to 11:00 p.m. now, and the cars and crowds were beginning to thin out fast. About the time the twins were ready to call it a night, a car rolled into the spot right next to them. Shon and Ryan looked over to see Mandy and Beth smiling at them. Ryan and Shon smiled back and then turned to each other. Ryan whispered, "Are you ready to find a tattoo?"

Shon quickly replied, "Do we look alike?" He then said to Mandy in the driver's seat, "We need to head for home, but can you girls follow us for a little stop-off before we get there?"

The girls were smiling and whispering to each other. Soon Beth replied with a giggle, "Lead the way."

The Nova started with a roar. Ryan looked at them and said, "Try and keep up." They headed back toward Alliance and turned onto an abandoned oil-well lane that was right off the road and secluded behind a grove of trees. They quickly shut off the car's engine and turned off the lights. The girls pulled in next, and as they swung in, Mandy hit the lights off and parked next to them. Ryan then said to Shon, "Go to their car and send Beth over."

Deep down Shon was relieved that Ryan made the decision for him. Of the twins, Ryan was definitely known to be wilder, and from what everyone knew, Beth would match him pretty well. Shon knocked on Beth's window and motioned for her to go over to Ryan. Her door opened and she told Mandy, "Have fun!" Then she ran and jumped into the Nova.

Shon and Mandy sat there quietly watching the commotion going on over at the other car, and then Shon said, "How about a little music?"

Mandy quickly answered, "Yes," and turned a couple of knobs. On came a pretty good make-out song, "The Next Time I Fall" by Peter Cetera and Amy Grant.

Chapter 7: Muscle Cars and Making Out

Shon looked at Mandy and said, "Perfect timing," and went in for a kiss.

After she accepted his initial offer, she responded with one of her own. After that, no one could really tell who started the kiss, but neither one of them wanted to be the one to end it. As the windows began to steam up, Mandy all of a sudden felt her neck and chest start to get chilly. Without her even realizing it, Shon already had a couple buttons of her blouse undone. Mandy quickly separated herself and said, "I'm sorry Shon, but, but . . ." and then started to cry. She quickly apologized to Shon.

Shon said, "Mandy, I was having a good time with you before I did that. I'm sorry. Are you okay?"

She said, "Yeah, but I've been going through a lot of stuff with the divorce of my parents. I am just not ready for anything else major right now." In many ways, Shon knew exactly what she was talking about, and he was relieved that she listened to herself.

He then asked her, "Do you like to sing at the top of your lungs in your car?"

Mandy said, "Of course. I'm the best!"

Shon laughed and said, "Let me be the judge of that."

She turned the station and found some rockin' tunes. For the next half hour, Shon and Mandy screamed songs ranging from AC/DC to Lover Boy and Def Leopard to Van Halen. They had a great time. They finally wiped some fog off the window and noticed the Nova rockin' out on its own. Mandy and Shon looked at each other, and Shon quickly said with a laugh, "Well, let's sing another."

Finally, Beth knocked on Mandy's car and said, "Take me home before I turn into a pumpkin."

Shon opened the door and said, "I think if the princess had a glass slipper in that car, it would've been shattered in many pieces."

Beth just smiled and said, "What you see is what you get." She closed the door and they took off back to town.

Shon got back to the car and Ryan said, "Bro, the tattoo was just the start. It was crazy. As she was getting in the front seat, I told her to follow me, and I jumped over the driver's seat into the back.

"I then said, 'Just think—when I went to your dad's church, I thought you had cooties.'

"She said, 'I hope you still don't think I have cooties.'

"I almost started hyperventilating, but said, 'I doubt you do, but let me check for myself and make sure.'"

Shon said, "And then? And then?"

Ryan just smiled and started the car. "It was quite a night. Let's go home."

Shon continued looking over at Ryan as they headed down the road to their driveway on the outskirts of town with a much quieter rumble. "Quite a night, alright," Shon said. "Quite a night."

Chapter 8:

THE PLAN

(Joel with Ryan and Shon—early years: 1979)

JOEL BRUNNER TRIED TO be secretive as he dialed the phone frantically down in the dark basement, but it was hard waiting for the phone's rotary dial to finish before he could spin the next number. All the while, he was wishing his parents wouldn't be the last ones in the world without a push-button phone, microwave oven, or color TV. Finally, the last number was dialed, and then—a busy signal. It was one of those annoying tones like a fire alarm in your ear to tell the people calling that they are just going to have to wait.

Making a phone call back in the late 70s and trying to reach the actual person you wanted to talk to was not for the faint of heart. With no instant voice mail or texting, you had to be strategic to set up phone calls to someone if you wanted the odds to favor your success. Joel had told Ryan and Shon at school that he would call them after he finished watching Get Smart, doing his homework, and before supper. That was a pretty narrow window, because as far as he knew, all families ate supper at 5:00 p.m.

when the dads got home. That is why he was frantic when the phone was busy. Joel dialed again (from the start, because there was no redial). It was still busy. He started dialing again, feeling a callus starting to take root on his index finger.

"Darn it," Joel said in a hush.

He thought that the whole plan was in jeopardy. Then he had an idea to change his luck. Joel went outside, ran around the house three times, and then called again. Sometimes even with a well-constructed plan, a little of the black arts was in order. Out of breath and with his finger a lot shakier, Joel dialed the twins' number. Now there were only five minutes before his father would pull into the driveway, and then it was all about the mashed potatoes, roast beef, and green beans. Fortunately, Joel heard that sweet sound of the telephone ringing. Shon picked up and asked, "Is that you, Joel?"

Joel said, "Yeah. I am about ready to have supper. Meet me at the playground to finalize the plan. Bring Ryan and Scott."

Shon immediately said, "No way. Scott will screw something up. We aren't letting him in on this one."

"Okay, fine," Joel said. "I guess the three of us can do this."

Just at that time, someone from Joel's house picked up the phone upstairs, and in unison, Shon and Joel very quietly had the secret agent's touch to hang up the phone without a trace. Joel bolted upstairs and offered to set the table as he blended in with the commotion of the kitchen. Joel looked in the refrigerator for milk, but the carton was nearly empty. Before he could say anything, his mom anticipated his very question and said, "Go out in the garage to get more from the milk box. The milkman should have been here today."

As Joel pulled the cartons out of the small metal box, his dad pulled into his space and said, "How's my champ doing? Anything new happening in sixth grade?"

Joel thought, *Not yet*, but said, "Oh, Dad, nothing exciting ever happens at that place."

Chapter 8: The Plan

"Come on, let me help you with that milk and let's go in and wash up for supper."

The Brunner family took their usual seats. Steam wafted up from all the dishes as everyone looked at Dad to make the next move. He was the quarterback at the table. One of two things was going to happen next. Either Dad would nod to Joel's little sister to say her prayer, followed by Joel, Joel's older brother, his mom, and finally his dad; or sometimes their dad would just start in and say a prayer for everyone. This time, the anticipated wait was over, and Joel's dad began to pray for the meal by saying, "Dear Lord, thank you for this food. Thank you for the hands that prepared this food. Be with each one of us as we live for you. Please forgive us when we fall short with our words and actions. Thank you for your grace. In Jesus's name, Amen."

Joel loved when his dad said the prayer. He always said the perfect thing. Joel was especially glad that his dad had prayed this time, because Joel knew he was going to need forgiveness after tonight. Joel ate faster than normal. Usually it took as long as his shoveling, chewing, and milk drinking allowed, but today he saved a step and just let the milk wash the food down. His plate was clean and time was wasting, so with one motion Joel pushed back the chair and accidentally burped out, "Got to go meet the guys for a game of football at the paarrrrrrrk."

The Brunner family busted out laughing, except for Joel's mom, who said, "Say 'Excuse me.'"

Holding his stomach after a little indigestion, Joel said, "Excuse me," and ran out the door. He jumped on his bike (it used to be his brother's bike—a metallic blue Schwinn Stingray chopper bike with a banana seat and gear shift on the middle bar), peddled down the road three blocks, and turned onto Basic Park Drive.

Joel always got a chuckle from the name of their park. He thought to himself, *Someone named it Basic Park. Really?* There was no one famous in the history of the town to deserve to name the park after? Wow! That was sad. So what we have was your ho-hum, run-of-the-mill, average-at-best-place-to-let-your-kids-run-off-some-energy type of park, basically. So aptly named, Basic Park.

Joel scanned the playground area as he pulled up to the shelter house. He noticed the slide. It was a sheet of military-strength aluminum, polished by the rumps of toddlers (and sometimes parents) who got whisked to the bottom in no time flat. This highly polished metal sears your hands and legs from the intense sun that has been cooking it all afternoon. And what happened when you got to the bottom? Well, only the most jolting way to get off a ride. Before you could get your feet under you, gravity harshly threw you on the hard ground with a thud. As you picked yourself up and waved away the dust cloud, you realized that you absolutely wanted to do that again!

There was also the merry-go-round. This was one of the best pieces of playground equipment ever thought of. You could get spun around so fast that you either threw up on yourself or on the person behind you. The other thing you had to manage was how you got off the ride if it was still spinning at a high rate of speed. You had to be part cartoon character and part Evel Knievel stunt performer.

The part that was a cartoon character had to jump off the merry-go-round while your legs were running in midair, like Wile E. Coyote before he fell into the canyon. This head start in midair provided you a way to literally hit the ground running. The part that was Evel Knievel had to work up the courage to jump off, unless you were thrown off involuntarily.

If the rider didn't land on his feet, he would hit the ground hard, but hitting the clay-packed ground may have been the best thing that could have happened. As the merry-go-round was brought up to speed by kids running around before they

Chapter 8: The Plan

jumped on, a little trench was created. And then there was always that one bully kid who stood in the trench and slapped the bars and made it go around faster and faster until everyone could feel the G-forces on his body. For those who tried to jump or were thrown off, they faced the real possibility of hitting the trench and ricocheting under the bottom of the rotating monster, which ate up skin and bones without thinking twice. What a ride!

But now it was time for Joel to get on with other things. He parked his bike and looked around the shelter to make sure no one else was there. As he sat on the picnic table, he saw the twins approaching. They parked their bikes and ran to the table to find out what Joel had on his mind.

Shon said, "Joel, what is so important that it couldn't wait until . . . ?"

Joel interrupted him before he could finish his question. He said, "Listen, we are in sixth grade. This is our last grade in this building. Next year we start all over at the junior-high building." (It was the time when kids from all over the district got placed together and started their journey toward high school.) Joel continued simply and as a matter of fact: "Guys, I want to pull the biggest prank in school history."

The twins looked at him as if frozen, without even a blink. Then, as if someone snapped his fingers to free them from a hypnotic state, they in unison turned their heads toward each other. Joel noticed that their stoic faces began to show signs of life. Their upper lips began to rise from the middle, under the nose, creating a very giddy point. At the same time, as only twins can do, they said, "We're in."

Joel told them, "Good, because we're going to begin the epic plan in less than two hours." Ryan and Shon moved in closer, as if to hear the quarterback in the huddle give the next play. Wishing there was a Cone of Silence like *Get Smart* had in the secret-agent world of CONTROL, Joel said quietly, "Guys, the first thing we have to do is stay out all night. To accomplish this, we have to go out on a limb and tell a little story to our parents."

Shon looked at Joel and rolled his eyes and asked, "You mean lie?"

"Yeah, okay; but believe me, it's going to be worth it! You guys go home and tell your mom that you are staying at my house, and I will go home and tell my mom that I am staying at yours. Grab a few snacks and meet here in two hours."

Ryan interrupted and said, "Please tell us the *what* and the *how*."

"Okay, okay," Joel said. "We are going to stack the entire gym with desks from all the rooms in the school to create a pyramid. What do you think?"

Shon didn't have to say anything. He just put his flattened hand into the middle of the huddle. Ryan's hand followed, and Joel's hand was third. Just because it was an extra great event on which they were embarking, Shon thrust his second hand on top of Joel's, and they went around again. With all their hands stacked, Joel knew it was his place, as the quarterback, to say something to break the huddle.

He said, "Listen. Janitor Jim will be finished up and ready to head home in about two hours or less. We have to sneak in before he locks the doors. Take care of what you need to at home and meet back here at 6:45. Is everyone ready for the night of their lives? All for one and one for all." Joel wished he had said something better at the end, but if it was good enough for the Three Musketeers, then it was good enough for them. The boys threw their hands down and left the scene of the conspiracy.

Joel peddled like mad toward the house. Racing in the driveway, he came within feet of crashing into the side of the car, when he slammed the peddles in reverse, turned the handlebars, and leaned over at the same time. Joel laid the perfect skid of

Chapter 8: The Plan

rubber down with his stop. He hit the kickstand and ran into the house. Then he yelled, "Mom, where are you?"

A voice from the basement said, "Down here doing laundry."

Joel collected himself and bounded down the old creaky basement steps. It sounded and felt like a board would crack and the unlucky person would be stuck dangling amid the spider webs that were at home in the dark dank rafters. At the bottom of the stairs, Joel said, "Mom. I am going to Ryan and Shon's to sleep over tonight."

She said, "Uh, what, mister?"

Just then, Joel knew he had made a serious mistake. He told his mom what he wanted to do instead of asking for permission. Did the "quarterback" just blow the play? Quickly, Joel said, "What I meant was, 'Is it okay if I stay overnight at the twins' house tonight?'"

In the middle of her giant pile of clothes that she was folding, she looked up and said, "Yes, it will be fine; just be home by 10:00 a.m. so you can help Dad with chores and then go to Scouts."

"Oh yes, of course. Thanks, Mom." And with that he flew up the stairs, skipping every other step, and running out the door with a slam. "Whew! That was close," Joel said as he headed for his bike. He knew he had a little time, so he decided to ride to AJ's, a little carryout store. Joel wanted to get a few snacks to take on the overnight mission. AJ's was one of those off-the-side-of-the-road places where someone could get a deli sandwich made while they waited or a couple dozen night crawlers for a fishing trip. And if anyone wanted some packaged dry snacks like Cracker Jacks or a box of cookies, they better accept that it came with a layer of dust, because the housekeeper hadn't visited for a very long time.

Joel went in picked up some peanut butter crackers and a pack of baseball cards. He couldn't help himself. He had to get a pack. Joel knew he would eventually get Ricky Henderson. It seemed like all his friends had a Ricky Henderson card except him, and he didn't want to give up what they would ask for to get theirs. Joel put the two things on the counter and waited for the lady to punch the price into the cash register. Hearing the paddles and dials banging around and the bells going off, someone would think Joel hit the jackpot, but unfortunately, the sounds resulted in him owing fifty-five cents.

Joel put his supplies in his jacket and went outside. He hopped on his bike and pedaled toward Basic Park. He did not have a lot of time now.

In the middle of the ride, a voice popped into his mind all of a sudden. *Was it God?* he wondered. It was unexplainable and unprovoked. He was startled by the inner thought he was having, as if the thought wanted to have a conversation. Instead of freaking out, Joel put his head down and peddled faster.

In no time, he turned the last corner and entered the park and made it back to the shelter. He was the first one there, so he jumped off the bike and strolled to the shelter house. As he walked, Joel put his hands into his jacket pockets, thinking he was the coolest thing around. Then his hand felt that pack of baseball cards. Joel grabbed it out of his pocket and screamed like his little sister. He wondered if today was the day he would get the card that he had been dying for.

Joel jumped onto the picnic table and peeled off the plastic wrapper. Immediately he flung the nasty pink piece of pressed flavored cardboard that some people refer to as bubblegum as far as he could. Joel thought to himself that he had chewed a lot of bubblegum in the past, and he wouldn't let a good sugar rush go without a fight, but the sugar from that bubblegum was definitely not worth the flavor that spoiled your whole mouth.

Also, that so-called bubblegum was the worst when it came to blowing a bubble. Your tongue would go through it half the time, and the other half of the time you would blow a pen-

Chapter 8: The Plan

ny-sized bubble. Whoa! Don't even think about getting into a bubble-blowing contest with anything of real value on the line if you put that garbage in your mouth. Joel knew he would put his entire piggy bank on the person with Hubba Bubba, Bubble Yum, or Bazooka for that matter.

The cards…the cards . . .

Joel began talking to himself, "What did I get? I got him already, got him too, got him, and him. Oh good, a Nolan Ryan and another Reggie Jackson. I hate the Yankees; I can use it for trades. Cool, got a George Brett and finally . . . a Steve Garvey. I have so many Steve Garveys, and so do my friends. I think he had a deal with the Topps baseball card company. Oh well, maybe next time I will get my Ricky Henderson. I won't give up."

Joel looked up and noticed the twins on their bikes closing fast and said, "Are you guys ready to make history?"

"We sure are," they said in unison.

"Any problems with sleeping over at my house tonight?" Joel asked, and then broke out in laughter. The twins followed his lead with snickers of their own, and they all road off toward the grade school.

Chapter 9:

THE PRANK

(Joel with Ryan and Shon—early years: 1979 continued)

ONCE THE BOYS GOT a block away, Joel veered onto the cemetery drive near the school. He said, "Come on, guys; let's ditch the bikes in the bushes at the back of the cemetery. It's time to go to work."

As they walked toward the school and by the gravestones, Joel hoped it was not a bad omen at the start of their mission. These people died of various things, he thought, and he hoped they don't get caught, because Joel knew he would die at the hands of his father.

Shon said, "Hurry, guys; this place freaks me out."

Ryan replied, "What do you mean? These people aren't going to be any trouble," and he began to laugh.

The boys crossed the road and made a beeline to the playground. From there they saw Janitor Jim's beat up Chevy pickup. Joel knew that his plan still had a chance. Now in a whisper, he said to Shon, "Go to the far side of the school, by the art room. When you see Janitor Jim in that area of the school, run back toward us. When Ryan and I see you, we will meet at the back gym door to go in."

As Shon ran off, Joel was hoping that the door would still be unlocked. He knew that some old guys played basketball after work on Fridays, and Janitor Jim may not lock the door until the end. It seemed like it took forever, but then they saw Shon crouched down and running along the side of the building. Ryan and Joel took off and met Shon at the back gym door, all out of breath. As Joel put his hand on the door and his thumb on the latch, he wanted to be as quiet as possible.

Ryan said with a frantic hush, "Hurry, you doofus. Open it!"

"I'm trying," Joel said with his own frantic hush. His thumb would not budge the latch. "It's locked!"

As soon as he said that, he got shoved aside by Ryan. "Let me try," Ryan said, followed by, "Oh no. Now what?"

Then Shon said in defeat, "Time to go home."

The boys all looked at each other, and Joel said, "Not yet. Let's try the front door." Joel knew the twins thought he was crazy, but he quickly said, "If Janitor Jim is still by the art room, then we have a chance at the front door. If it's locked, then we will head for home. Come on. Follow me."

Joel showed the very confidence of one of those generals in a WWII movie that played on his snow-filled black-and-white TV set on that obscure UHF channel 43. They hurried along the perimeter of the building and past the art windows, and sure enough, Janitor Jim was still working on a massive paint spill. What a perfect diversion, Joel thought. He wished he would have thought of that as part of the plan.

There were tall bushes all along the front of the school. The three boys dove into the bushes to catch their breaths. In single file, they made their way undercover to the front door entrance. Joel, still out of breath, said, "Let's make sure no cars are coming before we pop out of the bushes and try the door." Looking both ways and listening very intently, he didn't sense a thing, so off he

Chapter 9: The Prank

went. Grabbing the door handle and latch, Joel pressed down, and with a click that the boys thought echoed loudly enough to wake the dead across the street, the door could now be opened wide. The boys all shuffled in and headed down the back hall to the gym, where they could easily hide.

Joel quietly opened the gym door, and they went in. He let go of the door and turned to catch up with the twins, and like a grenade going off in his head, he realized the big old gym door was about ready to slam with an explosion of noise. At the last second, Joel dove back to the door and threw his hand in the remaining crack. He was ready for the shooting pain to set in, but luckily there was none.

Wow! Joel thought to himself. *That was close. Got all this way just to break my fingers or hand and scream out in pain. We would have surely been caught.* Joel closed the door with all the precision of a bomb specialist doing his job.

He caught up to the twins and whispered, "Let's hide on the stage behind the curtain where they keep all the extra mats."

They all did their best jump slide and rolled right under the closed curtain, settling in behind the big stack of mats. The only light that illuminated anything was a dimly lit emergency exit sign on the opposite side of the stage.

Shon whispered, "Now what?"

"What do you mean?" Joel said, with an irritated whisper.

"Let's go and do something," he replied.

"We have to wait for Janitor Jim to leave. Did you think he was going to help us?" Joel asked.

"Okay. I guess I'm just a little nervous and want to get this over with," Shon let out.

"Hey," Joel said, "remember—we will be a part of school history. That will definitely be worth the wait. Just sit back; it won't be long."

It wasn't long after the boys all settled down and settled into their own quiet thoughts that Joel heard that voice again. *From*

God? he wondered. Then, before he gave it another thought, Joel started hearing popping sounds. A few would go off, then nothing, and then a few more. Joel whispered to the twins, "Janitor Jim is turning off the lights. Soon this school will be ours." The boys all sprouted a huge smile. There was a lull of any noise, and then they heard a few more pops with a major door slam.

A few minutes passed by with no additional sounds, so Joel told the twins, "Stay put while I check and see if the coast is clear." He went to the gym door and opened the latch without a noise. Looking through the crack of the door and down the hallway, he noticed it was every bit as dark as the gym, with the same red glow from the exit signs.

Joel crept down the hall and rounded the corner. He had to go down the kindergarten hallway before he could see if Janitor Jim had indeed left. Joel continued to stay low and move real slow. Joel finally got to the ideal spot and slowly raised his head to see . . . nothing! The truck was gone. Joel turned and tore off like a wild animal busting through the door. Noise echoed from everywhere: from Joel, the door slamming, and then from the twins jumping off the stage and letting out their pent-up feelings.

Joel looked at the twins and said, "Let's get the table cart that is kept down by the art room." They hustled down the hall, turned the corner, and proceeded down the even longer hall to the end, where the art room was. There the boys found the cart and pushed it into the first classroom next to the art room.

They began to fill up the cart with desks. They managed to get eight desks on the long cart. After a quick calculation in his head, Joel knew it would take them three trips to wipe out this room, and most rooms for that matter. The boys pushed the cart back to the gym and began designing the "great pyramid of desks." They began to set the bottom/base row. After emptying two whole classrooms, the base row was completed. It was a good start, but they had a long way to go to complete their great wonder of the school world.

Chapter 9: The Prank

As they took the cart up and down each hallway and helped themselves to the "pyramid bricks," Joel had known for a while that they would have to go to the second floor for more desks, but he didn't want to break that detail to the twins quite yet. They finished up the last classroom, and were two desks short of completing the fourth row.

The boys sat back to admire their work. "Time for a break," Joel announced like the boss of a shop. Then he said, "We're only halfway done."

The twins said, "Oh, really? There are no more desks around here."

Joel replied, "It's time to go to the second floor. We have to go higher and finish this thing right. We'll start to bring the pyramid in, so we won't need quite as many desks, but I have a plan to make it easy on us. Follow me."

Feeling a second wind, they stormed out the gym doors and Joel led the way up the stairs to the second floor. "Guys," Joel said, "let's find three tables. We are going to use them as ramps."

The twins let out an, "Alright!" and went to work. In no time, they found their tables and brought them folded up to the edge of the steps.

Joel said, "We have to carry two down to the lower stairs first." The boys laid them down to where they became a perfect ramp for their plan. Next, they laid the other table on the upper stairs. It was a little short, but workable. Joel said, "Let's go into a room and carry the desks to the edge of the stairs."

This part of the plan came together better than the first. In no time, they had twenty-five desks ready. Just like a fire brigade, Ryan stood at the top, Joel was in the middle, and Shon stood at the bottom with the cart. Ryan slid the desk down to Joel, who caught it, carried it to the top of the bottom flight, and put it down for the next slide. The extra distance meant extra speed, which Joel didn't factor (math and science weren't his best subjects). The desk headed right for Shon at a faster clip than expected, but he lunged out of the way just in time. He hit the floor, his ball cap flew off, and he bit down on his lip. He immediately tasted blood. The desk hit the cart with a crash!

Shon yelled, "That was too close!" Ryan and Joel did not see what happened, but rushed down to see if there was any damage to the desk, and of course, to Shon.

Shon picked up his cap and started walking away. Joel asked, "Are you okay?"

"Yeah, but I bit my lip," he replied. "I have to get a cold drink from the water fountain. Give me a minute."

As he left, Joel said, "Let me be at the bottom."

Shon quickly answered, "Sounds good to me."

Joel thought it was only right that the captain of this mission should put himself in the greatest risk when the outcome was on the line. The boys got to their posts and the next desk was ready to come down toward Joel. Instead of letting it get a full head of steam, he quickly leapt up four or five stairs to guide it down to the bottom. It worked perfectly, and Joel loaded it onto the cart. They had the system worked out now, and soon six more desks were ready to be taken to the gym.

The boys had cleared out a total of four rooms upstairs, and all of the desks were down in the gym awaiting the final touches of the pyramid build. This final part was going to be the most time consuming, and this is where they had to be most careful. One by one, the boys hoisted each desk up to each level and carefully walked over and lifted them into place. They worked as a precision team, making sure the building blocks were locked in place. Hours went by, but the end was in sight.

Ryan suddenly stopped and said, "That's all we can do. It's getting too hard. I don't want to have an accident and ruin it. It looks super cool." Shon wiped the sweat from his forehead and nodded in full agreement.

Joel looked at them both and said, "We only have three more desks to do. We're not going anywhere tonight. Let's take

Chapter 9: The Prank

another break and do the last three before we finish." Hoping that was a convincing enough pep talk, the twins let out a loud deep breath and collapsed on the stage. Joel joined them on stage and began to admire their work under the red glow of three emergency exit signs.

Then, Joel popped up and said, "Guys, we have to check out the teachers' lounge and the girls' restroom."

"You know it!" exclaimed Ryan. Shon quickly agreed.

They jumped off the stage and headed to the teachers' lounge. As they approached the door, Joel felt like an explorer heading into a mysterious tomb with all sorts of hidden treasures and secrets inside. They were about to expose them, but unfortunately they wouldn't be able to tell anyone. *Rats*, he thought. *That's not fair.*

Turning the knob, he opened the door and immediately smelled the remnants of cigarette smoke. "Wow!" Joel said. "Must have been quite a smoke-out a few hours ago!"

Ryan said, "Oh, yeah. I heard that even Mr. George (the health teacher) comes in here a lot to puff away." It was pretty dark, but Joel could see a flashlight next to the refrigerator.

"Guys, check this out," he said, and with a click of the flashlight the room was further revealed. There were a couple of tables and some couches—not exactly what Joel would call hidden treasures. He thought maybe the good stuff was in the cabinets. Opening each one, he saw what amounted to school and cafeteria supplies. What a complete disappointment. It was much cooler in his head. He said to the guys, "No big deal here."

Then Shon said, "Race you to the girls' restroom; now that's where there are some real secrets!" The boys all took off with a flash.

Rounding the corner, Joel got to the door first. Again, he turned on the flashlight and gazed at this alien environment. His mind was racing with questions and thoughts: *How could this place be so different? We basically do the same things in the* restroom, don't we? Look at that mirror; it is so big. I'm not even sure if our restroom had a mirror. It probably did, but I couldn't tell you where it was. Theirs stretches the whole way across two walls, and under it was a countertop that could pass for another cafeteria table. I know. Maybe at lunch they get up from the table in pairs to go to the restroom so they can get a better lunch to eat! It's crazy.

In the dimly lit restroom, Ryan said, "Look, guys. They have a vending machine on the wall. Wow, the girls are so lucky!"

Shon said, "Yeah. It probably has gumballs or sweet tarts in it." Without hesitating, Shon dug in his pocket for a dime and turned the handle. Out popped something shaped like a marker wrapped in plastic.

Joel said, "That is definitely not candy. It makes no sense. Ditch it." Shon threw it like a dart toward the wastebasket and made it in.

Next, Joel shined the light on the actual stalls. He knew girls wouldn't have a trough to pee in with six of their closest buddies. Instead, there was more privacy, which he thought was quite a good concept; but what were those mailboxes attached to the inside of the stalls?

Again the questions and thoughts flooded in his head: *Do girls actually have a private place to write letters to their friends, and some restroom mail person sorts and secretly makes the deliveries for them? Wow, that is totally unfair. I am definitely going to expose this somehow, some way. But how? I know. I will write a letter from here and mail it to the office, saying that it would be a good idea if some mailboxes were put in the boys' restrooms. You never know when you might want to put in an anonymous suggestion or letter to the school newspaper.*

So with all the confidence in the world, Joel threw open the mailbox lid to grab the paper and pen that he was sure were at the bottom; but to his horror, there were bandages that someone used who must have been mortally wounded. He freaked out and screamed, "What is happening in here?"

Chapter 9: The Prank

Joel said to the guys, "Come on. Let's get out of here. This place is weirder then I thought. It's the boys who always come in from recess with bloody knees and elbows. The girls just sit around talking. Let's get back to the gym."

Back in the gym, Joel decided it was time to get back in gear and finish the pyramid. He hopped up on the first level, went to the second level, then the third, and finally the fourth. He told the guys he was ready for them to hand up the last three desks. The twins worked carefully and steadily until they had some extra desks in place to get the last three up.

The first went up with no problem. The second was in place; good. Finally the pyramid's cap desk was in place, and wow, it was quite a sight! They all retreated very carefully off the amazing structure. Back on the stage, where it felt safe again, the boys collapsed. *Better us then the pyramid*, Joel thought.

Exhausted and tired, Ryan said with a sleepy slur, "I'm gonna clooz my eyes fur a min-i-ant." They were all out . . .

Joel woke himself up rolling over on the mat, noticing some dim morning daylight coming through the upper windows. He yelled out, "Guys! Wake up! We've got to get out of here. It's morning!"

In a frantic scene like from the Dukes of Hazzard with *Boss Hog* closing in, they quickly raced out of the gym to the back hallway and to the back entrance of the school. Joel opened the door and all three of the boys ran into the bushes for a quick scan of their surroundings. Joel said, "Let's head to the back tree line and follow it to the next road over, and then backtrack to the cemetery to get our bikes."

"Sounds good," Shon said, with his heart pounding.

Following the course, they made it back to where they ditched the bikes. As the boys were about to go their separate ways, Joel spoke up and said, "Hey guys, we go to school Monday just like a regular day, and this is our secret—forever." They all nodded in agreement, and with a smirk on their faces, the twins road off to their house and Joel headed back to his.

It was now Monday morning and time for school. Little did any of the students know that the teachers had already discovered that the desks were missing in most of the rooms. There was general confusion among the teachers and the principal. To make matters worse, the buses were dropping off kids and the lines were forming to go into the building. Before the teacher's aide blew the whistle to start the march in, Principal Morgan came out with a stern look on his face.

He spoke very loudly and said, "We had a situation happen over the weekend. I am going to need the help of the fifth and sixth-grade boys." He continued, "Many of your rooms do not have any desks. The desks are currently in the gym. I want everyone else to go to the playground and hang out there until we have all the desks back in the rooms." The aide blew the whistle, and kids scattered and screamed their heads off as they ran to the playground.

The fifth and sixth-grade boys stood frozen in their lines as the principal waved to them to come closer for instructions. He looked each of them up and down for a sign of guilt. Not sensing anything, he knew he had to put the school back together.

Talking in a very stern voice, he said, "Fellas, we need your help to take the desks back to their rooms. But first we have to take them down from a pyramid." All the boys gasped. Ryan, Shon, and Joel did their best to follow along. The principal took the group into the gym. All the teachers were standing around shaking their heads in disbelief. Joel noticed all the jaws that were dropped open as they gazed on this enormous prank. Mr. Brock (he was the youngest and most athletic teacher) volunteered to climb the desks and begin handing them down. After a couple of hours, all the desks were back in the rooms and the school day got back to normal.

Chapter 9: The Prank

As the week continued, the kids were still talking about the prank. Joel didn't go anywhere without hearing the topic being whispered by students and teachers alike. He would love to be a fly in the teachers' lounge now!

It was finally Friday. School started out very normal, nothing unusual in the least, until Joel was on his way back to class after lunch and recess. Passing the office with a group of friends, out of the corner of his eye he saw some commotion. As he continued around the corner, he heard his name called by the office secretary. He stopped walking. She said, "Joel, the principal needs to see you."

Joel immediately felt like his lunch was coming up, as his stomach quickly tied itself into a knot. He peeled off from the group and went to the office, trying to find his confidence for whatever was before him. Joel was led down the hall to Mr. Morgan's office. As he entered the doorway, he saw his mom and dad staring back at him.

Mr. Morgan said, "Joel, please sit down."

Joel's dad very firmly added, "Yes, sit down."

Mr. Morgan said next, "Joel, tell me about your weekend."

Joel quickly answered, "I stayed over at Shon and Ryan's house and then came home and went to Scouts."

The line that was uttered next "sank Joel's battleship," and it came from Mr. Morgan. "Oh, Shon and Ryan said they stayed at *your* house."

The stern look from his father became one of disappointment and rage—mostly rage. Joel regularly got in trouble with his mom and dad for fighting with his brother and sister or for not doing his chores on a timely basis, but this was the first time he tried to pull a lie on his mom and dad, and he didn't think it was going to end like those other offenses.

Mr. Morgan said, "You see, Joel, we found a ball cap on the stage. Many of the teachers knew that it belonged to Shon. We talked to him and his parents earlier today. Shon said that he and Ryan started the weekend off by staying at your house Friday night. When I showed him the ball cap that was found, he said he must have lost it during gym class. I then immediately called your mother to check the overnight sleeping arrangements."

Now Joel knew why he had not seen the twins at lunch and recess today. He thought they had a doctor's appointment. Boy, was he wrong!

"Joel," Mr. Morgan said, "because this prank didn't vandalize the school or hurt anyone, it has been discussed with your parents and the twins that you guys will not be suspended, but you will have a very heavy dose of detention. It will be a new type of detention. I'm calling it Work Detention. After school for the next month you will help teachers and Mr. Dudley (Janitor Jim) with any chores they have. Is that understood?"

In his head, Joel knew this was probably the best of all possible outcomes, and he immediately responded with, "Yes, sir."

"Good," replied Mr. Morgan. Then he said, "Now go home for the rest of the day. I'm sure you have a lot to discuss with your mom and dad."

At that point, any blood that was still in Joel's veins ran ice cold. He was afraid to even look at his dad. But Joel's dad answered Mr. Morgan's comment with, "You bet we do."

Joel got up and started the death march home. His dad's punishment lived up to the torture he felt inside. With one crack of a well-worn paddle that had been handed down from several generations of no-nonsense disciplining parents, he understood one thing: lying to your parents was never worth it.

Then, he heard the voice again. It quietly said in his head, *Lying is never worth it.* Then the comedian in him also said to himself, *but pulling epic pranks is definitely worth it!*

The boys did their hard time after school for a month, and things at the house eventually got better. This month was also

Chapter 9: The Prank

when Joel noticed that the Huff family stopped going to church. When they missed several weeks in a row, Joel asked Shon one day why they didn't go to church anymore. He just said that his dad was done with it, and if his dad was done with it, his whole family was done with it. From that day on, Sunday school was less fun.

Chapter 10:

EPIC CHRISTMAS PRANK

(Joel with Ryan, Shon, and Colleen, briefly—early years: 1984)

RYAN AND SHON CONTINUED to be Joel's best friends. They hung out all the time. Any pranks they did were class-clown tame stuff compared to their epic sixth-grade adventure. But when Joel finally got his driver's license in December of his sophomore year, he began to look for the next big prank. He couldn't believe his parents let him get his license so soon after turning sixteen. He guessed they needed help getting his sister to all her dance practices for the Nutcracker that she was in every year.

Then all of a sudden it happened again, this time while he was waiting in the car for his sister to come out of dance practice. Joel looked over at the town square and noticed the Christmas tree. Decorated with hundreds of lights, it was the pride and joy of the town. Even then, Joel had little doubt what he had to do; he had to steal the Christmas tree. It was time to get with the twins and hatch the plan.

Joel rushed home, dropped off his little sister, and made a quick trip over to talk to the twins. When the feed mill was closed, the only other place Ryan and Shon would probably be was in their garage working on their car. Walking up to the door, he knew this prank would be their grand finale. He rang the doorbell and their mom came to the door. Joel said, "Hi, Mrs. Huff. What are the twins up to?"

She answered, "Not sure. They took a break from the garage a little while ago. Go ahead upstairs to their bedroom."

"Okay. Thanks," Joel replied.

Passing the living room, Joel gave Scott a wave and headed up the stairs. He knocked on their door and said, "Hey, open up." Shon opened the door.

Joel said, "I have an idea that I need your help with." Even though it had been five years since their last major prank, Shon knew by the look in Joel's eye and the tone of his voice that there was another adventure to plan. Joel entered the room, jumped on Ryan's bed, and rolled onto the floor near where Ryan was playing Atari video games.

"Hey, loser," Joel said. Ryan was only half paying attention, making sure not to miss the aliens coming down.

"I need to talk to you," Joel said a little louder. Still no response, so Joel stood up in front of the TV. Ryan scrambled off the floor to push him aside. He took his eye off the TV for a split second, when the alien fired the fatal shot to take him out. Ryan threw down the controller and tackled Joel. They immediately started laughing, and then Shon jumped on top and kept the scrum going until the boys heard their dad yell, "Knock it off up there!"

Ryan said to Joel, "Okay, what's up?" Joel just grinned and looked at Shon, who grinned back at him. They both looked at Ryan. Ryan didn't say anything, but just jumped back on top of both of them. The wrestling match started again until they heard a knock on the door. Shon said quickly, "Sorry. We're done

Chapter 10: Epic Christmas Prank

horsing around." Everyone froze until they heard the creaking of the floorboards and footsteps walking away.

"Okay, this is what I have in mind," Joel said with a whisper. "We are going to steal—no, more like move—Alliance's Christmas tree to a new location."

The twins began to rub their hands together. Ryan said, "Tell us more," as they moved in a little closer to hear the details of the plan.

"Well, it's going to involve a stakeout and a fast getaway."

Ryan said, "Whose car are you going to borrow?"

"Funny man," Joel replied, and then asked, "When will that awesome muscle car of yours be done?"

"Hey, we will own the road by this spring," Ryan emphatically stated.

"Yeah!" Shon said to back him up.

Then Joel said, "Well, my Vette can get the job done right now."

The twins cracked up and said, "You mean your Chevette?"

Joel quickly snapped back, "Yeah, whatever. This Friday we need to meet at the Pizza Oven and watch the movement of Roscoe." Roscoe wasn't his real name, but the kids called him that because of the doofus cop in the *Dukes of Hazzard*. He was frequently caught sleeping in his car on a warm summer day or scarfing down plenty of donuts to start the morning off. There was no doubt that Roscoe would not be able to pass a police academy physical unless it involved an eating contest.

Joel continued, "Once we know when he passes the square, then we can make our move to relocate the tree. We'll have plenty of time to talk about the actual heist. I've got to get home."

Every chance the boys had at school to talk about the heist, they did. Whether it was at library or at lunch, they found little secluded places to work out the details. They didn't want anything to go wrong or to leave anything behind.

Joel's parents let him borrow the Vette anytime. They figured it wasn't a car he could get into too much trouble with. For the most part, that was correct. It was ugly, rusting, and sputtered when you pushed past 50 mph; but for this situation, it would have to do. Joel picked up the twins at 7:30. They decided to cruise the Strip for a little while, go to the arcade, and then stop at the Pizza Oven for surveillance. While at the arcade, the boys started to play their favorite games. Joel really liked the shooting games like Asteroids, Galaga, and Centipede. Ryan and Shon were really good at the driving games like Pole Position and Hard Drivin'. After a couple dollars of tokens, Joel decided it was time to go. As they said goodbye to some of their other friends, three girls from the neighboring rival school, Jackson High, walked through the door. They were wearing their school jackets. It didn't matter that they wore the wrong-colored jacket; they were girls, and Ryan, Shon, and Joel were boys. Anything was possible.

Ryan said, "Guys, can we put this heist off? They're babes. Let's invite them for pizza."

Shon echoed his brother's sentiment with, "Oh, yeah. Oh, yeah!"

Joel was just about ready to give in, because let's face it, a chance to steam up the windows won every time over a prank. Then three of Jackson High's largest senior athletes came walking in. The three Alliance boys looked at each other and said in unison, "Time for pizza."

They got to the Pizza Oven and grabbed the booth by the front window. They ordered a large pizza with everything on it. The boys knew they needed their nourishment if they were to succeed with this prank.

While waiting for the pizza, the bells above the door rang out, announcing a new guest. It was Colleen Newcome, who had come in to pick up a to-go order. As she approached the counter, she grasped for her thick glasses so she could wipe off the steam due to the temperature difference. She didn't look

Chapter 10: Epic Christmas Prank

around to see if she knew anyone. She just wanted to get the pizza and head home. Ryan leaned in and said, "I know she is in band and is a total brain, but I would like to take her glasses off and get tutored."

Joel said, "Come on, relax. She's a great girl and is in the youth group with me at church."

Ryan quickly said, "Shut up. You guys were thinking it."

Joel then quickly added, "God help you when Colleen and your brother Scott join *The Revenge of the Nerds*."

Colleen got her pizza, turned, and headed for the door. She saw the guys and gave a wave on the way out. Ryan quickly spoke up. "Did you see that? She wants me."

Shon just laughed and said, "Yeah, stud, she totally wants you."

The guys devoured their pizza as they looked out the window for Roscoe. When they only had two pieces remaining, Roscoe drove by. Like in the middle of a "Leggo my Eggo" Kellogg's commercial, the boys grabbed for the last two slices, leaving Shon empty-handed. Then, Ryan and Joel ran out the door, leaving Shon to pull ten dollars from his pocket, which he threw on the table as he ran out to catch up with them. Just as they talked about all week, Joel pulled up right next to the tree. The twins jumped out, found the power cord, and unplugged it. So far, so good. Joel popped the Vette's hatchback and noticed the twins struggling with the tree. He asked, "What's the matter, you weaklings?"

Ryan quickly said with a grunt, "It . . . is . . . not . . . budging," as he tried again.

Joel thought fast, pulled a rope out of the back, and said, "Well, I guess we'll have to get it loose this way." He threw the twins the rope. They knew where it could be tied to the car without pulling off the bumper or leaving other evidence. In no time, the guys piled back into the car.

With those famous words from the movies, Ryan said, "Hit it." The rope's slack was taken up quickly, and then with a jolt and a crack, the boys saw a Christmas tree being dragged behind them. Joel stopped, and the twins quickly jumped back out to wrangle as much of the tree as possible into the hatchback. They got back into the car and sped off to the tree's final destination—"The Hill."

The Hill was the place where all of Alliance went for great sled riding. At the top was a burn barrel that got used for some nighttime sled riding by the older kids whom parents and police let have fun. The quickest way to the top was to drive up the small lane right next to The Hill that led to a baseball field where there was just enough of a flat spot to be used. Luckily, there wasn't enough snow for a sledding party. The Vette made it all the way to the top. They carried the tree to the burn barrel and dropped it in. They knew that at the light of day, everyone would see this mischief, and a new mysterious legend would begin. It was definitely time to hurry out of there before Roscoe made his way to that side of town. The boys left The Hill and made a clean getaway safely home.

Chapter 11:

BUILDING ON WHAT LASTS

(Colleen—early years: 1986-1987)

PASTOR RUSSELL WAS PREACHING. Colleen Newcome was trying to pay attention, but only noticed how small the congregation had become compared to the days when she loved running upstairs with all her friends during the mass exodus to children's church. She thought to herself, *Joel and I are still here, and of course, Beth. Wow! Things have really changed. We're the only high school kids here.* There were more middle school kids at the church, but it was sad to see that the high schoolers were down to three.

As church ended, Colleen saw a rush of mothers running to ask her for babysitting help after school this week and/or next weekend already. She was always in high demand. After the rush was over and she collected all her upcoming assignments, she thought, *I'm a high-schooler who doesn't have a social life, and this babysitting job isn't helping.* She chuckled to herself and then started to hum the song from *Snow White*, "Someday My Prince Will Come." She thought, *But until that day, I will have a good time earning babysitting money for college and hanging out with my band friends when I have time.*

Even though things seemed fine in Colleen's family, there was a secret that made her grow up fast. Colleen was the baby of the family, and there was an eight and a ten-year gap between her and two brothers. They were well out of the house by the time Colleen began to have more awareness of the family dynamics. It was at this time that any fond memories of her childhood were muted by a new reality. Colleen's dad was a hardworking industrial-cleaner salesman. He sold soaps, detergents, and degreasers to everywhere from car washes to warehouses, and he was very good at it. He was such a natural salesman that he could give Ron Popeil a run for his money with his Pocket Fisherman and Ginsu knives.

Mr. Newcome's personality was infectious and always held a stranger's attention. He made them feel like they'd known him forever, even if it had only been five minutes. His sales territory was expansive. He covered all of Ohio, West Virginia, and western Pennsylvania. His job kept him on the road most of the week, but he came home on weekends. Colleen loved and respected her dad a great deal, but missed him a lot.

It was because of his absence that Colleen's mom was lonely and searching. What she found was a companion in a clear bottle. Her mom was an at-home weekday alcoholic, never ever stepping into a filthy bar. She was repulsed by the idea of rubbing shoulders with others from that world. She was content dealing with her loneliness one glass at a time by herself at home.

Because of this, Colleen never invited anyone over to the house for sleepovers. Her mom's routine would be to finish cleaning the kitchen and checking on any laundry that needed to be started, and then pass out on the couch with housecoat and slippers not always positioned where they should be, with a *National Enquirer* still on her lap. Colleen's nightly ritual, which began when she was ten years old, was to finish her homework

Chapter 11: Building on What Lasts

in her bedroom and then go downstairs to cover up her passed-out mom for the night.

Because her mom was inside the house all the time, Colleen loved being outside. During her middle-school years, she would rush home, grab her bike, and meet her friends down at the woods beside Basic Park. There she would walk the trails and climb the trees. Colleen even convinced her friends that they should have a clubhouse. It would be a secret clubhouse, for girls only.

Someone used part of the woods as his personal dumping pit. As much of a littering mess and eyesore the trash pile was, it sure was perfect for Colleen and the girls to pick through and carry pieces of wood and metal scraps out of the pit to make their girls-only clubhouse. After a week of working hard after school, they had completed their clubhouse. They had a great time using it for about a month, when one day they showed up to find a litter of raccoons and their screeching momma ready to protect them. The girls left screaming, never to return to their prized clubhouse again.

Even when Colleen's friends quit meeting down at the woods or hanging out at the park, Colleen still loved going. It got her out of the house to think and to do the other thing that she loved to do—draw. She would draw everywhere—at the park, in the woods, at school, and in her bedroom. She loved to draw. She could draw horses, dogs, and cats, but she really liked drawing buildings and bridges. She would check books out of the library, not for the stories, but for their pictures. She would search out any that showed scenes of Paris, Rome, or Greece. There were so many great structures over there; and unlike people, once a building or bridge was created, it never changed. She loved the permanence of the form. She could not wait until she was old enough to visit all of them, but until then, she would continue to escape with her pencil and paper.

Besides becoming a very good artist, Colleen loved school and band. She definitely wanted to turn her attention to other things besides her home life, so when she got to her high-school years, she stayed busy with not only babysitting, but many school club activities. Even though she was involved in these activities and was well liked, she wasn't very vocal in any of them. She just loved being a part of the group, but did not want to get too much attention.

It was the same in band; she played the clarinet, but didn't want to stand out. Eventually she had to come home, and when she did, it was all she could do to have a quick supper and head upstairs again to do her homework and draw.

Just like Mandy and Beth, Colleen was ready for high school to be over. Her dream was to be accepted at the University of Cincinnati and study architecture, not only because it was the best college for architecture that was still in the state, but it was also one of the farthest away from her home. She knew she couldn't count on her mom for much during the week, but both her mom and dad heard her loud and clear about her plans on the weekends. She would show them her latest sketches of historic buildings and bridges, along with some of her skyscrapers of the future. Even though they were designed to be taller than anything ever built, they kept a classical appearance and looked amazing. Her parents knew she had a God-given talent, and they were thankful that she had found her passion.

One early November Sunday after church, Colleen noticed her dad driving in the opposite direction instead of driving straight home to watch hours of football and take a nap.

She said, "Dad, where in the world are you going? Don't you have football to watch?"

He smiled at Colleen's mom and said, "No, we have something more important to do," but he wouldn't say another word.

Chapter 11: Building on What Lasts

Colleen was now very curious and was sitting up straight trying to figure out where they were going. About forty minutes into the trip, Colleen held her stomach and asked, "Is anyone else hungry?"

Her mom spoke up and said, "Only a little bit, dear."

Then her dad interjected, "We're almost there."

By this time, they were heading straight for downtown Cleveland. Colleen jokingly said, "Dad, you can't go too much more north or we'll be swimming in Lake Erie, and I didn't bring my swimsuit." They all laughed as they finally exited the interstate.

Before long, they were driving next to Cleveland's gorgeous and iconic Terminal Tower. Colleen's dad said in a matter-of-fact manner, "If you're going to design special skyscrapers and buildings, you really should take a look at them up close."

Colleen screamed for joy. She couldn't believe what they were about to do. This was far better than anything else she had ever done with her parents! As they parked the car and started walking underneath the Terminal Tower's 771-foot shadow, Colleen's dad said, "Oh, by the way, we're having lunch up there on the observation deck."

Colleen screamed again, took her mom's hand, and started running. Her dad said, "Wait up; I have the money."

Like a gentleman from long ago, Colleen's dad opened one of the five heavy blazing-bright brass doors that signified you were someplace important. Not only did they pass through one of those impressive doors, but there was a second one waiting. Colleen's little round face was instantly transformed into an elongated shape of wonderment.

"Colleen, we'll have time to look at everything down here after lunch. I thought you were hungry," her dad said as he pushed the button to the elevator. As the doors opened, Colleen ran through them even before her parents could react. She searched the large panel of buttons that had everything from a G to 52.

Her dad said, "Go ahead and push 52. We're going to the top." She screamed again, but this time it echoed and even hurt her own ears.

She quickly stopped and said, "Sorry," with raised eyebrows and a sheepish grin.

They traveled up for what seemed to be several grueling minutes, until the light went off on the "52" button and a bell went off. The shiny metal door opened, revealing a lavish penthouse floor lobby. Colleen couldn't get enough of what she was taking in visually, but her dad pulled her over to the observation area and the rooftop café.

He chuckled and said, "Colleen, remember you're hungry."

The three of them had a quick sandwich and bag of chips and then began to enjoy the view. It was a crystal-clear day, and Colleen was in awe every place she looked. To the north over Lake Erie and into Canada, and in all other directions, she saw a vast amount of what looked like little model homes and buildings. Her perspective was like that of the creator of a toy train diorama. She didn't want to leave, as all her senses were trying to take everything completely in.

Her dad finally said, "Colleen, let's go to the ground level so you can see all the great architecture there." He didn't have to tell her twice. She raced toward the elevator doors, leaving her parents behind.

After the door opened to the ground level of the building, they walked out and around the corner, slowly taking in every extraordinary detail. The granite blocks that made the walls and columns were perfectly placed and finished to a polished luster. A beautiful hand-chiseled crown molding adorned the top of the walls and transitioned the eye to the crowning jewel—the ceiling. The painted plaster masterpiece had a spectacular pat-

Chapter 11: Building on What Lasts

tern of yellow rosettes inside a blue octagon that were inside a red octagon.

All these rows and rows formed an archway down the long grand entrance to this once-bustling train hub. Any weary traveler would have been instantaneously revived after walking down this corridor. Colleen's mom and dad slowed their walk, letting Colleen set the pace. As she finished meandering through the grand lobby, she stayed equally focused on the layout and design of the passenger terminal concourse floor. It had staircases coming from above on the outside walls and going below to the railroad platforms from the middle. The majority of the lighting was from bulbs hidden behind lattice work, giving off a defused light. This single line of lattice ran along the ceiling from column to column, creating a web effect with just the right amount of light from above and a glorious reflection on the highly waxed floors.

As Colleen was clearly enthralled by every detail, a custodian noticed her concentration and asked if she would like a rare behind-the-scenes view. Startled, Colleen looked back to her parents for reassurance, and then quickly responded, "Yes, I would love that." She motioned for Colleen and her mom and dad to follow her. There was a door at the end of the hallway where a narrow hallway awaited the group. At the end of that hallway was a beautiful carved wooden door.

The custodian said, "Inside this door is the private meeting room of the Van Sweringen brothers, who built this masterpiece."

When the door swung open, it showed a room that had the best handcrafted wood panel work she had ever seen. From the huge custom fireplace, moldings, turnings, and exquisite rafter work, to the beautiful shelves that reached halfway to the vaulted ceilings, this room became her favorite.

Colleen's dad couldn't believe this bonus tour. They all thanked the lady and went back to the main concourse. As they went from the main concourse to the awe-inspiring lobby again, Colleen took one more look to sear the image in her mind. She reluctantly pushed on the first heavy brass door leading to the breezeway and then the next, which led to the outside. She knew they had to leave, but leaving meant the best day of her life would be over—or was it?

Her dad asked, "Does anyone want dessert?"

Colleen's mom answered, "Of course we do!" and taking Colleen's hand, began to run back to the car.

Dad yelled, "Hey, you're going the wrong way. It's around the block over this way. We're going to walk." His girls stopped in their tracks and changed course. They rounded the corner and walked along the great Higbee's department store. The store had already started to showcase their world-famous Christmas window vignettes.

Mr. Newcome said, "Here we are. Higbee's."

The girls said in unison, "Shopping okay."

"No. This is where we are having our dessert," her dad answered.

Colleen saw Higbee's famous revolving door and jumped into a section, pushing it faster and faster with delight, like she was six again. The door let out a whoosh sound, followed by a dull bump every time a panel would pass by the bright brass curved side enclosures. Colleen's parents went through and waited for her to finish her circular fun.

Once inside, Colleen began to take in all the Art Deco forms throughout the store. She couldn't begin to get enough of the wonderful bold shapes. The Newcomes reached their dessert destination, the Silver Grille. Stepping inside this place took one back to the lavish era of when people tried to forget about the Great Depression and were encouraged to start anew by the elegant Art Deco modern movement.

Colleen and her parents were shown to their table by the hostess. Among the fluted painted columns was a platform in

Chapter 11: Building on What Lasts

the center of the room with an ornate pedestal that rose up to meet a massive chandelier. The walls were muted-green with metallic silver trim everywhere. The Newcomes were taken to a small table next to a gorgeous water fountain trimmed with copper. The well-padded crushed velvet chairs were flanked by the same silver trim that Colleen saw throughout the room. Colleen thought to herself, *This is far different than the squeaky wooden chairs at our kitchen table.* Everything in this place was in perfect symmetry and style, and Colleen loved it.

When the waiter arrived, Mr. Newcome immediately said, "We are here to have dessert only." The waiter left, but instead of returning with menus, he brought out a cart loaded with all the different desserts. He parked it right in front of Colleen. She had never seen anything like it, and could not have felt more special.

The waiter started off by pointing with his open hand to the first dessert and said, "This is our three-tiered Black Forest Cake with a cherry and cream filling between the heavenly chocolate cake layers. Next is our French Profiterole, or cream puff. It has a wonderfully whipped pastry taste with custard piped into the middle and then finished with a chocolate ganache. Next is a Crème Brule flambé. This is a rich custard base delight that is topped with a shell of caramel. It will be a real show stopper if you decide to get it," he said, as he winked at Colleen's parents.

He continued and presented the next dessert, saying, "This is our Apple Charlotte. It is a sweet sponge cake filled with a wonderful medley of apples and puree for the season drizzled with custard and topped with a cinnamon-sugar dusting."

Next, he gestured to the cheesecake, but before he could describe it, Colleen's mom blurted out, "I will be having that!" Everyone laughed.

The waiter cleared his throat and said, "This is our Pumpkin Cheesecake with a gingersnap crust. It is very delicious and is my fall favorite. And finally, we have a Caramel Apple Pie à la mode with a big scoop of vanilla ice cream." The waiter took a deep breath and said, "Good luck."

Colleen had never seen an apple pie with so much filling between the crusts and the oozing caramel syrup, not to mention the ice cream that wasn't even on top yet. She spoke up and said, "The Caramel Apple Pie à la mode, please."

Then Colleen's mom said, "You know which one I want." Everyone laughed again.

Colleen's dad said, "Well, I might as well get a piece of that Black Forest Cake so we can get our chocolate fix. I have a feeling we'll be sharing with each other." The waiter left with the orders and came back in no time with the wonderful delights.

Colleen's mom quickly said, "Before we try our own, let's try the other two." Everyone had the same reaction to each bite: "Mmmm," which was a great sign. Then they each took a bit of their own dessert, and the "Mmmmmmmmmm" went on much longer and was repeated again and again with each bite.

As Colleen took her final bite of the apple pie, she once again realized that this perfect day would soon be over—or would it?

Her dad took his final bite of his chocolatey goodness, reached for his coffee, and said, "Last week when I was down in the Cincinnati area, I stopped in at a certain college to show a certain dean some sketches from a certain girl from Alliance." Colleen's face froze, and those wide-open beautiful brown clear eyes became filled with tears that began to stream down her face.

Her dad paused and then said, "Well, if you were to ask me what he said, I would tell you that he told me to tell that certain girl to hurry up and get her application in and mark it to my attention."

Colleen didn't speak, but just put her hands up to her face, got up from the table, and followed the contour before collapsing in her dad's lap. There she began to sob, which seemed about as loud as the nearby fountain, and contained about the same amount of water, too. When all the emotions settled down,

Chapter 11: Building on What Lasts

Colleen and her mom were arm in arm, walking swiftly back to the car. They gabbed the whole time about their plan to get the application sent in by Tuesday so it would arrive at the university before the end of the week.

Colleen had never felt more special in the eyes of her parents, and she thanked God for everything that had happened. She especially treasured the moments that she noticed her mom and dad holding hands and enjoying each other's company. It had been a long time since that had happened. As Colleen's dad drove away from Terminal Tower, he could see his daughter staring back to get the final glimpses of the outside architecture. His smile matched hers, and it remained for the entire trip home.

Not too long after, the calendar flipped into the new year—1987. Colleen received a letter from the University of Cincinnati's School of Architecture. She ripped it open to find out that she was officially accepted. She screamed and carried on for days, until she realized she still had to finish four and a half more months of high school, which brought her back to reality. She made the best of those last few months in high school, but her heart was ready to move on to the next chapter of life—her college years as an architecture student.

Chapter 12:

SUMMER 1987 (REAL WORLD: REAL SHOCK)

(Ryan, Shon, Joel, Mandy, Beth, Colleen, and Scott)

IT WAS A SENIOR class tradition to have one last party before everyone went on to the next chapter in their lives. Someone came up with the name the "Three-Month Reunion," and it stuck. The Three-Month Reunion was always on the first Saturday night in August out at Alliance Lake. Kids would drive out to get the party started as the sun was beginning to hide for the night.

Mandy and Beth got there first, knowing that Ryan and Shon would be there. Beth couldn't pass up the chance to show Ryan her tattoo one more time. Colleen arrived with a bunch of her band friends. One of the last cars to show up was heard as it roared around the last couple of turns to emerge in a cloud of dust. Of course, it was Ryan and Shon's red Nova. Beth perked up as she headed over to greet Ryan. Also with the twins was the third wheel, Joel.

Scott had made it to the lake much earlier. After supper, he borrowed the family car and drove to the lake. It gave him some extra time before dark to walk around the lake and think. Then he just stayed for the party.

Everyone who showed up had a great time. There was plenty of music, snacks, and drinking available to go along with the memories that were flowing that night. It was getting close to 11:00 p.m. when people were pulling out to head back to town. As Scott made a mental inventory of who remained around the fire, one person, Colleen, seemed to be out of place. Why would she still be there? He remembered seeing her most of the night having fun with her band friends, but now she was sitting next to Ryan.

Scott got Joel's attention. Joel walked over and said, "What's up, Scott?"

Scott answered, "What's that all about?" as he motioned with a nudge of his head in Ryan and Colleen's direction.

Joel quickly and quietly said, "He asked her to stay, and guess what?"

"What?"

Joel answered, "Shon and I may need a ride home."

Scott rolled his eyes and followed Shon back to the fire. Before he had a chance to sit down, Ryan yelled at him to get more wood. Scott left the six of them with their own thoughts around a dying fire as he went to get more wood.

As Scott returned to the fire circle, everyone was much closer together, because the heat was no longer as strong. He also noticed that Ryan and Colleen were gone, and he heard the Nova start up. Scott dropped some wood on the low-crackling fire. Joel looked at Shon and Scott and said, "Told you."

Shon followed that comment with, "Bet you they don't make it past The Overlook." The Overlook was a bluff about thirty feet high where cars could be driven to get off the main dirt road. It was a convenient place for cars to find a short-term parking spot and watch the submarine races.

Chapter 12: Summer 1987 (Real World: Real Shock)

Joel responded, saying, "Well, they'll be joining about five or six other cars that I saw with their headlights on up there." Sure enough, another set of headlights emerged and then were quickly shut off at The Overlook.

Beth got up and said to Mandy, "Time to go home. Nothing left to do here."

"Wait," Scott said. "Stay and hang out a little longer. Let's not let a perfectly good fire go to waste." The girls shrugged, asked for another can out of the cooler, and sat back down.

Shon laughed and said with a sarcastic tone, "Boy, I've never heard you take a stand like that. Good for you, bro." Joel agreed, and they all laughed.

Ryan turned off the key to quiet the Nova's rumbling engine, letting the car coast to his spot at The Overlook. This was happening all too fast, Colleen thought. One minute she was laughing with her friends, and then the next minute this popular guy wanted to spend time with her. She knew it was close to the end of the summer and time was growing short before she was going to leave for college, but this could be her *Prince* moment she had always dreamed about when she was up in her room drawing by herself.

An inner voice had been seeking her attention in the car all the way up to The Overlook. She quickly redirected her mind to wonder if Ryan could hear her heartbeat that was pounding with anticipation. As she swung her head to let her hair fan the heat that was rising on her neck, Ryan slid over on the bench seat and pulled her close. He looked into her eyes, pulled her glasses off, and pressed his lips on the very spot that needed quenched. Before she knew it, they were in the backseat and other fires were beginning to burn. When Colleen didn't stop for any reason, he sure wasn't going to. Then it happened; it happened so fast. Ryan's fire might have been put out and was smoldering, but Colleen just lay there feeling cold, reaching for her clothes.

Ryan, feeling proud of himself, looked over and saw Colleen scurrying in the dark for her glasses and more of her clothes. He said, "I'll give you some privacy. I have something I've always wanted to do." Not hesitating one bit, he pulled on his shorts, opened the door, and took off running.

Colleen, still overwhelmed with what had just happened, sat up in time to see Ryan's last few steps look out of control, and he was not slowing down. She let out a scream, "Ryan, no!" He didn't even think twice. With a scream of courage, he dove off The Overlook bluff and into the lake. Again, Colleen let out one scream after another until those people in the cars around her came to her aide.

Shon looked at Scott and said, "Did you hear that?"

"What?" he replied.

"Someone's screaming Ryan's name," he said. "Listen." There it was again. That time Joel, Shon, and Scott all kicked dirt on the fire and ran toward the car. The girls got in their car and quickly followed them. They tore out of the party spot and headed toward The Overlook. Once they got there, people continued to scream Ryan's name.

Colleen ran up to them and said frantically, "Ryan just took a leap off the bluff like he was Superman, but he stumbled, and I don't know if he cleared the rocks below. I couldn't stop him. I couldn't stop him." She fell in a heap on the ground bawling. Mandy and Beth collapsed on the ground with her.

Shon, Joel, and Scott ran cautiously to the bluff's edge with the others, screaming out for Ryan over the thirty-foot drop into the dark. After they started getting hoarse, Scott yelled out, "Ryan this is not funny anymore. Please come out. Your prank is over. You got us good."

Everyone stood in silence. There was no reply. There was no Ryan. Shon sprinted to the Nova and yelled back to Scott that he was going to get help. He threw the car in reverse and the tires spun backwards, throwing dirt in every direction. Shon

Chapter 12: Summer 1987 (Real World: Real Shock)

slammed the gearshift down into first, peeling more dirt out toward the group.

He had no regard for this precious car any longer. He hit every rut, rock, and stump on the way out of there. There were several times that the combination of loose gravel and extreme horsepower almost put Shon into the ditch. He knew he had to get control of the car and of his state of mind if he wanted to have a chance to rescue Ryan. The car continued to take a severe beating as he drove back to town for help.

Entering the village limits, Shon knew he was almost to the firehouse, where he could get help. He rumbled into the station and slammed on the brakes. He was going much too fast to stop quickly. The brakes locked up and let out a resounding squawk. As he was sliding toward the massive fire engine doors, he spun the wheel and let off the brakes in time to go up on two wheels like a stunt show performance. The car hopped, stalled, and finally came down at rest. Shon was just glad he made it. Before he got out of the car, all the volunteer firefighters that were there came running to the Nova to find out the emergency. Shon's mind and mouth were still going way too fast. Janitor Jim helped Shon out of the car and said to him very calmly, "Shon look at me. Take a deep breath." They locked eyes and both took a long breath in and out.

He then asked Shon, "Where are you coming from?" Shon quickly but clearly said, "I came from Alliance Lake by The Overlook. I think Ryan had an accident. We didn't see him in the water after he dove off." As Shon was finishing the last two words, Jim and the other volunteers were already backpedaling toward the station to grab the emergency gear for the rescue. He hit the alarm to sound the call for help from others in town. He also put out a bulletin on the fire and police radio that there was a possible 10-32 out at Alliance Lake by The Overlook.

The emergency vehicles, one carrying a small flat-bottomed rescue boat, rushed out of the station. Jim yelled to Shon, "Get your mom and dad and meet us back at the lake." With sirens blaring, the vehicles left the station. Quickly, more of the town's posse emerged to follow behind and lend a hand. Shon didn't hesitate, but followed Jim's orders and drove home.

As he parked and raced in the door, the family already knew from the alarms that there was a serious emergency. Before Shon could say anything, his mom asked, "Where's Ryan?" There was silence. She did not ask about anyone else, but again repeated, "Where's Ryan?" Whether she just knew as a mother that it was Ryan and not Scott, or whether she just automatically went to that place that Ryan and Shon always thought was cute when they played favorites over Scott, he did not know, but his mom was right. It was Ryan.

By this time Shon was oddly calm, and he said to his parents as he was staring into space, "Yes, Ryan had an accident out at the lake. He did not surface after diving off The Overlook bluff. The emergency squad is responding now. Scott and others are still there. I was really hoping he was playing a trick. He likes playing tricks and pranks." Immediately Shon's mom and dad left him staring as they were getting dressed and gathering things together. They all piled into the pickup truck and sped out to the lake.

They came upon the scene with vehicles, people, and lights everywhere. People rushed toward them when they saw Mr. and Mrs. Huff. Mr. Huff asked in a hopeful tone, "Any news?" Everyone shook their head and looked concerned.

As he approached the edge of the bluff, Mr. Huff yelled down to Jim Dudley and the other volunteer responders, "I'll be right down. I'm coming to help."

Mr. Dudley said, "Please, Mr. Huff, you can best help by watching from up there and being with your wife and sons. We have divers in the water and we are checking everything systematically so we don't miss anything. It's dark, and I don't want any other accidents. I have sent all the kids back up to the top."

Chapter 12: Summer 1987 (Real World: Real Shock)

Mr. Huff felt very helpless, but he understood. Soon many teenage boys began appearing through the bushes into the car lights. Scott approached his mom and dad, not having any words. They put their arms around him and gave him a loving embrace. Shon saw his family in silhouette and was stirred to get up and join them. He wrapped his huge arms around everyone, and they began to sob.

It was getting close to three full hours since the accident happened, and the divers had completed their sweep of the areas that were mapped out for them to check. Mr. Dudley was visibly upset with this rescue-turned-recovery and said to his crew, "Guys, up top we have some of our Alliance family hurting terribly. What are we missing? Where is the boy?"

Jacob, one of the youngest members of the volunteer squad spoke up and said, "I have gone fishing plenty of times in this very spot, and I have always wondered if there was an underwater cave near the bluff. My line would always go deeper than I thought it should."

That information gave the two experienced divers just enough energy to change their tanks in a hurry and plunge under again. The people from the boat and the bluff could see the divers with their floodlight along the bottom, and then as they got closer to the craggy bluff wall, they disappeared. Everyone gasped and freaked out, as they knew a discovery could be made very soon.

Minutes later, the floodlights came back into view. The dive team surfaced on the far side of the boat with the lifeless body. They took their masks off, using the other hand to hold onto the boat. They looked at Jim and just nodded their heads, confirming the tragedy. Jim looked up on the bluff to what now seemed to be half the town still in hopeful vigil. He locked eyes with the Huffs, and with a disappointed and exhausted look on his face, he motioned for them to come down to the bottom. The spotlights in the water and in the boat quickly shut off before they lifted the body into the boat. It was the signal that turned hope into instant despair. People let their emotions loose, weeping and crying so loudly from The Overlook that it echoed for miles in the valley.

The Huffs were waiting on the stony shoreline when the boat approached. The body was under a wool blanket. The blanket was lifted back to reveal Ryan, who looked very peaceful. There looked to be very bad head trauma, but Mrs. Huff was strangely relieved that her son had been found. By this time she was in the water up to her knees, and Mr. Huff was holding her at the waist. She leaned over to give Ryan a kiss. She whispered something in his ear and then walked away with Mr. Huff guiding her onto shore. Shon threw his hat to Mr. Dudley and asked, "Can you please let Ryan wear this?"

Mr. Dudley said with a comforting voice, "That's a great idea." Scott stepped back with Shon, and each of them began wiping tears from their eyes as they started up the overgrown path to the top.

Throughout the beginning of the new week, funeral plans were being made and a constant stream of family and friends were stopping by. There were so many meals from the old church that Mrs. Huff had to tell Pastor Russell to let the ladies know she couldn't accept any more. They had run out of freezer space. Alliance did have a small funeral home, but arrangements were made to have the visitation in the morning and the funeral service in the afternoon at the church on the same day. This allowed for the needed room to accommodate the large crowd that was expected for both.

On the morning of the service, the four Huffs got into the car and drove to the church. Scott couldn't help but think back to those days when he was left alone in the middle seat and his brothers were the backseat victors. What he would give to have that feeling again instead of this one! No one said a word in the car.

Chapter 12: Summer 1987 (Real World: Real Shock)

As the family walked into the church, they were greeted by Pastor Russell. He led them down to the front of the sanctuary, where the casket was positioned. He told them to take their time and he would let people in when they were ready. Dad opened the casket and saw his precious son there. He couldn't help but remember all the times he and Ryan were the last ones in the garage working together on the family car or the Nova. He gave his son a kiss on the forehead and took a seat in the front row. Shon and Scott stepped forward to say their private goodbyes and then they sat next to Dad. Finally, Mom went to Ryan's side, stroked his hair, and gave him a kiss on the cheek. Once again, she leaned over and whispered something in his ear. Then she walked back to the first pew and joined her family.

For the next three hours, people streamed into the church and walked past the casket to pay their respects, and then they went by the Huffs' pew to express their condolences. Most of their high school classmates and parents came out to support Shon and Scott. They thought it especially comforting to see Mandy, Beth, Joel, and of course, Colleen, who was the last person with him, and who must have been dealing with her own struggles.

The church had a lunch prepared down in the basement fellowship room. There everyone was able to eat, relax, and visit with family and friends from out of town. By 2:00 p.m. it was time to go back to the sanctuary for the funeral service. The church was completely full by the time the Huff family sat down in the front pew. The piano softly played the final refrain of "It is Well with My Soul," as Pastor Russell got up and walked to the pulpit.

He looked directly at the Huffs and said, "I am so sorry for your loss."

He then looked out at those gathered and said, "I am so sorry for our loss. Ladies and gentlemen, we are here today to remember a great son, brother, and friend. After talking with many of you, I know each and every one here has a special story or memory about Ryan that you will hold dear. My own memory was when I would see that little guy tear out of the sanctuary for children's church. It seemed like he always had to be the first one up to class. He was always so excited and full of life. Whether he was working on his Nova or hanging out with friends, he always had fun, but he also cared about others and had a big heart.

The wisest man who ever lived summed up his own journey through life the following way in Ecclesiastes 3:1-14:

> There is a time for everything, and a season for every activity under the heavens: a time to be born and a time to die, a time to plant and a time to uproot, a time to kill and a time to heal, a time to tear down and a time to build, a time to weep and a time to laugh, a time to mourn and a time to dance, a time to scatter stones and a time to gather them, a time to embrace and a time to refrain from embracing, a time to search and a time to give up, a time to keep and a time to throw away, a time to tear and a time to mend, a time to be silent and a time to speak, a time to love and a time to hate, a time for war and a time for peace.
>
> What do workers gain from their toil? I have seen the burden God has laid on the human race. He has made everything beautiful in its time. He has also set eternity in the human heart; yet no one can fathom what God has done from beginning to end. I know that there is nothing better for people than to be happy and to do good while they live. That each of them may eat and drink, and find satisfaction in all their toil—this is the gift of God. I know that everything God does will endure forever; nothing can be added to it and nothing taken from it. God does it so that people will fear him.

Chapter 12: Summer 1987 (Real World: Real Shock)

I think we can all say that Ryan got the most out of the days that he had on this earth. It was his time, his season. I am struck by the words in verse eleven: 'He has made everything beautiful in its time. He has also set eternity in the human heart.'

Within our hearts, we understand that there is an eternal place for us. In Paul's second letter to the Corinthians, he wrote in chapter four and verse eighteen, 'So we fix our eyes not on what is seen, but on what is unseen, since what is seen is temporary, but what is unseen is eternal.'

Folks, it is so important that we heed these words and look to the important things of God—like faith, hope, and love. We have to fix our eyes and life on those unseen things. Seek after God. Seek after God's Son, Jesus, and those things will endure forever. They are eternal. For us, we have many days of mourning ahead, and that is to be perfectly expected. I only ask that we are there for each other and that in our quiet times, we ask God for His comfort and grace."

Pastor Russell stepped aside, and the pianist played a couple more songs while everyone reflected. The pastor then got back up and closed the service with a prayer. When the prayer concluded, Pastor Russell said, "We will be going immediately to the cemetery. For those who want to attend, it is located across from the elementary school. I would ask the pallbearers to please meet here in the front." After the announcement, the pianist began to play "Blessed Assurance," and those who were in attendance were dismissed.

Immediately, Shon, Joel, and Scott, along with three of their cousins, came to the front to receive instructions on carrying the casket to the hearse. The ride to the cemetery only took minutes. The pallbearers lined up at the back of the hearse to pull the casket out. Shon, who was directly across from Joel said to him quietly, "Hey, we know Ryan isn't freaking out about this place, don't we?"

Joel caught himself covering up a snorting laugh before giving Shon a dirty look and rolling his eyes. The pallbearers walked the casket to the gravesite under a small open tent. Once there, Pastor Russell offered another quick word of encouragement to everyone by saying, "Most of us know the story of Moses and the burning bush, when the Lord God appeared to Moses to send him back to Egypt to deliver the Israelites from the oppressing hand of Pharaoh. In the New Testament, Jesus commented on this story in the book of Mark when He was asked about our resurrection after this life. God said to Moses, 'I am the God of Abraham, the God of Isaac, and the God of Jacob. He is not the God of the dead, but of the living.' You see, Jesus is making the point that these Hebrew forefathers who died hundreds of years before are still with God in heaven. We can be comforted by that."

Pastor Russell asked everyone to bow their heads, and then he prayed, "Lord, today we grieve, and tomorrow we grieve, but You also want us to know that Your power is real and that resurrection after this life is real. We will see our loved ones again. May You watch over Ryan until we see him again. In Jesus's name, Amen."

People began to back away from the tent and head back to their vehicles. Joel, Beth, Mandy, and Colleen, who were standing together, walked up to Shon and Scott and gave them a hug. Shon immediately reached over to a blanket of roses on the casket, pulled some roses out, handed one to each of them, and thanked them.

They all shared another hug, and Joel, Beth, and Mandy left. Colleen, who was still crying and having a hard time, remained. Scott walked up to her and said, "Colleen, it will be alright. I'm sorry you had to go through this, but thanks for coming today. Will you be okay?"

Colleen said, "Thanks. It has just been so crazy, but I guess I will . . . I mean I will be . . ." Then she ran off to her car, leaving

Chapter 12: Summer 1987 (Real World: Real Shock)

Scott looking on.

"Scott. Scott, please come here."

"Yes, Dad," he replied.

Mr. Huff turned to Pastor Russell and said, "I wanted our whole family to be here to thank you and the rest of the church, Pastor, for all your help. It has meant so much."

Pastor Russell said, "It is our pleasure and purpose to care for those hurting and in need. Just know we are still here for you. Please let me know if there is anything else we can do for you. Anytime, okay?"

The entire family nodded, and Mr. and Mrs. Huff said, "Thank you very much."

The day after the funeral, without telling anyone, Shon went down to the Navy Recruiting Center and enlisted. He told the recruiter he was interested in Special Forces. The recruiter told him some of the physical and mental demands he would need to meet, but boot camp was first. Shon would have to make it out of boot camp and pass some very high minimum standards before he could make the cut for additional training. The recruiter signed Shon up to be in the United States Navy.

Shon got back to the house as his mom, dad, and Scott were sitting down at the table eating more leftovers from the meals that had been given to them. Shon sat down at his usual spot and the food was passed to him. He put one huge helping after another onto his plate until it resembled a casserole dish. Shon began to shovel the food into his mouth, occasionally picking up his milk to wash it down. The three others began to stare.

Scott finally asked what everyone else had to be thinking, "Wow, Shon, are you eating for two?" His mom and dad laughed. Scott quickly thought that was probably the first time they laughed at something he said.

Shon didn't miss a bite when he began to speak and eat at the same time. *Chew, chew,* "Navy", *chew, chew, gulp, chew, chew,* "need to be ready," *gulp.*

The family froze and looked at each other. His mom harshly asked, "You did what?"

Shon put down his fork, took a big drink of milk, cleared his throat, and said very calmly, "I have joined the Navy."

His mom asked, "Where did that come from?"

His dad and Scott quickly followed up with, "Well, Shon?"

Shon calmly replied, "I'm eighteen and I'm ready for something new."

His dad piped up and said, "Well, you'll definitely find it there."

Scott laughed, but Mom sighed and asked, "Do you have to do that for something new?"

Shon replied, "I'm going to start my conditioning here until I'm called for boot camp."

His mom started to say something, but was cut off by Shon who said, "Mom, I have enlisted and I'm waiting for their call to go to boot camp. It should be in two or three months."

She abruptly got up from the table to take her plate to the sink. She thought, *Great! Now I have lost two sons.* It may not have been rational, but that was how she felt.

Shon went on and said, "My goal is to join the Special Forces—the SEALs."

Upon hearing that, his dad changed his tune. He replied, "That's my boy! You go for it, the toughest challenge. Great job!" That comment from his dad made him feel good and secure about the future. His mom would still need time to get used to the idea.

Summer was over for the class of 1987. Parents and teachers always talked about "Wait until you get out in the real world." Well, for them it was time, and time doesn't wait for anyone.

Part Two:

AFTER HIGH SCHOOL—
LOOKING BACK FROM
SEPTEMBER 2002

Chapter 13:

ANCHORS AWEIGH

(Shon—after high school: 1987)

SHON CLOSED HIS MAGAZINE and looked out the window at 32,000 feet. He was in the middle of his flight traveling back to Ohio for the class reunion. He reclined his seat and closed his eyes. He began to think about his last fifteen years and remembered how it all started when he dropped the bomb on his family about joining the Navy. He couldn't help but smile when he remembered his mom's reaction, but that was the only thing he could smile about for a while. He drifted off thinking about the memories.

After he told his parents that he had joined the Navy, he wanted to get in top physical condition. Every morning, Shon got up before anyone else in the house and ran five miles. He continued to work at the feed mill. He begged the plant manager to let him do any heavy lifting jobs to allow him to get a workout in during the day. After his hours at the feed mill, he continued to work out by doing a variety of calisthenics, including push-ups, pull-ups, and sit-ups.

He wanted to be the best in his boot camp so he would get recommended for Special Forces training. Without telling anyone, Shon also went to Alliance Lake two days a week. There he could get stronger in the water and also have some quiet time with Ryan. It just felt right to be there as he prepared for this next adventure, and he wanted Ryan to know that he was taking him on this journey, too.

This became his daily routine until he received the call. He learned he would be leaving for boot camp in two weeks. He believed that he was in great physical shape, and he was not intimidated by anything mechanical, including guns. Only time would tell if he had what it takes to make the cut for an elite fighting group like the SEALs. It was a Saturday afternoon when Mom, Dad, and Scott said goodbye to Shon at the bus station in Canton. They watched him board the bus with several other recruits. The bus was headed to Cleveland to join up with more recruits from the area who were all beginning this new adventure. Shon's mom turned and walked by herself, trying to hold it together. Shon would eventually be heading west to Great Lakes, Illinois, to the site of the Navy's boot camp.

The trip to Cleveland would take less than an hour, but for the majority of the guys on the bus, they acted like the party needed to begin then and there. The recruiter was on the bus, but he knew he couldn't do anything to them until they were officially U.S. Navy property. He just sat in the front seat behind the bus driver with a big grin on his face. He knew their world might not change today, or during the day tomorrow, but their world would sure change tomorrow night!

Shon looked around at the others on his bus to size everyone up. He saw all shapes and sizes. He couldn't believe that he even

Chapter 13: Anchors Aweigh

saw someone who was extremely overweight. Shon thought to himself that that guy must not have known that there was physical training in the Navy. The recruiter definitely did not get his message across to him.

The guy who really stood out on the bus was Mark Chandler. He was the instigator on the short trip up to Cleveland. When there was a girl outside the window to whistle at, he was the loudest. When there were stories and exploits to talk about, he had one better than anyone else. By the end of the trip, it was quite clear that he talked his way into the Navy, and Shon wanted to stay as far away from him as he could.

The bus doors opened and the recruiter gave instructions where they should go next. Guys rushed by Shon looking to get this small stuff out of the way. Shon was a lot quieter and had a good measure of caution. This small group from Canton couldn't help themselves. They were making fun of everybody and everything. Their remarks and actions were attracting the like-minded. Shon could see the other Navy recruiters talking to each other, and he thought it best to stay as far away as he could from this overconfident eighteen-year-old bunch.

One of the recruiters took the group to the processing center and showed them where they would be spending the night. He made it very clear that none of them would have another night like this one for a very long time. This only gave permission to the fool-headed guys to begin planning their escapades.

On that fall night in 1987, Cleveland experienced the rowdiest group of soon-to-be naval recruits ever. There wasn't a bar in The Flats from which they didn't get thrown out. Several of Cleveland's finest would cut them one break after another, knowing this was their last night before the uniform would go on. It was later found out that Mark Chandler even tried to set the Cuyahoga River on fire again. Shon could not believe his bad luck with this bunch, but he ultimately knew that there would be even more guys like this up in Chicago who would become part of his Division.

The next morning came quickly for most. They dragged themselves down to see a very elaborate breakfast spread. The stories from the previous night along with echoes of laughter and the chimes of metal flatware against stone plates could be heard throughout the cafeteria and dining hall. Everyone got his fill, at least as much as hangovers would allow.

After breakfast, everyone went down to get his physical—a full physical. When the doctor asked Mark to turn his head and cough, he replied "What? I don't even have a cold." Again he got laughs from those around him, but Shon knew it wasn't going to be good for this clown if he hadn't gotten serious yet. After the physical, there were informational classes to attend. Everyone was provided with another excellent meal for lunch. It got to the point that Shon was beginning to feel pretty comfortable with this decision and he liked all the food choices. Once lunch was over, everyone was asked to stand up and take the oath of enlistment.

Shon repeated, "I, Shon Huff, do solemnly swear that I will support and defend the Constitution of the United States against all enemies, foreign and domestic; that I will bear true faith and allegiance to the same; and that I will obey the orders of the President of the United States and the orders of the officers appointed over me, according to regulations and the Uniform Code of Military Justice. So help me God."

With that, Shon and his group in Cleveland were officially Navy property. They were taken to a bus to board a plane headed to Great Lakes, Illinois. Shon looked out the plane window to see that his local recruiter was being given a hard time by the other recruiters. He didn't like the look of that, and boy, he couldn't have been more correct.

Chapter 13: Anchors Aweigh

When the plane landed in Chicago, it was already dark outside. All the Canton guys and several others who lit up the town were assigned to Bus #2. There were a total of twelve buses. As expected, those on Bus #2 were carrying on like they were going to step off the bus and find the local clubs or bars waiting for them so they could do more damage.

Shon just knew there would have to be one more shuffle to get the more serious guys together. They had to know that he ultimately wanted to be a SEAL, right? Shon almost lost his temper when Mark passed gas on his head. Shon just ignored it, because he didn't want to be seen as having anything to do with this group. He endured an hour-long bus ride with all kinds of these practical jokes going on around him.

It was nearly midnight when the bus slowed down and made a long turn past a sign that read "Navy Recruit Training Command, Great Lakes, Illinois." Everyone on Bus #2 let out a cheer, except for Shon. He took a deep breath and flipped a switch in his head.

No sooner did the bus come to a stop then a very serious naval officer with a lot of colorful ribbons on his uniform and a red rope draped over his shoulder, but under his arm and by his side, came aboard. He was of shorter stature than what most of Bus #2 expected, so many of the guys began to relax. That was a mistake.

Before he even said a word, he looked intently at each person; when he got through, everyone knew who was in charge. His stern stare and his rock-hard clenched jaw were locked and loaded. He began with a very matter-of-fact presentation of the facts in a subdued but calloused voice: "I am Petty Officer First Class Rhoades. Recruits, you were placed on Bus #2. That was no accident. You have been assigned to me, because you have not given this process any respect. I have not had to be a Recruit

Division Commander (RDC, or drill instructor) for over a year, and I learned from several very capable USMC DI's how to get maggots like you ready for the Navy. I am going to treat you like the #2 you are."

Then he let out a scream that can only be described as coming from the devil himself: "GET OFF MY BUS! GET OFF MY BUS! GET OFF MY BUS!"

There were guys jumping up running into each other. No one wanted to go out the front where he was, so someone opened the back emergency door and people threw themselves out. Bodies were in a pile like a goal-line play in a football game. When RDC Rhoades stepped off the front of the bus, more people streamed out the front, including Shon. Shon had a fleeting thought go through his mind: *If Mark screws with me from here on out, I will take him out. So help me God!*

The RDC barked orders and insults at the same time. All the buses were dealing with the screaming, but there was something very different about Bus #2. It was mayhem as the guys on Bus #2 tried to form four lines like they were told. The screaming and the filthy language did not stop. Shon heard references to whale droppings and mommies and girlfriends who weren't there. People were getting smacked in the head if they weren't looking straight ahead. Then the RDC launched at one of those fun-loving guys right next to Shon and screamed, "Are you eyeballing me? No one eyeballs me. You are nothing. Just give me a reason to throw your scrawny butt to the ground and stomp on it."

Suddenly Shon's leg felt wet. He took a quick look down without moving his head. His pants were wicking the urine from the guy next to him. The RDC caught Shon's glance, and at once began yelling and degrading him. He moved on to the next recruit who had screwed something up; it never ended. The RDC kept screaming, barely taking a breath, yet his voice never once cracked or lost power. Shon immediately knew that it was

Chapter 13: Anchors Aweigh

time to keep the switch flipped on and make an impression. He would let all the others get punished, but he soon found out that it didn't work that way, either. Usually when one screwed up, everyone was punished.

After a mixture of standing there getting yelled at and doing push-ups, Shon thought the worst was over, until the RDC screamed, "March!" The marching looked a lot like running. As the group ran, the RDC screamed more insults. He had everyone run inside a building that had a narrow hallway. The RDC was going up and down the line making crude comments about all the guys' hair. He was laughing and screaming at the same time, saying that Erik Estrada and Tom Selleck wouldn't have to worry anymore. Everyone's perfect pretty hair would soon be a memory.

As Shon got closer, he heard someone saying, "Next" about every ten seconds. Shon knew there were some guys with full manes, and he couldn't understand how this could be. Maybe there were three or four barber chairs. Shon soon discovered that he wasn't at Doug's Barber Shop in Alliance, Ohio. There was one "barber," or to be more accurate, a "shearer," using industrial-grade clippers. The guy in front of Shon had one of those long feathered-back hairstyles that was parted in the middle. Ten seconds later, he looked like a white cue ball. Ten seconds after that, Shon looked exactly the same, and his head was immediately sensitive to any chill. There were many shades of cue balls now, and most of them were walking around even more in a haze than before. Everyone was issued utility clothes that were thrown at them, shower and shave gear, and a sea bag for travel. The RDC's screaming continued all the way to their barracks, called a "ship," which was the USS Hopper.

Bunks or racks were assigned, and then the RDC decided to tell everyone a bedtime story. It went something like this: "Once upon a time I had a bunch of dirty, stinkin' pieces of filth. They couldn't even stand in a straight line. Then one day a wizard came down and cut off all their pretty little locks. Their world started to get better when it was time to hit the rack! I want you recruits to know that you are nothing right now. Go to sleep and dream about what you think it takes, but right now you are nothing to me or to the Navy. Remember, this is day one of boot camp. You have a long way to go, so you better get your butts to sleep. I better not hear anyone cry or you will be running until the sun comes up. Oh, and you better know something else about your RDC: I don't need sleep." With that, the bedtime story was over and the lights were snapped off.

Even Shon, confident, but not cocky like the other ones in his section, laid there in the dark wondering what he had gotten himself into. No sooner than he felt himself drift off to sleep, the lights were turned on and the chaos began again. The RDC screamed for everyone to get out of their racks and to line up outside. All the other barracks were silent. This section got to start their day when it was still very dark and still very early, and Shon was convinced it was because of the actions of those in his Canton group. As it turned out, he was correct, and this only made him more determined to be focused. The running and the calisthenics began and didn't stop until the recruits from the other barracks started to join them on the grinder (asphalt pavement).

Training was under way. Everyone learned the Navy way to do everything. From shaving to making the bed, there was only one way. As the training went on, the RDC began to call us less four-letter names and started to assign everyone nicknames. People fell into one of three areas when it came to nicknames. The first were those who were making progress while nothing in their personality stood out, so the RDC gave them names that resembled their own last name. For instance, Nelson was Nelly, Thompson was Tommy, Buchtel was Buck.

The second category were not screw ups, but something in their personality or actions contributed to their nicknames. These

Chapter 13: Anchors Aweigh

included names such as Giggles, who had the most annoying girly laugh, Rooster, who annoyingly woke up every morning with a very loud yawn and clearing of the throat, and Crusher, who was that heavy guy who was very quickly getting into shape.

The last group of nicknames were given to the screw ups. Some of the names in that group were Fungus, Fuzznuts (later shortened to Fuzzy), Gronk, and Noodle. Good old Mark Chandler would fall into this last group. His nickname became Skid Mark, for obvious reasons.

RDC Rhoades of Division #052 didn't let up. Only two weeks in, and Shon knew that any inspection they had would result in torture and/or punishment. There were many of the sixty guys who were not getting the details down. After a hard day of marching and working on the USS Never Sail, the group went back to their USS Hopper and found the RDC ready for a bunk and locker inspection.

Shon knew that there wasn't going to be any free time for him to write letters. Normally, making a bed would be one of the easiest chores to accomplish, but when the RDC got done with the room, more than half the mattresses were thrown off their racks, and just as many footlockers were spilled onto the floor, mostly belonging to the same people. Those who passed inspection got to go outside and run the grinder until everyone had passed inspection and got to join them on the run.

When it was all over and everyone was feeling very beat down, the RDC assembled the group and said, "Recruits, you came in last week and you guys were full of yourselves. I came out of RDC retirement because we knew how worthless many of you were to the Navy. We have had barrack and dress inspections, along with PT scores, and you have finished dead last among the twelve divisions here. Listen to me right now. You better get your $!+%!#!%* together right now or I will tear each and every one of you into $%#@%&$&&& and ^$@^$*#%%&@^. I have never ever placed lower than third by the end of graduation, and

I better not this time, either. We have six more weeks. I am done taking it easy on you. You recruits are going to start to sweat and work. And when you screw up, you're going to pay with more. And just like my RDC told me back in the day, the more you sweat now in peace, the less you bleed in war. Are you ready to start winning around here?"

The entire division let out a loud "Yes, sir!"

Over the course of the next five weeks, Division #052 marched for hours at a time on the grinder in the rain, shine, and even some snow. They became so improved that RDC Rhoades allowed the recruits extra time to write letters. In one of the letters, Shon wrote,

> Mom, Dad, and Scott,
>
> I know that my first couple letters were vague regarding Navy training and some of the guys in my division. Also, I said not to worry about me because I was having loads of fun. Well, now I can tell you that this has been the hardest thing I have ever done, but it has been completely worth it. I can't wait to see you for graduation so I can tell you more.
>
> Love, Shon

Week three was the first week that Division #052 was presented with the winning flag for marching. They never gave it up. As far as the other inspections, there were some hiccups along the way, and DI Rhoades made sure Division #052 paid with extra physical training (PT), which Shon actually accepted as a challenge to get stronger and faster.

By week four, Division #052 was becoming a much-focused unit. They worked together to accomplish their firefighting training goals and all the ship deck tasks. In week five, Division

Chapter 13: Anchors Aweigh

#052 was carrying all four competition flags (Academic Achievement, Weapons and Military Drill, Compartment Readiness, and Physical Fitness). The guys' confidence was at an all-time high, which was good, because it would soon be time for the "Confidence Chamber" and another test involving a thirty-foot jump into the water with a flotation device.

First, the Confidence Chamber. Shon's heart rate began to increase as he recalled stories from others who had gone into the Chamber. The division walked into the compartment, sat down, grabbed the gas masks, and secured them properly, just as they were taught. The final instruction given was, "Gentlemen, do not panic. This is tear gas. What you learn here could save your life later. The lights will go out, and the gas will be released. You will be given some time to ensure that your equipment is working properly. When the lights come back on, everyone needs to take their masks off and stay calm before we open the doors for your release. And I do mean *stay calm*."

Shon and the others prepared themselves before it went dark and the gas could be heard. Shon did his best to concentrate on his breathing. He quickly thought of being under his Nova in the cramped tight space with little to no light. He began to find a better pace and rhythm to his breathing. When the lights came on, he was in control and the tear gas was manageable for him. Some of the other guys, including Skid Mark, failed. Those who failed heard about it from RDC Rhoades, and they had to repeat the Chamber.

At the beginning of week six there were many more drills and tests, but the one that made Shon and others anxious was the thirty-foot water jump. One by one, recruits ahead of Shon in line took turns making the jump and catching wind in a pair of utility pants to create a last-resort flotation device. This, too, was a test that needed to be passed, and many of the recruits who made the jump had trouble making the flotation device work.

When it was Shon's turn, he approached the edge, but then

he froze, with the utility pants in hand. A flashback to that awful summer night at Alliance Lake paralyzed Shon. The instructor by his side said, "Recruit, this is easy; it's only thirty feet, and gravity will help you. Now jump." Shon snapped out of it, took a deep breath, and jumped. He successfully inflated the pants and passed the test.

As week six came to a close, RDC Rhoades pulled Shon aside and asked, "Recruit, are you wondering why you were kept with this division?"

Shon answered, "Yes, sir. I have been wondering that since the beginning of training."

"How about now?" Petty Officer Rhoades asked.

"Sir, I couldn't do anything about it, so I chose to focus on the training."

"Yes, and you have done exceptionally well, recruit. But the reason you were originally left with this group was because you put down that you wanted to be in the SEAL Special Forces, so we had to know what you were made of. Recruit, I want to personally invite you to go in front of the RTC (recruit training command) board for inspections and an interview. Each division offers up its best for this review and awards."

"Thank you, sir. It will be my honor to represent Division #052," Shon confidently replied.

Shon returned to the USS Hopper and told the guys what he had the opportunity to do. They all agreed with the choice. Soon after, RDC Rhoades entered the barracks and everyone quickly stood at attention. He said, "Recruits, you have come a long way. I have never told you that I am originally from Ohio. When I heard that a bunch of cocky partiers were going to try and pull one over on this Navy, I gladly took the assignment to straighten you out. Tomorrow is Battle Stations—the final test. You will be up all night performing all the exercises you have learned and have been training to do without thinking. You all must do your individual jobs in order for the team to have suc-

Chapter 13: Anchors Aweigh

cess. If you pass Battle Stations, you go from miserable recruits to having the honor of becoming sailors in the United States Navy. Recruits, this is your ultimate test. Get in your racks and begin to think about everything you have learned. Run through it in your mind. Make it automatic. I have faith in each and every one of you. Good night."

All sixty recruits responded with, "Good night, sir."

Battle Station had the intensity and agony that everyone described, but Division #052 responded, and not a single person in the group was held back. Everyone passed. Standing in formation after the grueling twelve-hour hands-on test, RDC Rhoades had everyone take off their ball caps that said "Recruit," to be replaced with ones that now read "Navy."

They all continued standing at attention as they recited the Sailor's Creed:

> I am a United States Sailor. I will support and defend the Constitution of the United States of America and I will obey the orders of those appointed over me. I represent the fighting spirit of the Navy and those who have gone before me to defend freedom and democracy around the world. I proudly serve my country's Navy combat team with honor, courage and commitment. I am committed to excellence and the fair treatment of all.

Even through their exhaustion, the men of Division #052 celebrated with a burst of energy. Even RDC Rhoades cracked a smile for the first time. He then told his men, "You have some time to make phone calls to let people know the graduation details that have been placed on your rack back at the ship. Also, use this time to get some rest, because for the next week we are going to continue to drill so we can look sharp for the final Pass-In-Review/Graduation. You will also be given your orders for your next assignment, your A School (apprentice school) training."

The guys knew they were on the home stretch with boot camp, and they relaxed a little more. Even RDC Rhoades made a point of pulling back on any tough love and just razzed them about their few screw ups. One by one, RDC Rhoades invited each of the guys into his office and gave them their A School orders. Nelly opened his letter and saw that he had received his first choice of the Aviation Tech program. Buck went in to find out he was going to be part of the Seabee Engineering group. Noodle wanted to be on a submarine and got his wish.

Crusher went in next and only talked about doing one thing, and that was diving. He opened up his orders to find out he was accepted into the Navy diving school and would be going to Panama City, Florida, after graduation. Skid Mark was next. He was hoping for the diving school like Crusher, but instead, his orders put him on top of a ship for combat training. He definitely walked out a little dejected, but he knew he didn't score quite as well as Crusher on the underwater testing.

Finally, Shon entered the room and saw the last envelope on the table. RDC Rhoades said, "Son, let's see where you'll be going." Shon approached the envelope and looked at his RDC to see if he could read his face. "Come on. It's time to see what's next for you," the commander encouraged.

"Yes, sir," Shon said as he slid his finger through the sealed envelope and pulled out the letter. It didn't take him long to scan down to see the important parts.

Shon Huff
Next report: BUD/S (Basic Underwater Demolition/SEAL) Training.
Location: Coronado, California

Shon took a deep breath and then immediately closed his eyes, thinking, *We did it, Ryan. We did it!*

Chapter 13: Anchors Aweigh

RDC Rhoades quickly said, "Congratulations, sailor. Don't let the location fool you. You better be ready for more than I gave you. Go make us Ohio boys proud!"

"Yes, sir. I sure will," Shon replied.

Graduation day came, and Mr. and Mrs. Huff were there with Scott. Scott had been able to get out of his Friday classes at Ohio State's Agricultural Technical Institute in Wooster, Ohio. Along with the Huffs were thousands of others in the stands anticipating their first glimpse of their overhauled loved ones. They were treated to see these perfectly-in-unison marching groups dressed in perfectly fitted dress blue uniforms. As each division came into the drill hall, they were announced. They were each carrying the flag or flags they had earned. Division #052 carried all four flags, along with the most exemplary achievement division flag during the current training groups, called the Chief of Naval Operations Honor Division Recognition, or Battle E flag.

After the military band and choral performances, a few officers made speeches. The sailors knew the last speech was going to end with finding out who the best of the 850 recruits was, and each was hoping he would come from his own division. The greatly-decorated naval officer ended his speech with, "After accomplishing everything in the classroom, during training exercises, and showing leadership at all times, the one recruit to receive the Navy Club of the United States Military Excellence Award is—Shon Huff."

The Huff's all looked at each other as all the sailors gave him three cheers. Shon approached the four-star admiral, gave a salute, received the plaque, and stepped back in place with Division #052. A final song was played, and then a booming voice said, "Liberty call, liberty call. Fall out!"

After that command, the sailors relaxed and began to hunt for their loved ones. People poured out of the stands and into the sea of navy blue. Hugs and kisses were exchanged liberally and tears were being wiped away. Shon found his mom first, and she threw her arms around him. Shon said, "We did it. Ryan and I did it. We did this!" as he held up the plaque and began to cry.

Mrs. Huff choked back her tears and whispered in his ear, "You're my very sweet boy. I love you." They continued to hug as Mr. Huff and Scott walked up to give their hugs.

Mr. Huff said, "So proud of you, son! And I know Ryan is, too."

Scott quickly said, "You bet he is. You two are unstoppable."

Shon replied, "Thanks, bro. He definitely helped me out a lot over these last seven weeks. And now I am going to BUD/S training to hopefully be selected as a SEAL. I will definitely need more of his help!"

The Huffs left the base and traveled to Chicago for the entire next day before Shon needed to leave for California and A School. On their way into the city, Shon told his dad to pull into Sizzler. Shon ordered the biggest steak with all the sides to go with it.

As he sat down with his side of beef, he made the first cut and . . .

(Memories faded as an announcement was made.)

"Ladies and gentlemen, please buckle your seat belts and secure your trays. We are going to start our final approach to the Akron-Canton airport. Thank you." Shon felt like he was coming out of his clouds as he began waking up.

Shon got off the plane and was waiting for his bags when he heard a voice call out, "I thought Navy men knew how to travel light."

Shon immediately recognized his dad's voice, turned to him, and gave him a big hug. His dad said, "Welcome home, Son."

Chapter 13: Anchors Aweigh

"Thanks, Dad. It's been way too long. I'm so glad for this extra-long leave."

Mr. Huff then said, "Come on. Let's go home. You have time to see your mother for a little bit before the class reunion. Oh, and I'm supposed to tell you about your arrival at the Hall, but I'll do that on the ride. Come on. Let's get to the car."

Chapter 14:

BEST FRIENDS, BUT BIG CHANGES!

(Mandy and Beth—after high school: 1987-1988)

MANDY'S CELL PHONE RANG as she got in her car to leave for home. She recognized the number, flipped open her phone, and said, "Hi, Beth."

Beth, giving her the third degree, asked, "Are you still at your school?"

"Yes, but I'm leaving now," Mandy replied.

"Good. It's Friday night, so give yourself a break."

"I know, I know. You're right," said Mandy.

"I can't believe how much time you spend there, and to think how much we wanted to get out of high school! I have to laugh every time I think of that," Beth said.

"I know. I do the same thing. But, speaking of things unexpected, what about you?" She paused and then said, "You married a rock star!"

They both laughed uncontrollably, and then Beth said, "Listen, I wanted to make sure you were still going tomorrow. I definitely do not want to go alone."

"Why is that?" Mandy asked, laughing.

"Let's just say I changed a lot," Beth replied.

"Wow! That's the understatement of the decade," Mandy quipped.

Beth then answered abruptly, "Okay, enough crap from my best friend. Just promise me you'll be picking me up Saturday at 6:00 p.m. so we can get there at 6:30."

"Yes, I promise, but you have to promise me one thing," said Mandy.

"What's that?"

Mandy quickly screamed into the phone, "No tattoos!" and then pinched her phone shut and laughed hysterically.

Beth just shook her head and then burst out laughing. "I'll never live that one down," she said out loud.

Mandy, still laughing and driving away from the school, thought about how she and Beth had come full circle to stay best friends.

You know what they say about a woman's prerogative to change her mind? Well, when it was time for Mandy, Beth, and Joanne to begin their after-high-school plan together, Joanne backed out. She backed out of the job, of being a roommate—of everything. She became serious with a boy and didn't want to move away from him.

Undeterred, Mandy and Beth stuck to their plan and became even closer best friends. It was always a matter of fact that when and where you saw Mandy, you saw Beth. They worked the same shift at the box factory, they partied at the same bars and clubs, and of course, they were roommates. However, six months into this carefree routine, things began to change for Mandy. She was becoming more restless. Night after night of going out with Beth

Chapter 14: Best Friends, but Big Changes!

was becoming a chore. It felt forced. It was hard to explain, but it was just not what she wanted any longer. As was mentioned earlier, it is always a woman's prerogative to change her mind.

Mandy stayed home after work more often. She played the mother role in her friendship with Beth. Mandy kept track of her and made sure she knew where Beth's plans were going to take her. And yes, they even got into a few fights because Beth did not call Mandy to tell her when things changed. They were always able to patch things up, but it was increasingly hard for Beth to accept. It became more convenient to drive to work separately on many days.

On one of those days when Mandy drove separately, she had just finished her shift and pulled out of the parking lot to go back to the apartment, but for some reason she decided to go a little different way. She found herself taking the bypass around town. Next to the new school that was being built, she saw little girls playing soccer in the field. She was drawn to pull in, park, and watch. Mandy got out of her car, sat on the hood, and just stared at them. She saw the joy in their faces as their little ponytails and pigtails bounced with each step. It looked so pure, so innocent, so freeing. She couldn't take her eyes off the scene, and she got lost in remembering how things used to be for her. Mandy didn't realize that someone was approaching her.

A lady said, "Excuse me. Are you Mandy McConnell?"

Startled, Mandy replied, "Uh, yes, I am."

The lady quickly said, "I'm very sorry to have startled you, but I thought that was you. You don't know me. We've never met, but I've watched you a lot. My name is Deidra Kopley. First, my daughter is one of those little ponytailed girls out there playing, and secondly, I'm the new coach for the Mount Union College women's soccer team."

Mandy nodded her head and said, "Oh, that's great. How's it going?"

Alliance Lake ~ Be Still

Coach Kopley said, "We had a pretty good first season this past fall, but we have a long way to go. What are you up to now?"

Mandy replied, "Well, I'm working at the box factory."

The coach was a little surprised, but said, "Nothing against working there, but is that what you want to do for the rest of your life?"

"Yes," Mandy said sarcastically. "I mean, no; I don't know. I've never really thought about it."

Then Coach Kopley said, "Well, let me give you something to think about. I have room for one more assistant coach on my staff. I would like you to come work for me and pursue an education in something that will help you in your future."

Not believing what she just heard, Mandy said, "You want me to be your assistant? I am the same age as your players. Why would that be a good idea?"

"Trust me; it is," Coach Kopley said. "You were an elite player like I have never seen before, and I have also seen you as a coach on the field. You can do it. My girls will respect you. They all know your story, and you will make them so much better than they know they can be. Please think about it and call or stop by my office sometime soon to tell me your answer. You could start classes this summer, and of course we will have the new team in for conditioning." The coach smiled and started to run off toward her daughter's game.

Mandy went back to the apartment. As she changed into her night shirt, sweats, and slippers, she began to think about everything the coach was offering her. She was definitely not happy with how her life was going. She only knew of one person she needed to talk to at this critical point in her life—Coach E. It had been over six years, but she really needed his advice.

Mandy quickly ran into her bedroom, and in one motion she kicked off her slippers, flung her top off with one hand, and pulled her sweatpants off with the other. They got stuck on her

Chapter 14: Best Friends, but Big Changes!

heel, so she finished them off with a karate kick that sent them flying overtop the dresser. She grabbed a pair of Calvin Kleins and put a white t-shirt on. Then she put on her favorite flannel shirt and ran out the door.

Fifteen minutes later she was pulling into the Canton Public Library, about forty minutes before it closed. She quickly went to the reference desk and asked the librarian, "How do I find a phone number in Columbus, Ohio?"

The librarian answered with "Follow me." They went to an area where the shelves were full of nothing but phone books from all over the state of Ohio and some other larger cities across the U.S. The librarian stopped and said, "Here it is—the latest White and Yellow Pages for the Columbus area.

Mandy thanked her, and then she took the massive bound books to an empty table and began turning pages. She found the area of the White Pages that had some of the Ohio State University phone numbers. She jotted down several possible numbers, left the library, and went back to her apartment. It was too late to call the numbers today, but Mandy thought it was important enough to use a personal day tomorrow and call off work. She felt real good about her decision, which made going to sleep a lot easier.

As she thought about her day, she said a prayer for the first time in a long time: "Lord, what a day! I'm not sure what to make of it, but I ask for your help deciding about these opportunities I have. It's thrilling, but scary. Please let Coach E. be the help I need right now, like he was for me so many years ago. Amen."

Mandy was still excited and wanted to stay awake until Beth got home from the club so she could tell her the news about everything, but exhaustion won out and Mandy fell asleep. At the first morning light, Mandy enthusiastically popped out of bed, ran to Beth's bedroom, and jumped on her bed. "Beth, wake up! Wake up! You have to start getting ready for work, but I don't."

Beth answered Mandy's annoying outburst with a morning monotone, "Why aren't you going to work today?"

"Because I'm going to track down my old soccer coach," Mandy replied.

Beth yawned, stretched, and asked, "Why do you need to do that?"

Mandy told Beth everything that happened after work yesterday. She ended by telling Beth that she was seriously thinking about it, but quickly jumped a little closer toward Beth and said, "But I will never leave my roommate."

Beth cracked a smile, gave her a hug, and said, "Thanks, roomy."

Mandy then threw a pillow at Beth and said, "Now get up and get to work. I need some peace and quiet around here."

As Beth was in the bathroom getting ready, Mandy used her personal day and called off work. Beth left, and Mandy settled in on the couch. With a deep breath, she made her phone call to the Ohio State University. A woman at the main switchboard answered and said, "What college, please?"

Confused, Mandy asked, "Is this Ohio State?"

"Yes, miss. What college, please?"

Mandy replied, "Ohio State."

"No," the operator said abruptly. "I am asking you to tell me the college you want, like Business, Education, or Science."

Mandy was now very flustered and said, "I'm sorry. I don't know. I am trying to locate a Mr. Cliff Epolaski."

There was silence. Then after about a minute, the operator came on the phone and said, "Miss, I have checked all the colleges, and there is no one by that name here at Ohio State."

Mandy was very upset, but said, "Thank you," and hung up. It was only 8:30, and Mandy convinced herself that she wasn't ready to give up. Getting off the couch, it hit her that she had to go to the University of Akron next. After taking her shower and getting ready, she drove to Akron to talk to the current soccer coach to see if he could tell Mandy about Coach E's whereabouts.

Chapter 14: Best Friends, but Big Changes!

Mandy arrived on campus and walked to the James A. Rhodes Arena (The JAR), where most of the athletic coaches had offices. She found the door with a picture of a soccer ball next to it on the window, and she let herself in. There she saw a man on the phone behind another small office door waving her in to see him.

Mandy thought, *This is no time to be intimidated,* and she walked through that door. The man who motioned for Mandy to have a seat as he finished his phone call happened to be the men's soccer coach.

He hung up and quickly said, "You're Mandy McConnell, aren't you?"

Mandy was now a little intimidated and taken aback, being recognized two days in a row. She answered, "Yes, I am."

"I thought so," said the men's coach. "Are you looking for the women's coach?"

"No," she said. "I need to ask you something."

"Me? Okay. How can I help?"

Mandy said, "I'm trying to find Cliff Epolaski."

The coach began to laugh and said, "Well, if you were here last year at this time, you could have talked to him face-to-face."

Mandy got a shocked look on her face and exclaimed, "What? Really?"

"Yes," he said. "Cliff was working on his master's degree in exercise science here at Akron. He graduated just last year. He was accepted to continue his research and pursue his PhD at a school in Texas.

Mandy, still excited, asked, "Can you tell me which school in Texas?"

The coach replied, "No, but I can send you to someone in his old department who will know." Mandy began to jump around in her seat eagerly waiting for his instructions. He quickly jotted a map on a piece of paper and handed it to her.

Mandy shook his hand and said, "Thank you."

Off she went, walking briskly across campus with the next clue in hand to find what she was looking for. She found the building and raced up the stairs, missing every other step. Rounding the corner, she saw the door with #317 on it and a sign that said "Exercise Science."

Mandy opened the door and was greeted by someone who asked, "May I help you?"

Out of breath, Mandy answered, "I hope so. I really need to find out what school in Texas Mr. Epolaski went to. He used to be my soccer coach, and I really need his advice right now."

"Oh, sweety. That's easy. Mr. Epolaski went to Baylor College of Medicine. I even have a direct phone number for him."

Mandy couldn't believe how things were coming together. She gratefully said, "Thank you so much. What a relief."

The lady pointed behind her and said, "Honey, why don't you go into that conference room and make your call?"

Mandy couldn't believe what was being offered. "Are you sure?" Mandy asked.

The lady said, "Yes. We call long distance so much, we have a monthly charge. Believe me, it's just fine."

Knowing how much long distance calling costs per minute were, Mandy wasn't going to refuse. She went into the conference room and took a seat in one of the high-backed leather swivel chairs. All of a sudden, she got real nervous. Her heart started to race as she knew this was it. She was about to call Coach E. She took a couple deep breaths and began to dial, whispering to herself, "Coach E. will help me. Coach E. will help me."

The phone was answered by a familiar voice saying, "Hello?"

Mandy said, "Coach E, this is . . ."

Coach E. quickly piped up and said in unison with her, "Mandy McConnell. What are you doing calling me? It's so good to hear from you. I wonder about you a lot. How are you doing?" He finally stopped and they both laughed together at his rapid-fire questions.

Chapter 14: Best Friends, but Big Changes!

Mandy said, "First, I had quite the time tracking you down at your current college. I am currently sitting in the Exercise Science office at the University of Akron." Coach E. laughed some more. She told him that she was doing okay, but wondered if he had a few minutes to speak to her now.

He immediately said, "Yes, of course."

Mandy told Coach E. about how things went downhill after her surgery, and that the rest of her high school career had not been a very positive experience. She told him that she was working at a box factory and paying the bills. Then she explained the amazing thing that happened with Mount Union yesterday, but told him that she was really scared about the opportunity. She had left high school not enjoying studying, and she left soccer broken and not able to play like she wanted to.

Coach E. let Mandy finish and then said very calmly, "Mandy, listen to me. This is an opportunity that God has brought before you. Trust me. I have seen things that happen that only make sense when you think of a heavenly plan. I know you are scared and unsure. You ask how the girls will accept you as their coach when you are basically the same age. I say that you will show them in a very real way how to play and love the game with all the intensity and fun that you always played with. This is just a beginning of the next great chapter in the life of Mandy McConnell. Will it be hard? Yes, probably. It will stretch you and make you uncomfortable at times. And you know, nothing is more worth it in the end than when you go through something like that."

Mandy said, "Yes, Coach, but my injury."

He said, "Mandy, you will be an excellent assistant coach. You are no longer an elite athlete. You have to accept that; but you can do wonderful things with this opportunity. You never know when you will leave a sport as an athlete, and most of the time the decision is made for you. Whether you are sixteen, twenty-six, or thirty-six, you never know what will happen. For you it was at sixteen. Okay, fine. Now what? Sometimes it is an injury or sometimes it is the next big thing—the next Mandy McConnell." Mandy began to laugh.

Coach E. continued, "Don't you want to inspire girls to see and feel the things you did when you were out there doing amazing things on the soccer field? Again, I believe God has brought you to this time in your life for you to trust Him as you take this ride. He won't abandon you. Can I also let you know that this old coach of yours won't abandon you either? I promise I will stay in touch with you from here on out. In fact, every time you have a championship game, I will travel to be there!"

Mandy said, "Well, I will be seeing you a lot then!" They both laughed and exchanged phone numbers before they said goodbye. Walking back to her car, Mandy knew that her next stop was at the campus of Mount Union College.

Once there, she sat down with Coach Kopley and discussed everything about the position. Mandy became more excited about this opportunity and even about going back to school. The assistant coach's position would pay for most of her college tuition costs and also provide enough to allow her to stay in her apartment. Coach Kopley walked Mandy over to the administration building so she could finish her paperwork for the assistant coach position and also register for summer classes.

After she completed a stack of paperwork the best she could, she brought it to an adviser assigned to her to help review and finalize everything. Once completed, it was time to schedule classes. The first thing the adviser wanted to know was what Mandy's major would be. Mandy reviewed her options and chose elementary education. She also wanted to take as many health and nutrition classes as possible. With a couple signatures and stamps, Mandy was not only a student at Mount Union, but she was now the new assistant coach for the women's Purple Raiders soccer team.

Chapter 14: Best Friends, but Big Changes!

Mandy made it back to her apartment in time to collapse on her bed until Beth got home from work. This time it was Beth who came running into the apartment and jumped on Mandy's bed. "Wake up, sleepyhead. How did your day go?" Mandy was still so exhausted and sleeping so soundly that she hardly moved. Beth tried jumping on the bed again and said, "Hey! It's after 5:00. Your personal day is over. Wake up!"

This time the pile of covers shuffled, and Mandy pulled herself up and asked, "What time is it?"

Beth answered, "About 5:15. Time to think about food. What did you cook for me today?"

Mandy looked through her squinted eyes and said, "Yeah, right." Then after a big stretch and groan she said, "I have so much to tell you, but I want to save it for dinner. I want to call my mom and see if she will join us."

Beth said, "Sounds good. Hurry up and make plans. I'm hungry."

Mandy called her mom and made arrangements to meet at Parasson's Italian Restaurant. After they arrived and ordered, Mrs. McConnell said, "Okay, Mandy, what's your news?"

"Mom," Mandy said, "I'm going to college."

Mrs. McConnell didn't ask any questions, but got up and went over to her and gave her a hug right in the middle of the busy restaurant. She said, "That's so wonderful. Tell me more."

"Yeah," Beth said. "Tell us more."

Mandy explained everything that happened to her in the past twenty-four hours. They laughed and cried as the story was shared. Mandy ended it by saying, "I just know this is what I'm supposed to do next."

Mandy's mom was very happy for Mandy and excited about her future. Beth, on the other hand, was glad for her, but somehow felt like she was getting left behind.

Chapter 15:
IT'S JUST A PHASE

(Mandy and Beth—after high school: 1988-1989)

AS SUMMER GOT UNDERWAY, Mandy became extremely busy learning how to be a dedicated student and a part of a college coaching staff. There was so much going on that she and Beth barely saw each other. Mandy went from the motherly figure who kept track of everything coming and going to someone focused on her own busy life. There were many times when Mandy and Beth didn't see each other for days. Beth knew things were very different when she ended up staying over at a guy's place back-to-back nights and Mandy never even said anything to her when they did finally see each other on Sunday evening.

Without Mandy being active in Beth's life on a regular basis, Beth began not holding back, and was now more out of control than before; however, this time she was not in high school and no longer did she have to consider her dad, the pastor. For the first time in her life she felt like she had no one looking over her shoulder judging her. Her behavior became very destructive very quickly.

Beth was now an even better actress than at any other point in her life. Yes, she was happy for Mandy, but she wasn't ready to figure out what her own next chapter should be. She was content to explore the easy and the familiar. Just like water taking the path of least resistance, Beth went with the flow right into the dark and depressing world of the underground club movement.

In this underground subculture, all those who felt like society's outcasts felt accepted. Beth became more and more interested in people who were living out a Gothic/Goth lifestyle. She was transformed from a brown-haired girl next door to a waif of a woman with sleek coal-black hair and lips and eyeliner to match. Most of her outfits included a corset that was adorned with black velvet and black and leather lace combinations. Her accessories would include fishnet gloves that would reach past the crease in her elbows and the best leather and silver-spiked dog collar that an upscale pet shop could offer. This would break up her creamy white face with her pasty white shoulders, upper arms, and ample bosom that left nothing to the imagination. Gone were any type of girly pumps, flats, or heals. Beth had a variety of boots, most with leather straps and silver eyelets, and ranging from ankle-length to over-the-knee high. The black skirts were always cute. Some had lots of layers of fabric and frills with even longer and more tasteful formal trains. Let's just say Beth and her friends stood out. If the idea was to walk around looking all morose, melancholy, and full of angst, then they were nailing it.

Every night Beth was transformed into Lady Macbeth at one of the small clubs up in the Akron or Cleveland areas that supported the Goth scene. Lady Macbeth was always somewhere at night listening to the latest shock death metal sounds of Nine Inch Nails or Marilyn Manson. Then when they wanted to play a "slow dance" classic song they would play some Megadeth or Metallica. By the end of the night, everyone in the club left

Chapter 15: It's Just a Phase

with their ears ringing and their shiny black boots in lockstep to continue to hate anything mainstream.

Lady Macbeth and her new best friend, Lady Victoria, always found out where the after-club party would continue with more alcohol, pot, and an occasional LSD trip. This group didn't care for anything or anyone that wasn't Goth. Everyone at these all-night hangouts was definitely channeling his or her inner Dracula. Just before sunrise, people would scatter to endure the headaches and mandates of society. But as the sun set on another day, the Goth angst would take over for another night.

One Friday night as people were leaving The Chamber in Cleveland, someone suggested to have the after-party at a secluded cemetery on the east side. People, including both "The Ladies," packed the cars and drove twenty minutes to the cemetery. As people were enjoying a little different venue to express their "gothness," someone in a drunken state said, "Hey, we deserve a big metal concert here in Akron or Cleveland."

Then Lady Macbeth said, "I think I'll try and get Mutilated Heart." The group laughed (which was very "ungoth-like"). Lady Macbeth continued, "The lead singer was actually born and raised in the Canton area and attended school there. I think I could get him to come back."

No one was laughing now. They all chanted (which is "goth-like") Lady Macbeth's name as they became more excited (which, again, is "ungoth-like"). As the chanting died down, Lady Victoria asked Lady Macbeth, "Do you really think you can get them?"

Lady Macbeth replied, "I sure hope we can."

Lady Victoria said, "You'd better be able to now," as they both laughed (which is, being extremely redundant, very "ungoth-like!").

As dawn was quickly approaching, the two Ladies headed back to Victoria's apartment, where Beth began to plan her phone calls. She found Mutilated Heart's management group information in an article from one of Victoria's metal magazines. From there she called an operator for information on the name and city. Only seconds later, they had a phone number. Beth did not waste any time. Even though she was scared, she decided not to hesitate or think about it. She began to dial.

A very nice sounding voice answered the phone and said, "Hello, can I help you?"

Beth was shocked at how easy it was still going, but she quickly said, "Hi, my name is Beth Russell. I am from where Danny Rowel grew up in Ohio. We have a loyal group in the Goth metal scene and we want to invite him to come home for a concert."

Then the man with the nice-sounding voice said, "I am the manager. Thank you for calling. You have definitely given me something to think about. Give me your number, and I will be back in touch in a week or so."

After Beth hung the phone up, she let out a very happy squeal of delight (yeah, I won't mention the gothness or ungothness of that).

About a week later, the manager called Beth and gave her the details of the upcoming concert. He told her that the purpose was not going to be to get people to come out based on flyers in the underground clubs and alternative radio spots, but the purpose was going to be to shock the people. They wanted them to know that what was coming would be unlike anything they had ever seen in their community. They were looking to shock people into paying attention and wanting to check them out. The idea was to whip everyone into a frenzy and have word of mouth be the best fuel for ticket sales and exposure.

The plan worked to perfection as one mainstream radio program in the area after another promoted the shocking death-metal message that Mutilated Heart delivered. Within days, the preachers and politicians began to march in front of the

Chapter 15: It's Just a Phase

news cameras asking for a ban on this concert event. Then like a gift from the dark side, a group calling themselves Ohioans for Children and Families got national headlines and TV time when they announced that the Mutilated Heart concert would violate the Harmful to Minors Act. As news of the concert swirled, every curious non-conforming wannabe bought a ticket. From a one-concert show that would be modestly attended, they were now going to play to a packed theater on Thursday, Friday, and Saturday nights.

Beth received a phone call a week before the show. It was the manager. He said, "Beth, you were the inspiration for this show. Because you have given the band so much free press and notoriety, you and five of your friends can have all-access passes during all three nights." Beth was almost speechless, but managed to say, "Thank you."

Beth and her friends could not believe how well things came together. She was counting down the days before the best thing in her life was going to happen—being able to have full access to Mutilated Heart!

Mandy knew Beth was getting in very deep with this Goth stuff, but was glad she was finding some new friends and activities. Mandy always looked at this as a bizarre phase that couldn't last. She was very busy with her new opportunities at Mount Union.

During the three nights outside the concert hall, picket signs and cameras gathered as the band unleashed the dark message in an eardrum-piercing fury of sound from the microphones and amplifiers. Any voice that Lady Macbeth would hear in her soul now would have to scream as loud as a death metal band screaming toward her in front of the speakers against the stage. She couldn't get enough of the sights, the sounds, and the feelings as each concert went on, each one better than the last. Beth's mind was racing a mile a second trying to process the euphoria.

After the concert ended on Saturday night, the Ladies and four of their friends were once again backstage and in awe of the performances of their new idols. They were hanging out with the band as the equipment was being loaded into the buses, preparing to leave for Cincinnati and more controversy.

The manager called for the band to head out. They got on the bus and began to wave goodbye to the remaining group of gothic fans. Suddenly and without any warning, Lady Macbeth turned to Lady Victoria and said, "I need to leave. Come with me!"

Lady Victoria said, "Beth, No. Are you crazy?"

Beth said, "Maybe, but I'm still going. Tell Mandy I'm sorry about skipping out on her and the apartment and that I love her." Then the first official band groupie ran and jumped into the bus.

Victoria gave it one more try. "What about your job?"

Beth responded with a black-lipped smile, saying, "Just tell them I've decided to think outside the box." The doors of the bus closed and the air brake was released. The bus began to coast away, then it revved up and left with a thick heavy cloud of diesel exhaust to match the night air.

Victoria had the phone numbers for Beth and Mandy, but decided to wait until 7:30 a.m. before she called Mandy to tell her everything. At 7:30, Victoria called Mandy, who was getting ready for work. "Hello," Mandy said.

"Mandy, this is Victoria."

"Oh, yes. Hi. Do you need to speak to Beth?" Mandy asked.

"Uh, well, no. She's not there," Victoria answered.

"What, really? Where then?" Mandy said.

"On her way to Cincinnati with the band Mutilated Heart on their tour bus," she replied.

Mandy was still really confused but was waking up fast. She said, "Uhhhhhh, what? Okay, thanks for letting me know. I will call her parents right now."

Right before Mandy hung up, Victoria quickly added, "Wait! She wanted me to tell you to tell her employer that she

Chapter 15: It's Just a Phase

has decided to quit and think outside the box. Also, she is sorry for leaving you like this and that she loves you."

As Mandy hung up the phone, stunned by Beth's compulsive decision, she said a quick prayer for Beth and for her safety and then wondered what she would say to Beth's parents in mere minutes. After Mandy loaded up her car with her bookbag and soccer bag, she dropped onto the couch to make the phone call she was dreading. It was 8:00 a.m.

The phone rang. "Good morning. Pastor Russell speaking."

Mandy took a deep breath and said, "Pastor Russell, this is Mandy McConnell. I just got a call from Beth's friend Victoria." Mandy hesitated to find the words.

Pastor Russell said, "Go on, Mandy. Please tell me about the call."

"Well, she is now a groupie with Mutilated Heart."

Pastor Russell began to laugh and asked, "What is Mutilated Heart?"

After Mandy explained everything she knew about the band, Pastor Russell calmly said, "Thank you for calling and making me aware of Beth's choice. Please go on with your college classes and your coaching."

"But, Pastor . . ." Mandy said, before she was interrupted.

"Mandy, Beth has made this choice, and we are not going to chase her down. We are going to pray that she will hear the Lord's voice in this matter. She is not listening right now. But I pray that she soon will; and when she does, she will call one of us. When she calls, we will both drop everything and go running to her. Okay?"

"Yes, sir." Mandy replied, before she hung up. She left for class and went on to soccer practice. Days and then weeks went by. Mandy was into her routine with the Mount Union Purple Raiders. The games would start next week. She was making a difference to the team. Coach Kopley put her in charge of conditioning and drills. All she did was use the wisdom from Coach

E's "training manual," which, boiled down, simply meant that my team will be in better condition than yours.

Mandy made the girls run and run some more—sprints, mid-distance, and long distance. She even had a few players who said they may switch to the cross-country team, and she had to laugh. When they did run soccer drills, half the time was without the ball. Mandy made sure the team was going to be the fastest to the ball and have an extremely aggressive pace as they set the play toward the opponent's goal. Coach Kopley was very pleased with the results she was seeing at practice, and she knew Assistant Coach Mandy was an extremely talented coach.

Before the season started, no one thought that Mount Union would be in competition for the league title. Not only were they competitive, but they won two out of every three games and were in the hunt for the championship going into the last two weeks of the season.

Like most days, Mandy came home exhausted. The October sky was nearly dark. Mandy noticed a bright "2" flashing on her answering machine. She went over and pressed the button. The tape rewound and played back a soft and beaten down voice, "Mandy, this is Beth, and I'm ready to come home. Please call me back at the woman's shelter in Fort Lauderdale. I guess I'll call my dad, too."

Then the answering machine beeped and the second message was an exuberant voice that said, "Mandy, this is Pastor Russell. Our prayers have been answered. Beth is in Florida and will soon be coming home on a flight to Akron/Canton. Just wanted you to know. Thanks for being there. I'll let you know more after we get her."

And with that, the answering machine beeped again and all was quiet—until Mandy threw her hands in the air and cried, "Thank you, thank you, thank you, Lord!" and she fell onto the couch kicking her feet like she was peddling a bicycle.

Chapter 15: It's Just a Phase

The reunion at the airport was one the Russells had been looking forward to for a long time. As Beth came out of the gate tunnel, she looked worn down as she searched the crowd for her waiting mom and dad. People and their carry-on bags were bumping into her as they passed. When the crowd cleared enough to create a small opening, Pastor Russell darted in to wrap his arms around her, and he helped her to the side, where Beth's mom joined the huddle.

Beth said in a very tired and hoarse voice, "I just want to go home."

Her mom gave her a kiss on her greasy matted hair while her dad just continued to hold her to the point that all of her weight was now in his arms. Mrs. Russell took the one small leather bag that Beth was carrying so Pastor Russell could completely lift Beth's body in his arms and carry her to the car. Beth slept the entire trip back to Alliance. Pastor Russell parked the car and carried Beth into the house and into her waiting bed. She slept until the next evening.

As she awoke, she could smell her mom's famous cinnamon rolls. Beth stretched, smiled, and walked into the kitchen to see the steam rising off the simmering pot of homemade chicken soup. Beth didn't say anything, but just gave her mom a hug from behind as she was stirring the soup. Bayla, the loving Australian-shepherd mix, wanted to offer her welcome home to Beth, also. Beth bent down and gave Bayla a squeeze and said, "I missed you too, girl. But right now, I am so hungry."

Her mom laughed and said while she was pointing to the cinnamon rolls, "Good. We need to eat some of these before your dad gets home."

Beth grabbed the gooiest one from the cooling rack and said, "I'm going to take a quick shower."

Beth's mom lovingly smiled and said, "Please don't rush your shower, honey."

A long silence was broken when their eyes met and they both laughed out loud. "Thanks, Mom," Beth expressed dramatically as she left the kitchen.

Beth stepped into the shower and let the warm water pour over her head. She felt the dirt and grime literally washing away, and she hoped it was washing away figuratively, too. She breathed in the hot steam as she took her time washing her body and hair. A shower never felt so good to her. It definitely helped her come back to life. Beth decided to step out of the shower as the nearly hot water was turning on the cool side of warm by now.

She got dressed and returned to the kitchen to see her dad with a big smile. Beth returned the smile and slipped into his outstretched arms. "Hi, Daddy."

"Come on. Let's eat," Beth's mom insisted.

"How about a prayer first?" asked Pastor Russell.

They sat down and grabbed each other's hands. Pastor Russell began to pray: "Lord, thank you for bringing our Beth home. We are so glad you answered our prayers to protect her and guide her back to us. We ask for nourishment from this food. Let us always look to You for our source of strength in this life. In Jesus's name, Amen."

"Amen," Beth repeated.

As Mrs. Russell gave Beth a huge steaming bowl of chicken soup, Beth took in a deep breath to revive her senses of comfort and security. She was again very thankful that the past three weeks were over. She filled her spoon to overflowing and put it to her lips, when all of a sudden the doorbell rang. Bayla let out a bark and Pastor Russell went to the door to see who it was. He came back into the kitchen with Mandy. Beth jumped out of her seat and ran to Mandy, throwing her arms around her and crying out, "I missed you. I missed you."

Mandy laughed and said, "I am so glad you are back. I missed you, too."

Chapter 15: It's Just a Phase

Mrs. Russell then said, "Come on, everyone. Sit down. Please join us, Mandy."

"Wow! Thank you," she replied.

Then Pastor Russell said, "Beth, I know you went through a lot and we were very worried about you."

Beth cleared her throat and said, "First, I want to tell the three most important people to me that I am really sorry for scaring them. I also want to say that I did some stuff that was very stupid. It will definitely take a while for me to work through and get over all that happened."

Mrs. Russell took the napkin from her lap and wiped her streaming tears. Beth continued. "That's why I had to get home. At this time, I'm not ready to talk about the specifics of what happened. I prefer to block it out. Maybe someday I will journal about it."

Mrs. Russell blotted her eyes and just kept thinking how good it was to have Beth back and that their prayers were answered. The evening went by fast as Mandy and Beth laughed and talked. When they walked into the family room where Pastor and Mrs. Russell were watching TV, Beth said, "Mom and Dad, I asked Mandy if she would have me back as a roommate. I told her I would get two jobs and work really hard to gain her trust back. And she said yes!"

"That's great, girls." Pastor Russell said. "Please let us know if we can help out with anything."

Beth started working at a truck stop during the day and at a video store at night. It didn't take too long for Beth to pay Mandy back. They were still both real busy, but this time they did not let that become an excuse. They made time to talk. Mandy filled Beth in on everything going on at Mount Union, including all the funny stories from her classes and some of the soccer drama. Then Beth had a chance to tell Mandy about how many more truckers asked her to hit the road with them.

Every time, they would both scream "Eewww, gross," and then she would give her rehearsed answer to them, which was, "Uh, I already tried something like that. Didn't like it too much. No thanks. More coffee?" There were a couple times she was tempted by a few young bad-boy bikers who came in and started sweet-talking her, but she resisted the urge.

Chapter 16:

TWO BIG BOYS

(Mandy and Beth—after high school: 1990-1992)

THE WOMEN'S SOCCER PROGRAM at Mount Union became better and better. In fact, during Mandy's third and fourth year of coaching, they won the league championship. As promised, Coach E. was right there to cheer them on. Mandy achieved much as an assistant coach, and she had Coach Kopley to thank. One day Coach Kopley saw Mandy enter the training room next to her office, and she called her in.

"Mandy, I want to know your plans for next year. You are student teaching right now and will be graduating in May. What's next for you?"

Mandy took a deep breath and said, "Well, I'm not entirely sure. If I knew of a high school opening for a girls' soccer coach, then I would probably check it out, but I'm just not sure how to go about any of that."

"Well," Coach said, "I know we have a great thing going with you here, but I wouldn't be doing my job if I didn't tell you about an opportunity that I just found out about." Mandy scooted the chair a little closer to the desk and leaned forward. "Mandy," the coach continued, "Medina Schools would like to talk to you about a gym-and-health teacher opening, along with their high school girls' soccer coach position."

Mandy flew out of the chair and gave the coach a big hug that almost knocked her out of her office swivel chair. Coach said, "I take it you want to talk to them."

"Yes!" she said, and then asked hesitantly, "If it doesn't work out, can I still coach for you?"

"Yes, of course. You had better," she answered.

They hugged again, and Mandy was given the contact information. Mandy hurried to get back to the apartment and tell Beth before she had to go work at the video store. With unleashed excitement, Mandy rushed through the door and yelled to Beth, "Hey, my dear, we need to celebrate!"

Beth met her in the living room and asked, "What for?" as she pulled her ponytail through her hairband for a final time.

Mandy replied, "I have a good lead on a teaching and coaching job."

"That's so great!" Beth shouted. "I have time to go to Big Boy right now and buy you a sundae to celebrate."

"That sounds perfect," Mandy said. Mandy grabbed the health test and some homework from one of her student-teaching classes so she could grade after Beth left. The girls had a great time finishing off their hot fudge sundaes before Beth had to leave to get to the video store.

As Mandy pulled out her papers to grade, she stopped the waitress and asked for a cup of hot tea. Mandy began to grade the papers, but looked up when her hot water and selection of tea bags were delivered to her table. She chose an English Breakfast tea and added the water and some honey. As the tea

Chapter 16: Two Big Boys

was steeping, she noticed a guy in the far corner with his head down and a pile of papers on his table. Maybe it was the good news she had received today or maybe it was that she wasn't ready to begin grading the papers, but Mandy got up and went over to the stranger's table and said, "Excuse me."

With a flip from his long dark hair, along with a nervous heel and a tapping red pen, the stranger looked up at Beth and said, "Oh, sorry. Am I being annoying? It's a habit. I'm a music major. I'm a student teacher and I have lots of papers to grade. I'm rambling. I'm sorry. Am I being annoying?" He picked up his coffee and took a sip.

Mandy began to crack up and then said, "No, you're not being annoying. I thought you might be a teacher, so I decided to find out. I'm a teacher, too. I go to Mount Union. I'm Mandy McConnell."

"Hi, Mandy. I'm Matt Griffith, and I attend Malone College. I'm so stressed-out right now with all these papers to grade and with graduating this May. I've been sending out resumes, but haven't found any leads on a band teacher job anywhere. How about you?"

"Well, I'll graduate in May, also, and I just got a real good lead on an elementary health and phys-ed position at Medina schools, along with coaching girls' soccer."

Matt immediately said, "Congratulations! Hey, do you want to bring your papers over and grade with me?"

"Sure. That sounds good." Mandy moved all her papers and hot tea over opposite Matt and then asked, "I know you can probably play a lot of instruments, but what is your favorite?"

Matt quickly picked up his silverware and banged out a little drum solo. When he finished, he said, "The oboe." They both laughed and began to grade their papers, asking each other a lot of questions and laughing back and forth. Soon it was approaching midnight, and the waitress began making subtle hints that they were closing.

Matt said, "Hey, can I have your phone number to call you?"

Mandy replied, "No."

Matt was a little shocked and dejected, but didn't say anything. Then Mandy quickly said, "You're going to have to meet me here tomorrow night for that."

He quickly flashed her a smile and said, "I'll have your hot tea ready."

The next night couldn't come around fast enough for Matt. He was on his third cup of coffee when Mandy walked in with quite a full bookbag. Matt didn't have anything to grade, so he offered to help. She pushed some papers his way, squeezed some honey into her tea, and said, "Thanks for your help. I found out my interview with Medina is in two days, and I'm starting to get nervous."

Matt said, "You'll do great. You are everything they want for a teacher and coach. Just be yourself. I really like who that is." After Matt finished saying that, he turned red. He then said, "Ah, you know what I mean, right?"

Mandy laughed and said, "And I like who you are, too. In fact, I owe you this." Then she opened her bookbag and pulled out a piece of paper with a phone number. Matt immediately ripped it in half and looked up at her reaction. She was unfazed. Matt started to laugh, and then he grabbed her red pen and wrote his number on the other half of the paper. They ended up being there at Big Boy's closing time again.

As they got ready to leave, Matt told Mandy that he had an ensemble concert the next night at the college. Mandy explained that she wanted to prepare for the interview and that talking on the phone would be best, but they promised each other they would meet again in two days and talk about everything then.

Matt's concert went well, and Mandy's interview went extremely well. In fact, the principal told Mandy that as soon as

Chapter 16: Two Big Boys

she looked over all the hiring information she would recommend her to the board of education to be hired. She was thrilled and grateful beyond belief. She drove straight back to Alliance and gave her mom the news. Her mom was very happy for Mandy, and even though she would be about an hour away, she knew that this first teaching and coaching job was a wonderful opportunity for her.

Quickly, Mandy went to the phone and dialed Matt's dorm phone. After Mandy hung up the phone, her mom said, "Was that Beth?"

"No," Mandy said. "I met someone who is going to Malone but will be graduating this spring, like me."

Mrs. McConnell, replied, "Oh, really?" and raised her chin and pursed her lips.

"Mom," Mandy said in a playful way, "we have already met at Big Boy a couple of times."

Then her mom said, "And?"

"And . . ." Mandy said with a smile, "I like him. I never would have thought he was my type, but there's something there, I think."

Mandy's mom gave her a hug and told her that she was proud of her. Mandy told her she'll see her later in the weekend, but that she needed to get back to her apartment before Matt got there.

Mandy's mom said, "Wait. He's going over to your apartment? Beth is at the video store, right?"

"Yes, Mom. It's okay!"

"Well, just in case, be ready to use one of your soccer kicks on him!" Mrs. McConnell shouted.

"Yes, Mom. I will."

Mandy left and got to the apartment just ahead of Matt. She quickly tidied up and waited for him. Not long after she sat down, there was a knock at the door. She opened the door to see an assortment of spring flowers and a card on the stoop. She picked up the bouquet. With a smile on her face, she quickly looked around and opened the card. It read, "Congratulations! You will brighten up Medina like you brightened up my life."

Mandy said, "Hello? If you're not out there somewhere, Matt, then I have a real mystery man to figure out."

Matt came around the corner and asked, "How'd you know?"

Mandy invited him in, and they sat on the couch and began to talk about their lives some more, from family to past friendships and experiences. They were in the middle of talking about Beth and roommate stuff when Beth got home from the video store.

As she walked in the door, Mandy said, "And here is that crazy roommate of mine."

"Hi," Beth said to Matt, as she closed the door behind her.

Mandy quickly spouted off an official introduction. "Matt, this is Beth Russell, and Beth, this is Matt Griffith. Hurry up and sit down. I haven't had a chance to tell you about everything."

Beth went to her room and changed clothes. She came out and sat down next to Mandy to find out that Mandy and Matt met at Big Boy the other day after she left. Mandy also told Beth that it looked very good that the Medina job was hers for next year. Beth delivered a big hug to Mandy and let out a squeal of joy. Both girls began talking a mile a minute, with Beth asking one question after another, and Mandy doing her best to keep up with the answers.

After things settled down, Mandy said, "Oh, Beth, Matt told me that he's a PK [preacher's kid] just like you."

Beth said, "Oh, really? Then I know he's trouble, and I am going to watch out for you."

The girls started to laugh, and Matt said, "Now wait . . ."

The three of them talked well past midnight, until Matt told them he had to get back to his dorm. Before he left, he asked them if they would both be up for doing something tomorrow night with his friends.

Chapter 16: Two Big Boys

Mandy said she was free, but Beth had to see if she could get the night off from the video store. Mandy pulled on Beth's arm and said with a smile, "She'll be there with me."

"Great," Matt said. "Park outside the student union around 7:00 p.m. and come on in. You'll see what's going on at that time."

Beth was able to get off work, and the girls drove over to Malone's campus. They parked near the student union and began walking toward the building. Before they got there, they could hear loud music booming. Mandy and Beth looked at each other and began to laugh, because Malone was a Christian college and they did not expect rock music to be blasting. When they walked into the student union, there were people everywhere. Over the stage was a banner that read, *1992 Battle of the Bands.*

Matt walked over to them and began shouting over the music about coming closer to the stage to meet the guys. He took them to a table closer to the front and off to the right of the stage. There he introduced them to four other guys in the band, just as they were called to go backstage. Mandy and Beth decided to just sit down there and talk to each other.

Finally, everything quieted down. An older man approached the microphone and said, "Welcome, Malone students and visitors to the 1992 Battle of the Bands." There was a roar of applause. He continued, "We have eight bands for you tonight. They will each play one song. Take the ticket you got when you came in, and at the end of the performances, put it in the jar of your favorite band. The top three vote getters will have a chance to play another song for everyone. From there, we will have another vote which we will tell you about later. So get ready and welcome the first band, Just Because." Everyone in the audience paused before they realized that Just Because was the band's name; then they began to cheer.

Seven bands played to a nice response, but when Matt and the other guys from Malone came to the stage, there was out-of-control screaming and applause. The announcer said, "Ladies and gentlemen, please welcome Hired Razor!" The music was intense, with two lead guitars, a bass guitar, a keyboard, and of course—the drums. The sound was alternative rock with a new edge called grunge. It was clear who was going to win the first round.

After the votes were counted, the top three bands were Hired Razor, Last Train, and Vision. The announcer told everyone that after the three bands played another song, everyone would have a chance to vote again by going to the table, having their hand stamped, and getting another ticket. Last Train played again, and the crowd seemed to like that song more than their first one. Vision played, and they drew a subdued response. But as soon as Hired Razor took the stage, the place blew up with people, including Mandy and Beth, jumping and pumping their fists in the air.

When the band finished, people got their stamps, tickets, and then voted. With an overwhelming victory, Hired Razor was awarded the Battle of the Band Champions and played a final song. The crowd continued to chant and cheer for another song they all knew called "Angel." As the song started out, Denny, the lead singer and keyboard player, began to sing a wonderful ballad that turned into a thumping anthem. Mandy was jumping around with the rest of the crowd when she noticed that Beth was no longer beside her. She spun around and made a complete scan everywhere, until she saw Beth leaning motionless against the stage, staring up at Denny as he belted out the song. The song wound down with a soft closing, and he was only noticing her.

The announcer thanked the crowd for coming to the event, and then he reminded them that because Hired Razor won the competition, they would be playing on the mainstage at the Alive Festival in June. Everyone cheered and began to leave. Matt got Mandy's attention and she joined him on stage, while Denny sat on the edge of the stage chatting and laughing with Beth.

Chapter 16: Two Big Boys

The band and some of the close friends decided to go to Big Boy for dessert and to hang out some more. Before Mandy could talk to Beth about driving over to the restaurant, Beth told her that she had a ride and would see her over there. Beth gave her a smile and said, "Don't worry. There is no bus to take off on. I'll see you in ten minutes."

Mandy looked at her and said, "I better see you in ten minutes, Lady Macbeth." With that comment, Beth put her index finger to her lips and said "SSSSShhhh. I like grunge rock way more than death metal, don't you know," and then she met back up with Denny to leave.

For the rest of the school year, until graduation, Mandy and Matt could often be found on double dates with Beth and Denny. After graduation, Hired Razor decided to stay together and play some gigs around town and prepare for the Alive Festival in late June. They wrote a couple more original songs, and they knew all of the popular grunge hits from Nirvana and Pearl Jam. They played in all the local clubs and were even asked by two different area clubs to be the main house band on Thursday, Friday, and Saturday nights. The guys were thrilled for the opportunity, but told the club owners that they wanted to finish out the summer making themselves available for traveling, and would let them know by Labor Day.

Alive was a Christian music event that took place at a local swimming hole and amphitheater. The festival was Wednesday through Saturday night, with a worship service on Sunday morning. There was music, camping, and beach and water fun for all who came. The newer bands played on stages throughout the park, while the nationally known bands played on the main stage beginning in the late afternoon all the way until 11:00 p.m. or later.

Hired Razor was given the slot to play on Wednesday on one of the smaller stages near the beach. So many people came out of the water and surrounded the stage to listen to the music and the guys' stories that they were asked to come back and play more days during those late morning hours. Also, because they had won the Battle of the Bands, they were given the 4:30 p.m. time slot on Saturday on the main stage.

Usually there were not too many people paying attention to that first band, as people were getting their spots picked out and getting settled in for the later concerts. More people were playing Frisbee than watching the bands. But when Hired Razor came to the stage at 4:30, they already had a hyped-up group of loyal mosh-pit kids who were ready to let loose. In front of the stage were more people than anyone had ever seen for a 4:30 performance. Hired Razor did not disappoint. Their energy, sound, and lyrics drew all the new people into their performance. Even though they only played three songs, they made a lasting impression. So much so, in fact, that one of the main band's managers asked to have a meeting with them on his tour bus right after their set.

The talks went well and the guys had plenty to discuss. They were given the chance to open for one of the most popular bands at the time on a year-long tour and to get signed to their first record deal. It was the break that any band dreams of, but right away Matt was not at peace. He talked to Mandy about it and had trouble explaining his feelings and why. He just knew that he didn't want to be on the road. He needed more roots.

The next time the guys got together, Matt told them he was going to have to step away, because his heart would not be in it like he knew it needed to be for their success. The meeting was hard and feelings were hurt, but Matt poured out his heart; they eventually understood where he was on his life journey. Matt told the guys he would be available to help get another drummer up and running so that Hired Razor would be as sharp as ever. That pun did not go over too well with the guys, and then Ben, the bass guitar player, said, "Ah, we're musicians; we never want anything to be flat or sharp."

Chapter 16: Two Big Boys

"Okay, okay," Matt said. "But I will help you goofballs out if you want me to." And he did. Within a month, the band had found another drummer who fit right in, and Hired Razor was ready to record their first record and plan their national tour. Matt felt a sense of loss, but he felt at peace with his decision.

Meanwhile, Mandy was preparing to start early summer practices with her Medina High School girls' soccer program. As she was busy with that, Matt knew that all the local teacher positions were filled and that he wasn't going to be able to have a permanent position as a band teacher anywhere. He was very discouraged, but joined the ranks of substitute teachers around the area. It would definitely give Matt exposure to many different school systems, and that was a positive thing.

Matt also gave private lessons to those wanting to get better with a host of instruments. With a reference from one of Matt's Malone professors, he started drum and guitar lessons with a son of a young dynamic pastor from the Akron area, Pastor Mike Landon. The more Pastor Mike was around Matt, the more he was convinced he needed to talk to Matt about an idea that he felt God was leading him toward. After his son's guitar practice one evening, Pastor Mike sat down with Matt and asked him, "Have you ever thought about being a church worship leader?"

Matt, who was a little blown away, said, "No, not really."

Pastor Mike began to tell him what his vision was for the music part of the service. It would be a multimedia-incorporated worship experience. The more he described everything, the more interested Matt became. By the end of the conversation, Matt and Pastor Mike were sharing ideas back and forth about how to pull this off.

Pastor Mike finally came out and said, "Matt, I want to recommend you to our church leadership for the position of worship leader. I understand if you need time to . . ."

Then with an outburst, Matt said, "No. I mean, yes. I want to be the church's worship leader. I would love to bring people closer to God through music and singing."

Pastor Mike said, "Great! I'll contact you for a meeting with everyone."

Matt replied, "Sounds good. What an awesome opportunity! Thank you."

"No," Pastor Mike said. "Thank you. I have been praying for the perfect person for our church, and I was drawn to you every time Jack had a lesson with you. You are a great young man of God."

"Thanks. I try to be. I have some great news to share with my girlfriend."

"Well, then, we should leave so you can talk with her," said Pastor Mike.

Right after he said goodbye, he dialed Mandy's phone and told her everything. She was so overjoyed for him, that she said with an honest emotion, "I love you." She then realized what she said and how awkward over the phone and in that moment it was. Mandy cringed and was silent.

It seemed like minutes went by, although it had only been a few seconds, when Matt said, "Oh, shoot! You said it first."

Mandy said, "Are you serious?"

"Yes, I am, Mandy McConnell. When I see you this weekend, I will tell you in person."

"Well," Mandy replied, "I will tell you back that I love you, too." They ended their conversation, and both had a smile on their face all the way up until each went to bed.

Love must have been in the air, because about that same time, Denny told Beth that he loved her. Hired Razor had finished writing all the remaining songs and was getting ready to go to Nashville to record their first album, and Denny said that he would be coming back with a little gift for Beth. Beth was overjoyed and called Mandy. Mandy and Beth were shrieking in delight as each told her story.

Chapter 16: Two Big Boys

Not only did Mandy feel excited and blessed to have Matt in her life, but she was very proud of her Medina girls' soccer program that first year. She had the girls playing very competitively. They won their league, but did not advance past the first round of the state tournament. During that same time frame, Beth waited patiently for Denny to return to Ohio after all their recording sessions were over and before the tour began.

It was almost midnight when Matt's phone rang and woke him from a deep sleep. He knocked his phone off the nightstand and fell out of bed trying to locate it and answer it. The familiar voice asked, "Were you asleep?"

"Yeah, Denny," Matt said. "I was."

"Not sure why," Denny replied. "You're in a band and should be rocking out like us."

"Uh, I'm in a worship band and we practice early in the evenings and play on Sunday mornings."

Denny just laughed and said, "Oh, yeah. Well, while you're up, what if you and I propose to our ladies on the same nights? Wouldn't that be cool for them? I just picked up a ring."

Matt said, "You might have a ring, but I don't yet."

"Well, get busy," Denny said. "I get back in two weeks, so we have to get things going. I then leave for the tour two weeks after that. I'll call you back in a few days to talk more about some proposal ideas. In the meantime, call Mandy's dad to ask for his daughter's hand. I am going to call Beth's dad. We are going to do this."

Matt answered him with, "I know we are going to do this. I am definitely ready, but please call a lot earlier next time, rock star."

A few days passed, and Denny called Matt back. Matt started the conversation by saying, "I have my ring; do you have yours?"

"Yes, of course I do," Denny said with a huff.

"Well, you rock stars are always changing things up, so I thought I'd ask," Matt quickly said in his comeback.

"Okay, good point. What ideas do you have for this dual proposal?" Denny asked.

"I've thought about it, but haven't come up with the perfect idea. How about you?"

After Matt asked his question, Denny described his plan in vivid detail.

※

Beth couldn't wait to see Denny. Her long-distance phone bill was as much as her rent. The plan for popping the question would be on that very first night back. The parents would even have a front-row seat to the proposal. Denny and his bandmates got back into town around 7:00 p.m. and dropped him off at the video store. He told Beth's supervisor prior to tonight that he would like to steal her away from her shift. He was up for Denny's plan. The store was packed with people when he slipped in unnoticed. Denny pulled an armful of VHS tapes off the rack and carried them in front of his face to the checkout counter. Beth said, "Sir, there is a maximum of four videos that you can check out."

Denny dropped the tapes on the counter and said, "Well then, ma'am, I don't want any of them."

Beth reached over the counter and latched onto his neck. "I didn't know if I'd see you tonight."

Beth's manager saw the whole thing and just shook his head and said, "Clock out and get out of here. We've got things handled." It took Beth thirty seconds in the back to grab her things. She then grabbed Denny's hand and out the door they went. They got into Beth's car and headed over to Big Boy, where Mandy and Matt would be waiting. They slid into the booth opposite Mandy and Matt and ordered a dessert and coffee. As

Chapter 16: Two Big Boys

Beth explained to Mandy what just happened to her, the proposal plan was already under way outside the restaurant.

It was about 8:30 when Denny spoke up and said, "It has been a long day. I'm ready to call it a night."

"Okay," Matt said. "We are, too. We'll walk out with you."

As they walked through the doors to leave the restaurant, Mandy noticed first and began cracking up. She said, "Oh my, Beth. Look!"

She quickly saw what Mandy was looking at and began laughing hysterically. Right in front of them was the iconic Big Boy statue with a hamburger raised, but it now had a guitar perched under his other hand like he was playing a big riff. The girls were now hugging each other in disbelief. Matt asked, "What's hanging on the guitar?"

The girls approached to see two rings. They went even more crazy. The boys untied the rings, got down on one knee, and each asked his girl the question. After both said yes, Mandy's mom and Beth's parents jumped out of their cars to surprise them. It was quite the celebration in front of the restaurant, that even the customers enjoyed.

※

Mandy couldn't believe she was already pulling into Beth's driveway. It was just after 6:15 p.m. Beth came running out of the house with a coat over her arm and was scooting across the sidewalk in her heels. She got in the car and said, "You're late. Let's go have some fun."

Mandy looked at her and said, "What? You aren't going to let me say hi to sweet little Grace or Mr. Rockstar?"

"Uh, no. This is momma's night out. Let's go!"

The two old friends drove toward Alliance Hall, only fifteen minutes away.

Chapter 17:

ONCE A PRANKSTER ALWAYS A PRANKSTER

(Joel—after high school: 1987-1991)

"JOEL," A NURSE CALLED out into the waiting room. Joel gathered his coat, got up, and followed the nurse. "Let's stop here and get your weight," she said. Then the nurse pointed and said, "Okay. Go ahead and have a seat right here in #4." She began to take Joel's blood pressure and ended by saying, "120/80, okay." Next she grabbed his wrist and took his pulse and quickly said, "65. Okay." The nurse then sat down and asked Joel for the names of all the medications he was taking. Joel spouted them off. "The doctor is running behind," the nurse told Joel. "Please make yourself comfortable. There are magazines right over there," she said as she pointed and closed the door.

"Great. Time to wait some more," Joel said under his breath incredulously, before he fell back onto the exam table. Even though Joel survived a life-threatening cardiac event only six months earlier, he only wanted to know one thing from his doctor. Could he go back to Alliance, three hours away, to his high school reunion? I guess the answer would have to wait. So

Joel closed his eyes, folded his arms, and began to think about the last fifteen years. He definitely knew no one at the reunion could top his story.

Even before Ryan's accident, Joel had been accepted to the University of Toledo to study engineering. He wasn't sure which type of engineering, but luckily, he didn't have to decide until the end of his freshman year. Toledo was about three hours away from home. Joel thought that was the perfect distance away, but it was not too far away. No one else from his class went to UT, so Joel knew that he was on his own, and that was fine with him.

Well, that was all well and good in his head, but the moment Joel's mom and dad pulled away from the sidewalk leaving him in front of the dorm, reality hit. Joel was all alone and felt alone. A voice deep from within reassured him that he was where he belonged. Throughout the first semester, Joel became involved in some different campus organizations, but he never was fulfilled by them. He even got really involved with the dorm hall leadership, but toward the end of the first semester he found that so many people were coming to him with petty drama instead of real issues, that he thought it best to quit the leadership team and focus on something more meaningful.

Joel had no idea what that was, but he remembered seeing a table tent in the cafeteria about an on-campus church service. Not knowing what to expect, he got up in the morning and made his way over to the student union. There he heard singing coming out of one of the meeting rooms like he never heard before, with guitars, a keyboard, clapping, and voices singing at peak volume. It was intimidating. Joel's church only sang hymns and a few worship songs.

About the time he was ready to turn and run, someone friendly spotted him and said, "Welcome to ACT. We just got

Chapter 17: Once a Prankster Always a Prankster

started. Here is a paper about the service today. Please sit where you're comfortable. It doesn't matter where."

On his way to the back, Joel was greeted by a short red-haired man with a fiery goatee to match. He said, "Hi. I'm Steve Schertzinger, the campus minister. What's your name?"

Joel answered, "Joel Brunner."

Steve said, "Glad you're here, Joel."

Joel, not being much of a singer, thought it best to find the back row and blend in. He quickly looked over the paper and found out that ACT stood for Active Christians Today. After that first song, the song leader said, "Let's take a minute and greet those around you." Joel wasn't ready for that, but he could see all the people heading his way. One after another, they introduced themselves and shook his hand. In that short period of time, he was asked about his major, his year, if he lived on campus, and where he was from. He was glad when the song leader started to strum his guitar again.

Joel caught his breath. He didn't know what it was about this place or more specifically what it was about these people, but again he had that feeling that he was in the right place. The rest of the service was inspirational, challenging, and comforting. It was exactly what he was looking for.

At the end of the service, Joel met more people. A tall, lanky, awkward guy from the other side of the room came over to him and said, "Hi, I'm J.R. Has anyone asked you to go to lunch yet?"

Joel answered, "No."

"Well," J.R. said, "A group of us are heading to the East Commons for something to eat. Do you want to come with us?"

"Sure," Joel said quickly.

As they headed out, J.R. introduced him to other people in the group. There was a Gary, CJ, John, and another guy named John whom everyone called Duke. At lunch, Joel found out that everyone in the ACT group called this little guy group the Lima Boys. It made sense because they were all from Lima, Ohio. As they ate their food, J.R. stopped abruptly, looked at Joel, and asked, "Do you like to pull pranks?" Joel nearly choked on his food. He couldn't believe what he just heard.

He smiled, cleared his throat twice, and then said, "Lima Boys, let me tell you a few stories while you finish your dessert." As he told his stories, everyone around the table was either laughing hysterically or looking mesmerized at what he was describing.

Then Duke said in his monotone, dry humor way, "Okay, okay. I think we know that you are pretty good at pranks." Everyone laughed.

J.R. said, "Well, this afternoon we are going into the campus house and Saran Wrap everything in Steve's office. When I say everything, I mean everything." When Joel heard the plan, not only was he in for the prank, but he had definitely found his home away from home.

He then said, "Who's got the car? Sounds like we need to go shopping." They all had final exams the coming week, so they needed to let off some steam and take care of the prank right away. Joel followed the guys back to their off-campus apartment and they headed out to get as much Saran Wrap as they could afford. They piled a bunch of cartons in the shopping cart and began to check out. It was pretty obvious that boys with Saran Wrap couldn't be up to anything good. The young clerk just shook her head.

Right before she gave the final total, Joel said, "Hold up. I'll be right back." He came back with a Christmas stocking full of candy and said, "Let's wrap this up and leave it on the middle of his desk."

All the Lima Boys nodded their heads in agreement and J.R. said, "That's a great touch, Joel." They made it back to the ACT Campus House, where it wasn't hard to break into Steve's office. Once in, they went to work. Every chair, lamp, piece of stereo equipment, and even every book got wrapped. The windows, the framed pictures, and all his office supplies on his

Chapter 17: Once a Prankster Always a Prankster

desk got wrapped. They placed the stocking in the middle of his desk calendar and wrapped it up. Then, they wrapped his entire desk. On the way out, they put a Saran Wrap barrier on the inside of the door before they shut it. The prank had been completed, and so they went back and began to study for their finals and wait for everyone's reaction. Steve would most likely see it Monday morning and then they would get to hear about it on Tuesday at the Tuesday night gathering.

Monday came and went, and finals were in full swing. Tuesday was a rough day of finals. Joel got out of his last one for the day at 7:30 p.m. and was brain-dead. He was ready to pop in on the ACT Tuesday night gathering and find out what Steve's reaction was to our prank. The meeting started promptly at 7:00. They had just finished some songs when Joel sat down next to J.R. and the other Lima Boys.

Steve walked up front and said, "I'll keep my message short because I know you all have studying to do. I thought I knew what I was going to leave you with before you went on to finish your semester exams and go home for the winter break, but then when I got to my office on Monday morning, I had another vision of what I should talk about."

There was a sudden and quick snicker beside Joel, but Joel didn't even flinch.

Steve continued, "The second Monday of the month, I have breakfast and prayer time with some of the other campus ministers. This week the prayer time was in my office."

Again someone snickered, and a few guys near Joel started to squirm in their chairs.

Steve continued, "We were so moved by our students in our ministries that we decided to stand and pray. In fact, I offered to say the prayer for the entire group so I could wrap up our morning together before we went our separate ways."

There was a bit more laughter as more people began to whisper.

Steve went on. "The verses I want to read are from Psalm 109:28-31. It says:

> While they curse, may you bless; may those who attack me be put to shame, but may your servant rejoice. May my accusers be clothed with disgrace and wrapped in shame as in a cloak. With my mouth I will greatly extol the Lord; in the great throng of worshipers I will praise him. For he stands at the right hand of the needy, to save their lives from those who would condemn them.

Much more laughter began to percolate.

Steve just as calmly as possible began to preach, "During this week of exams you may feel like you are under attack and that you didn't study and prepare as well as you could have. But just know that you did your best, and leave it all in the Lord's hands." Steve paused for dramatic effect and then continued. "Those not of the Lord will be *wrapped* in shame. Those who praise him will be saved from those who condemn . . ."

He couldn't go on anymore, but started laughing with a very characteristic Steve cackle. The rest of the group busted out laughing as word of the prank got around. Steve just looked in our direction shaking his head and said, "Thank you for the Christmas stocking. Does anyone need any Saran Wrap for their Christmas cookies?"

Once back from break, Joel really got involved in ACT. He loved all of his engineering classes, but he really looked forward to his time when he got together with those in the group for social time or Bible study. One of the outreaches was a nursing-home ministry. The students from ACT would provide the residents with a church service. They would also spend any extra time they

Chapter 17: Once a Prankster Always a Prankster

could with the elderly. This made Joel understand and empathize with those who may not have had any visitors in a really long time. Because of this, he asked Steve if he could begin another church service at another nursing home.

Steve said, "What are you doing right now?"

Joel responded, "Nothing. I'm finished with classes."

Steve said "Well, let's go over to Bancroft Manor and ask them together."

When they got to the nursing home and walked in, Joel immediately had a first impression that this place was a little less cared for than any other nursing home he had ever visited. His eyes told him that things were a bit messier and people were scrambling around everywhere. But it was his nose that informed him that the people at this place had their hands full.

Steve and Joel sat down with the manager and asked whether there was a church service for the residents on Sunday mornings. The lady said there was not, but there were individual clergy coming in to see the residents. Joel spoke up and asked, "Could you please post a note and get the word out to see if there would be any interest?" The manager said that she would, so Steve left the Campus House number with her so she could let him know the results.

When Steve saw Joel at the Tuesday evening gathering, he called him over and said, "Well, get your sermon ready. You guys start this Sunday." Joel could not believe it, but was thrilled.

An announcement was made at the beginning and end of the gathering for any students interested in helping. As people began to leave, Joel was suddenly surrounded by four others. They were J.R., Ruth, Jennifer, and Johnathon. Joel always noticed a lot of the other college kids hugging, but he had not grown up in that kind of environment. However, when he saw J.R. there, he stepped forward and gave him a big hug and said, "It's one of my Lima Boys!" Joel knew that J.R. and Johnathon would help out with the preaching, and Ruth knew how to play the piano. This was going to work out great.

Steve came over to the group and said, "Guys, you have a chance to be God's light to some very special people over there. I look forward to hearing wonderful things." Sunday rolled around and Johnathan picked everyone up. They walked into Bancroft Manor and headed back to the little chapel down one of the side hallways. As they turned the corner, Joel saw some nurse aides pushing some people to the edge of the door. Joel thought maybe that person was shy, and so he continued to walk toward the door. All the students greeted those in the hallway and then turned in to the chapel to see the place packed. The students looked at each other with wide eyes. Ruth fought back a tear and quickly took her place at the piano. J.R. did a quick count and held up his fingers to Joel: three-four. Joel went up front and looked out to everyone's face and thought to himself, *I bet Pastor Russell would be cracking up right about now.*

Joel said, "Hello, everyone. Thanks for coming to the chapel this morning. We are from the university and belong to a group called ACT. It stands for Active Christians Today."

About the time Joel finished with the introduction, someone from the back asked his neighbor, "What did he say?"

Joel looked at J.R., who began cracking up. He tried again, but this time mustered a little more voice at this early Sunday morning hour.

There weren't too many people on a college campus who would say they loved Sunday mornings, but Joel did. He looked forward to getting up while the campus was silent and walking to the Campus House and then out to the nursing home. He had some very special times of sharing and singing with the residents. He did not want to miss a Sunday service at the nursing home for the rest of his college days. Other than winter break, spring break, and sickness, Joel never missed. He also knew his parents understood why he never wanted to come home anymore on the

Chapter 17: Once a Prankster Always a Prankster

weekends. They were proud of him. The things that happened in that little chapel impacted his life forever.

Throughout the course of Joel's time at ACT, he was involved in many other activities, including Bible studies, weekend retreats, spring-break mission trips, and other outreaches; but by far, there was one thing that he did that made his faith real in his life. He portrayed Jesus at the crucifixion. The Campus House was set along Dorr Street, which was a main street where a lot of people walked back and forth to class just on the outskirts of campus. It was actually Good Friday when they did this portrayal. Steve had the audio story being narrated in the upper windows blasting out to the crowds passing by. They heard all the shouts and jeers at the Messiah, along with the ominous wind and thunder in the background.

Joel and J.R. took turns playing Jesus. John, one of the Lima Boys who was built like a college football lineman, and Eric, an avid weight lifter/bodybuilder, played the Roman guards. They had the pleasure of beating up J.R. and Joel and tying them on the cross so they could then hammer the "air nails" into their hands. They also cracked a whip in the air for effect. John once accidentally got too close to J.R. with the whip, and a very real welt was left. To make matters worse, it was an early April Friday that felt like February. Every form of precipitation fell, and they only had loin cloths covering them. Several of the girls in the group portrayed the women who gathered at the cross to mourn.

The music began, and Joel was led out to the front yard. The people passing by stopped and saw what was going on, as the Roman soldiers began to beat Jesus. The cross was dropped in a hole and Jesus was lifted up and tied in place. Using a big steel sledgehammer, one of the soldiers swung back and struck right in time with the stereo accompaniment as the hammer pounding began. When it was over, a crown of thorns was thrust on his head. The mourners were wailing down below. All the while, people were passing and stopping, not believing what they were seeing. The whole time, Joel and J.R. were into the character of Jesus, making eye contact with those who would stop. They would say to them in an exhausted and dying voice, "I love you." When Joel thought of that time, he was not sure how many people his portrayal touched, but looking into so many people's searching eyes, he prayed that the words, "I love you" would bring hope and healing to them. J.R. and Joel each took two shifts, but on J.R.'s last shift, the drama literally came to a crashing halt. As J.R. was making eye contact and saying "I love you" to the onlookers, a woman driving a car was not paying attention. Someone in front of her was still stopped as she was also looking at the drama. The next sound heard was a loud crunching of metal. The police were called and the crucifixion drama was over.

Joel's time with ACT was incredibly important into making him the man he thought the Lord wanted him to be. But he also valued the engineering education he was getting at UT. Joel decided on mechanical engineering and had many opportunities to excel in his classes with group projects. A professor took him aside his junior year and told him that he really should apply for the Owens Corning internship that summer. It would be a very good opportunity and would help start building his resume for the job market.

Just after spring break, Joel found out that he had been chosen as one of eight engineering students for the internship. Joel's parents were thrilled with his opportunity. Joel and his dad were able to find a very nice used Honda that was a perfect car for him to drive. Arrangements were made for Joel to live with Craig, an alumnus from ACT who lived and worked in Toledo. Joel was deeply involved with the development of a new product at Owens Corning that he could not talk about to anyone. Craig and others who came over in the evenings tried very hard to get him to slip up and tell them about the new product, but after

Chapter 17: Once a Prankster Always a Prankster

having no luck, they gave up and became convinced that Joel was really working for the CIA. It was a running joke.

ACT had a sister ministry right down the interstate about a half an hour on the campus of Bowling Green State University. All through the summer, the students who stayed to go to school or work would take turns and get together with the other group for a dinner and Bible study. One evening when it was UT's turn to go to BG, Craig drove those who were able to go. When Joel walked in to the house, he and the others were immediately greeted. Joel's attention was being distracted by a very attractive girl sitting off to the side and who was involved in another conversation. He couldn't help but feel like he was staring. He had to get out of there; no, wait. He had to introduce himself—but how? He didn't want it to be lame. So, he bought some time and went into the kitchen to pour a drink. As he was sipping the froth from his overflowing Coke, the girl walked into the small kitchen and said, "Oh, hi. My name is Lisa. What's yours?"

As Joel brought his head out of his cup, he said with a frothy mustache, "Hi. I'm Joel. I work for the CIA."

Stunned, Lisa said, "You work for who?"

Joel, knowing he was blowing it, snapped out of it and tried again, "Oh, I'm sorry. My name is Joel Brunner. I don't work for the CIA, but all my friends think I do." They both laughed and sat down so he could tell her the whole story. He also found out more about her. She was from the Findlay, Ohio, area, about half an hour away in the opposite direction from Toledo. Lisa's major was in elementary education, and she was there this summer to get a few more classes out of the way to prepare for her very demanding senior year. Dinner and the Bible study were over, and someone from the BG group yelled out, "Anyone want to go to DQ?"

Alliance Lake ~ Be Still

Joel said yes right away, hoping that Lisa would want to go, too, because he did not want to leave her yet.

Craig said, "No, I think I'm good. Time to head back to Toledo."

Joel was not sure why Craig didn't understand the loud and clear hint or pick up on what was going on, but he had to think fast. He looked at Lisa with wide eyes and a pout. She began to crack up and turn away. Joel hoped that would be enough until next week. On the way out, Joel asked Lisa, "Will you try to come up to our place next week?"

She nodded and said, "Yes, I hope to."

"Great," Joel said, and then added, "Make sure you pick a driver who likes ice cream." They both laughed as he went out the back door. The ride back to Toledo was quiet. Joel didn't want to make a big deal about going to DQ, but it was! He began counting down the days before he would see Lisa again.

Joel and Lisa never missed a Bible study. They made the most of their time together. Joel learned his lesson and always volunteered to be the driver when the Toledo group went to Bowling Green. He wanted to control the departure time. Joel and Lisa also made time on the weekends for dates. They went out to movies, malls, and the different parks around town.

Late in the summer, Joel got a call at work that his grandpa had a stroke, and that things didn't look very good. That evening right before the Bible study group was going to meet in Toledo, Joel got a call from his mom, who told him that his grandpa had passed away. Joel was crushed. This was the first grandparent whom he had lost, and he was devastated. As the BG people were arriving for the Bible study, Joel was too upset to stay in the group setting. He told Craig about the phone call and said that he needed to go for a walk around campus.

Lisa noticed that Joel seemed very upset. She went to him and asked, "What's wrong?" Joel couldn't answer her. He just grabbed her hand and they left. They walked across campus to

Chapter 17: Once a Prankster Always a Prankster

Ottawa Park. Every time he tried to say something to Lisa, the tears interrupted him. He finally decided to sit down on a bench next to the lake in a place that seemed very calming.

He had not cried like this since Ryan's funeral. After he felt settled down, he looked at Lisa and said, "Thank you."

Lisa replied, "Of course. What's going on?"

Joel took a deep breath and said, "I just found out that my grandpa had a stroke and passed away. I can't believe how sudden everything happened. It's hard to believe that I won't be able to talk to him ever again. I feel so bad for my grandma." Joel started to sob again.

Lisa leaned in to hug and hold him. Joel just thought how good that felt. After he finished his spell, he looked into her eyes and said, "Thank you for being with me tonight."

Lisa said, "I can stay with you as long as you want tonight; but I will need a ride home."

Joel found something very funny with what she just said and began to laugh like crazy. Embarrassed, Lisa asked, "What did I say? What did I say?"

He said, "You are so cute. Thank you. How about some ice cream at Netty's?"

Lisa sarcastically insisted, "It's not BG's DQ, but it will do."

Joel quickly said, "Now wait a minute. Netty's is the best."

Lisa replied, "Yeah; as long as you're paying, it is the best!" They got up from the bench and strolled along the lake back toward campus and Netty's.

Joel's trip home for the funeral was difficult, but meaningful. It really helped to be with his family during that difficult time. It wasn't long before school started back up and things got busy for both Joel and Lisa with their schoolwork. They were able to see each other either Friday or Saturday night throughout their senior year. Lisa was able to get a student-teaching job at Webster Elementary, which was fairly close to BG. Joel continued to prepare himself for graduation, hoping that his time with Owens Corning would allow him to get a permanent position with them.

On one of the last weekends before graduation, the UT and BG ACT groups got together for a big spaghetti dinner and game night. In the middle of everyone playing games, the lights dimmed and Gary ran down the stairs wearing a puffy white shirt and wielding a sword and saying, "Where did he go? Where did he go? Where did the six-fingered man go? My name is Inigo Montoya. He killed my father. He has to prepare to die." Then he ran out of the room.

Next, Big John came lumbering down the stairs with CJ behind him saying, "He got away. He got away. *Inconceivable. Inconceivable.*" They continued through the group and disappeared into the back room.

Finally, Joel came down the stairs and bent down on one knee where Lisa was playing Uno. He held out a ring and said, "You are more than my Princess Buttercup. I don't want to ever go away from you. I want to go on the journey that God has for us together." Lisa Evans, will you marry me?" Still stunned by the Lima Boys' performance, she put her hands on Joel's face and said, "As you wish, yes."

The room erupted in applause and laughter. As it began to settle down, J.R. came down the stairs wearing a long white robe and a tall papal hat and said, "Maaa-widge . . ." Everyone started to laugh even harder, knowing that the guys nailed their performances from the *Princess Bride* movie.

Before Lisa could ask Joel any questions, her parents came in from the back room. She ran to her mom and they both began to cry. Her dad gave Joel a handshake and a pat on the back.

Chapter 18:

REAL PRESSURE

(Joel—after high school: 1991-1998)

BOTH JOEL AND LISA graduated and were able to get jobs at the places where they did their student work. The wedding was small and personal. It was perfect for them. Joel and Lisa settled in the Perrysburg, Ohio, community, halfway between both of their jobs. They had a little apartment above a farmhouse, and it, too, was perfect. Their jobs were demanding, but they made time to go on weekend trips and visit college friends.

They got involved in a small church in Perrysburg. It reminded them of an adult version of ACT, and that made it perfect. Even though the church was small, there were quite a few young couples with whom they bonded and made some very special long-lasting memories. After a few short years, each couple began their journey into parenthood, which brought another layer of joy and fun among the couples. Joel and Lisa had their first daughter in 1995 and their second daughter in 1998. Between the two births, they moved into their first house.

Now with the two girls and a house, Joel felt more pressure than he ever did before. It didn't help that the project he was working on for more than seven years all of a sudden got cancelled, and rumors of Owens Corning going into bankruptcy began to be whispered. The uncertainty, coupled with the responsibility of his new family, began to take a toll on Joel.

He began to stay up late into the night worrying about how to make his job more secure, and how to make himself not so worried about things he couldn't necessarily control. During the day, things got more and more intense as corporate news was being released almost hourly. At night, he got less and less sleep. Lisa saw Joel acting more irrational and erratic. She tried everything to help him out and be supportive, but things got worse when he withdrew from church and from his friends. Joel forced himself to go to work, and then he would come home and find his dark bedroom the best comfort for his frazzled mind and body.

Unable to watch Joel continue to withdraw from all aspects of his life, Lisa decided to call Craig to see if his old friend could help. Craig agreed to try. Before Craig arrived, Lisa knocked on the bedroom door and waited for Joel's answer. Joel spoke slowly and said, "Come in."

Lisa quietly said, "Honey, I know you are hurting. I'm not sure what to do for you, but you know I'm here. I've invited Craig to come over for supper tonight. I think it will be really good for you to talk to him. You two are a lot alike in many ways."

Joel didn't hesitate, but answered, "You're right. It will be good to talk to Craig." He rolled over and said, "Please tell me when he gets here." Lisa closed the door and went back to running the house and family that included an active preschooler and an active toddler. Craig arrived a few hours later, and Lisa greeted him with a big hug.

She said, "I hope you can . . ." and began to cry.

He hugged her again and said, "He's a good man."

Chapter 18: Real Pressure

She looked Craig in the eyes and said, "He is, I know. Now we have to get him to know it."

Craig went to the bedroom, knocked on the door, and said, "Come out with your hands up. You're under arrest for impersonating a CIA agent." Joel opened the door and threw his arms in the air. He then wrapped them around Craig for a hug, but Craig could tell that Joel wasn't hugging back and that Craig was holding his entire weight. Craig compassionately said, "You have worn yourself out."

Joel responded, "I feel worn out."

Sitting on the edge of the bed, Craig went into the details of how a few years ago he had felt very frustrated with how things were going at work, and it messed up his stomach with an ulcer and his mind with worry. He was directed by his pastor to see a counselor and talk things out. Craig looked at Joel and said, "It was the best thing I could have done. I wasn't getting better. I know you feel like you don't have the energy for that step, but let me help you. You don't have to worry about a thing. I will have Lisa set it up and I will drive you there."

Joel knew he was in a very dark place, so he said, "Yeah."

"Good," Craig exclaimed as he gave him another hug. "We're going to get through this together."

They had supper together. Lisa and Craig did most of the talking. Just seeing his wife race around and take care of the kids without any of his help made him feel even worse, so Joel pushed his chair back and said, "Craig, thanks for coming. I'm really tired and I'm going back to bed." Lisa and Craig nodded and watched him walk down the hallway into the darkened bedroom before he shut the door.

After the children were wiped clean and sent on their way to play in the heap of toys all over the floor, Craig told Lisa what they talked about and agreed to. That made Lisa feel better. She would make an appointment right away.

Lisa was very happy that she was able to get an appointment for Joel in less than a week. Craig picked Joel up and took him to the counselor, who had a PhD. Craig introduced him to this short round guy with thick glasses. Craig and Joel sat down together to talk about how they were connected, and then the doctor asked Craig if he would sit out in the waiting room for the rest of the session. Joel began to talk about the stress and anxiety at work. He knew it was coming from there, but he couldn't find anything secure to hold on to. The future seemed very unsure, and that terrified him.

The doctor knew that Joel was a man of faith, so he said, "Joel, you are in a cycle that hasn't run its course. I'm not going to tell you at this time why the cycle started for you, but you are in it. We have to begin to break it. We'll do that by talking to each other a couple times a week. Also, I need you to start getting your rest both in the day and at night. I want to prescribe some medication. Your mind is racing to places it doesn't need to go. We have to slow that down. At night, you need your body to settle itself and get some good healthy sleep. Will you follow this program?"

Joel, knowing he was in a dark place, responded with, "Yes, I will."

"Good. Let's go out to my assistant and schedule your next session."

As Craig drove Joel back, Craig did most of the talking. Joel was very exhausted and knew he had work in the morning to endure. Joel followed through with all the doctor's orders, and in about three weeks he began to feel a little better. After two months, things were even better, and Joel was helping out around the house. Even playing with the girls became easy and no longer seemed like a chore to him. Lisa knew that she nearly had her Joel back, but not yet completely.

Three months into the treatments, Joel announced that he was going to church and that he didn't want to be late. Lisa about

Chapter 18: Real Pressure

spilled the Cheerios. She began running around with a big grin on her face getting the girls ready. He knew it was time. When they got to church, a lot of people greeted them. They began to sing the worship songs and Joel felt more of the darkness and fear leaving his mind and body. Before he knew it, he was crying. His glasses were full of tears and he could only see Lisa as a wavy figure. He took off his glasses and she reached for his hand and held it tightly. The service was healing in many ways: the songs, the message, and the friends who knew his struggle. Joel gave thanks for the Lord's patience with him.

The calendar flipped to a new year and a new millennium. All the computer angst about Y2K came and went. Unfortunately, work at Owens Corning did not get any better. In fact, early in the year a Chapter 11 bankruptcy was indeed filed, and the pink slips began to be passed out. Every Friday it was a different set of departments, first Finance and Accounting, next Marketing and Human Resources, followed by Computer Systems and Printing, and finally Engineering and Management.

When Joel's department manager gave him his pink slip, he handed him a box and told him he only had a few minutes before he would be escorted out. Joel had witnessed several Friday layoffs, so he knew exactly what to do as he went back to his desk and began putting things in his box. Two minutes later he was finished, all packed and waiting for his escort out the door for good. People were passing by his desk saying their quick undercover goodbyes and good lucks. He had nine years of corporate torture and a half-empty box of personal possessions. Joel knew that he survived his internal battle with the fear of the future, but now he was going to be facing a different kind of unknown.

Joel went home and told Lisa the news. It was something they were hoping would pass them by, but they had known it was a possibility. They still had her income, and Joel knew he was within an hour of many great manufacturing and engineering centers. To the north was the center of the American automotive, to the east and south was Whirlpool, again to the south was Marathon Oil and Gas and Cooper Tires, and to the west was one of the world leaders in prefabricated furniture, Sauder Industries.

Joel began the process of finding his next job. He filled out as many applications and dropped off as many resumes as a day would allow. He even got some very promising interviews. After five months of looking, Joel was really questioning whether he should still work in the engineering field or if there was something else that God had for him.

It was late in the summer of 2000, and Lisa was preparing herself to begin a new school year. One Saturday at noon Joel decided to go for a long bike ride by himself on the Rails-to-Trails path. He liked to do it at least once a year, and with all his job searching, he had not done it yet this year. The round trip usually took two and a half hours.

When Joel wasn't back home at 4:00 p.m., Lisa started to worry. This was the time she wished that they would have a cell phone like others she knew, but it definitely wasn't in their budget. She thought that if he was finished with his bike ride and was visiting someone, he would call. What in the world was going on? She decided to call Craig to see if Joel stopped in to see him.

Craig picked up and said, "Hello?"

"Hi, Craig. This is Lisa."

"Oh, hi, Lisa. What's up?"

Lisa hesitated, not knowing what to say. She didn't want to overreact, but still knew that Joel was dealing with a lot, being out of work for a long time now. Craig spoke again but said firmly, "Lisa, what is going on?"

Chapter 18: Real Pressure

Lisa finally said, "Joel went out at noon to ride the long bike trail. He should have been back by 2:30 or 3:00 at the latest."

Craig said, "There is still enough light in the day to get someone on that trail and check it out. I don't have a bike. Who do you know who does?"

Lisa responded immediately and said, "Kevin! Thank you, Craig, for helping me think this through. You are amazing. I'll call you back once I find out where he is. Thank you." Lisa's next call was to Kevin, two houses down. Joel and Kevin had gotten to be real close lately. They would help each other on various house projects and even take their daughters to the park together to have some playtime with them.

Kevin picked up the phone and said, "Hello?"

"Hi, Kevin. This is Lisa." He recognized her voice.

"Okay. Is Joel stuck in the attic or under a sink needing my help?"

Lisa didn't laugh, but said, "I'm not sure."

Sensing something was wrong, he asked, "Where is Joel?"

Lisa explained the situation. Kevin was very familiar with that bike trail since he rode it at least twice a month. Kevin was also a salesman and had a cell phone. He told Lisa that he would call her immediately when he found out what was going on with Joel. Kevin told his wife, Tracy, where he was going, threw his bike in the back of his pickup, and headed to the trailhead.

Kevin was in very good shape. He was always looking for the next 5 or 10k race to run in. There was no more heat left in the day and the shadows were getting long when Kevin began his ride. He knew he had to ride fast, but he also had to keep a lookout along the trail. Once Kevin broke through the woods after the initial few miles, he hit a relentless headwind. It pushed him back in his seat several times, but he kept peddling hard as if he was racing someone who wasn't giving up. Kevin knew in his mind that he wasn't giving up, either.

He hadn't passed anyone for twenty minutes now, and he was ten minutes away from the turnaround point. The winds had finally subsided, and he was able to go faster than at any other time during the trip. The final stretch of the bike path went right to the edge of the coinciding southern trailhead in a neighboring small town. There one could use the public restroom, fill a water bottle, and have a snack on a bench. Kevin ignored the signs to slow down, racing all the way to the restrooms before he dismounted his bike and began to run toward a lone bike parked up against the tree on the other side of the picnic area. As Kevin approached the bike, he definitely knew it was Joel's. *Why is it here, but Joel isn't?* he thought, as he quickly ran into the restroom and shouted out Joel's name. His answer came back as a hollow echo.

Kevin knew he had to check in with Lisa, but he wished he had better news. As he checked his phone, he saw that he had a missed call and a voice mail message. He figured he missed the call because of all the loud wind in his face. He pushed the buttons to bring up the message. In his ear was Lisa's voice saying, "Kevin, Joel finally called. He is at the Train Depot having a burger with another cyclist he met. Go there and meet him. He'll tell you more when you get there. Also, Tracy and I will be picking you guys up when you are ready."

Kevin was relieved, to say the least. He parked his bike next to Joel's and walked the block and a half to the Train Depot. As he walked in, Joel yelled out, "What took you so long?"

Kevin just shook his head and said with a grin, "Just don't ask me for any help on your house projects for a while. You owe me."

Joel replied, "How about I buy you a burger and a drink? Will that help?" Kevin just kept shaking his head.

After Kevin ordered his food, Joel introduced him to Mark, who owned a print shop in town. Mark was about ready to buy the most sophisticated piece of addressing and sorting equipment available. Mark explained how it would allow his business to

Chapter 18: Real Pressure

grow, as they could save other companies hundreds and thousands of dollars by doing the printing and the mailing. After his quick technical explanation, he said that he didn't know who he would have set up the equipment, until he ran into Joel on the bike trail.

Joel looked at Kevin and said, "Boy, I'm glad I went for a bike ride today!" They all laughed as Kevin took the first bite of his juicy burger.

Chapter 19:

THE HEART OF THE MATTER

(Joel—after high school: 2000-2002)

JOEL REALLY LIKED THE small-business atmosphere, and he thrived on coming through on jobs that had more of an immediate timeline. The fast pace and the fact that he didn't have to wait months or years for corporate decision-makers to approve ideas and products were extremely satisfying to him. A year into working for the print shop, 9/11 happened. The whole country focused on safety, security, and the military response. Mark did not lay anyone off during that slow period, and Joel and the others appreciated him for that.

At the end of October that same year, 2001, Joel was doing his favorite fall chore—raking leaves. Joel always laughed at the neighbors with their leaf blowers and pull-behind leaf collectors. He knew the fastest way to rake leaves was to actually use a rake and a tarp.

The idea wasn't to rake them from the farthest point of the yard to the street curb; it was to gather the leaves into concentrated piles and then rake them onto a tarp. Then simply pull the tarp to the front yard and the curb. A bonus of this approach was the fun it provided Joel's daughters as they rode the tarp on the bumpy yard in a pile of leaves to the front; then like a tidal wave, Joel would pull the back of the tarp up and over their heads into the street as the tarp and leaves rolled them up like a sushi roll. They would laugh and carry on and race back to the next leaf pile to be put on the tarp.

Joel's yard had the most trees in his neighborhood, but he would always get done before anyone else. He had a little bit of a "John Henry complex" (man vs. machine), and was proud of that. This particular fall, however, as Joel was enjoying racing back and forth with his daughters, he felt unusually tired. Normally, he would not ever think of stopping until the job was done, but now there were several times when he sat down on the stoop and took a break. He also noticed his heart beating very erratically. He eventually finished raking all the leaves, but without setting any new neighborhood records.

Throughout the holidays, Joel was aware of his heartbeat because it was skipping, pounding, and getting his attention. Finally, in January of 2002, Joel mentioned the symptoms to Lisa. She immediately called and made him an appointment with the family doctor. When Joel went in for his checkup, the doctor spent a lot of time listening to his chest with the stethoscope and feeling and looking at his hands and feet. The doctor sat down in front of Joel, who was still on the examination table, and said, "Joel, I hear something going on with your heart valve. It is definitely not working smoothly or very quietly. There is a heck of a murmur going on. Do you have any family history?"

Joel thought for a minute and said, "My grandfather had heart disease and several bypasses, but nothing with the heart valves that I know of."

"Well," the doctor said, "I am scheduling you to go directly to a cardiologist today. You need to be seen now, and also we need an echocardiogram done."

Chapter 19: The Heart of the Matter

"A what?" Joel said, shocked.

The doctor replied, "An ultrasound for the heart. It is like you see on the screen when the OB/GYN showed your baby in the womb, but this is seeing what the heart is doing. This is very important for the cardiologist." Joel felt a little better and agreed to it. He asked to use the office phone to leave a message on his home answering machine, because he didn't know how long he was going to be.

Joel arrived at the cardiologist's office building, checked in, and waited. After going through all the magazines and waiting some more, he finally heard his name called. The nurse got all of his vitals charted and then left. It was only a few short minutes until the cardiologist walked in and introduced himself as Dr. Schory. He was wearing a New York Yankees tie. Joel really hated the Yankees, but he didn't want to bring that up at this time.

Dr. Schory said, "Your family physician was concerned about your heart. Let me take a listen." He spent several minutes maneuvering the stethoscope on the chest and then on the back and then on the belly. He even put it on his ankles.

"Joel," the cardiologist said, "it's a good thing your doctor sent you in today. Something is going on. I'm going to make sure you get the last appointment next door for an echo. We need to get some pictures and measurements."

Joel ruffled his eyebrows and asked, "What do you think it is?"

The doctor said, "Something is going on with your mitral valve, but I need to know more. I'm not going home tonight until I get the results from the technician, and I will talk with you then. I would suggest you see if your wife can come in, so she can hear everything we discuss and decide."

Joel knew by the doctor's tone that this was serious, but he was a little surprised because he didn't feel that bad. He knew his heartbeat was a little wacky, but he certainly didn't think it was life threatening. He placed another call from the nurse's desk to Lisa. She was home from school with the kids this time.

As soon as Lisa answered, Joel said, "Hi, Love. I wish I had a cell phone. I'm tired of asking for a phone to borrow."

Lisa said, "Never mind that. What did the cardiologist say?"

"I have to stay here and get an ultrasound—right now! It is just like you got when we were looking at the babies; isn't that crazy? The doctor wants you to be present to hear the results."

Lisa said, "I'm going to ask Tracy to watch the girls, and I'll be on my way."

Right after Joel hung up the phone, the echocardiogram tech called him into her small lab room. The ultrasound was very interesting to Joel. He was amazed how the technician could capture everything like she was playing a video game—all the sounds and video of the heart from every sort of angle. Joel was finished and was waiting in the main lobby when Lisa rushed in. They hugged and began to talk about each other's day.

They were the last ones in the waiting room and office at this time. The doctor personally came out and said to Joel, "Please come back to my office." On the way back, he introduced himself to Lisa. He sat them down in an office that reminded Joel of the offices of many college professors he had at UT. There were professional journals and files all over the place. His inbox stack was going to tumble like a game of Jenga, if he wasn't careful.

Then Dr. Schory said something that not too many thirty-two-year-olds ever get to hear. "Joel, I am so glad you decided to listen to your body. Your heart has a leaky valve and is making the heart work very hard. As the heart works hard, it will begin to enlarge. That is not good. Fortunately, right now your heart has not enlarged in size, which is good. What the echo has told me is the mitral valve is prolapsed or bulged. I suspect you have some damaged tissue cords."

Lisa asked, "How does someone damage the valve tissue cords?"

Chapter 19: The Heart of the Matter

Dr. Schory answered, "Having a mitral valve prolapse is not very unusual, and people can live with a mild case of it without anything needing to be done. But what is unusual is that every so often the tissue cords that anchor the valve flap to the heart wall get stretched or suddenly tear. I am afraid Joel is someone in the 'every-so-often' group. I'm still not sure if you have stretched cords or a tear, but in either case we need to get more tests and then prepare for surgery. In my opinion, the surgery doesn't have to be next week or maybe even next month, but you are in the window for surgery, and we have to follow up with some additional tests to see how immediate surgery should be."

The doctor slapped Joel on the leg and said, "I'm not even going to talk to you about the different options for surgery. Let's get the other tests done first, okay?" There was silence.

He then asked, "Any questions for me?"

Joel asked, "Will you do the surgery?"

The doctor said, "Uh, no. That will be a cardiac surgeon."

"Good," Joel said. "I hate the Yankees!" Everyone began to laugh. The doctor walked them out of the office, talking to Joel about how the Yankees' starting rotation looked really good. Joel just said, "Hey, Doc, ease up. I'm a Cleveland fan, and you guys have won your share." They laughed again.

Driving home in separate cars, both Joel and Lisa were running scenarios through their heads about the follow-up tests and the foreseeable surgery. They didn't get enough information at that first visit, but they couldn't help their minds going in all sorts of directions at once. Joel went directly home, while Lisa stopped and got the kids. She updated Kevin and Tracy as much as she could in private.

Joel and Lisa gave the girls an extra-tight hug that night before putting them to bed. The house was finally quiet as they met on the couch. They looked at each other and Joel asked, "Why am I always the problem?"

Lisa threw herself at him and said, "Don't go there!" as she started throwing her shoulder into him.

"Okay, okay," Joel said. "Be careful. Be careful with me or you might make my heart explode or something," he said as he began to laugh.

Lisa responded, "That is not funny, mister."

Joel settled down and started to express to Lisa that he was fine going through this journey, and that he would not doubt anything that God had for him in this life. They hugged and talked more about the kids and funny stories about Lisa's kindergarten class. Hearing about some of the little troublemakers always put Joel in a good place.

The next day at work, Joel updated Mark on everything medically going on that he knew about. He told him he would need to take a half day off soon for more tests, but other than that no more time off would be needed until the surgery. Mark understood, and he knew there was enough cross-training to cover when or if Joel had to be off for an extended amount of time.

Two weeks passed before Joel got in for those other tests. They included several chest x-rays and a transesophageal echocardiogram. Basically, the same equipment was used, but the ultrasound wand had a small transducer that was sent down the esophagus to take a closer look at the mitral valve. Joel was very glad he had some anesthesia to get through this test. It was extremely uncomfortable. When it was over, Lisa took him home for some additional rest over the weekend. On Sunday at church, Lisa made sure that she wrote on the attendance card that they would like prayer for God's provision and help on whatever the tests would show.

The next day, Lisa went to her school and Joel went to the print shop. That afternoon, Joel received a call from the cardiologist's assistant asking him to come into his office before 5:30 that day. Joel's workday was finished at 4:45, so getting there by 5:30 wouldn't be a problem. He left a message with the school

Chapter 19: The Heart of the Matter

office to tell Lisa that he needed to go back to the cardiologist for hospital test results and that he would update her when he got home later.

Dr. Schory entered the exam room and asked, "Do you remember me referring to you as being in the window of needing surgery?"

Joel nodded and said, "Yes."

Dr. Schory shook his head and said, "Well, you are well in the window right now. Waiting too long will risk the heart enlarging and not being able to go back to functioning normally. You should not put this off too long."

Joel sat in the exam room stunned. He knew this very news had been a possibility, but he didn't feel sick or in pain. He was just in a daze. The doctor told Joel that he would be giving him a packet of information about the surgery to review and discuss with Lisa. He also told him that he hoped to hear back from him soon.

On the way home, Joel was still dazed. He wasn't sure how to approach this news with Lisa. He understood the importance of the situation, but still wasn't convinced about the urgency. He was not having a bit of trouble. At home, Lisa already had the kids over at Kevin and Tracy's house so that Lisa and Joel could discuss the test results.

Joel began by saying that the doctor confirmed that he was definitely in the window for the surgery. Joel went on to tell Lisa that it was up to them when the surgery would be, but the doctor wanted it to be sooner rather than later. Joel pulled the papers out of the envelope and began reviewing them with Lisa. After they finished reading all the pages, he told her, "I want to wait until summer. You will be done with school and it will just be easier on everyone. What do you think?"

"I guess that makes sense, but I will be watching you closely. I have all the symptoms right here," Lisa said as she pointed to the medical papers. She then put her two fingers out like snake fangs and pointed back and forth to both their sets of eyes. Lisa grabbed Joel's hands and started to pray: "Lord, you are in control. You know how important Joel is to this family. We ask that you watch over him in these months ahead and protect him and his heart. We are so thankful that you guided him to see the doctor. We trust in you and ask for the peace that only comes from you. Thank you for loving us. We love you. It is in Jesus's name I pray. Amen."

Joel called the next day to tell the people at the cardiologist's office that he wanted the surgery to be scheduled for the middle of June. They were pleased with his decision and told him they would be in touch in a few months with more pre-surgical consultations.

It was the middle of March, and the weather finally gave everyone a tease when it warmed up to 70 degrees for two days over that weekend. Joel and Kevin decided to take the basketball and shoot some hoops down at the school. Before long, taking turns shooting wasn't enough. Joel asked Kevin, "Are you ready for a little one-on-one?"

Kevin answered, "Always ready!"

Joel threw the ball to him at the foul line and said, "Let's play to fifteen baskets."

They began to play—running, jumping, and shooting. Most of the time they missed, but every so often the ball would go through the hoop for a score. After a while, Joel wished that they were only playing to ten, but he was determined to play through the exhaustion.

The score was 13-12 in favor of Kevin, when Joel rebounded the ball and began to dribble back to the foul line to clear the ball and set up his next shot. As he dribbled, his body began to list to the left, and then he staggered to the right trying to find

Chapter 19: The Heart of the Matter

his balance and regain his bearings. Every time he tried to take a step, he knew that his foot wasn't reacting the way it should. He heard Kevin beside him saying something, but there were only blurred motions and sounds everywhere. Joel knew he needed to sit down. He made his way to the side of the court and folded into the grass.

Kevin came rushing over and said, "What's the matter? Wow! You are completely white—like a ghost."

Joel said, "I'm not sure. My stomach really hurts. I had some fast food earlier, so maybe it was bad."

Kevin said, "I don't know, but we're done playing. Take a minute, and then we're heading back."

On Joel's arrival back at the house, he headed straight back to the bedroom and shut the door. Kevin peaked in the door and interrupted Lisa reading a story to the kids in the living room before their nap. He explained to Lisa everything that happened. She immediately asked Kevin if Tracy was busy. She needed someone to be over at the house when the girls woke up from their nap. She was taking Joel to the ER. Kevin said that he would go and find out and be back over.

Lisa put the girls down for their nap and went to the bedroom door. She slowly opened it to see Joel on the bed and to hear his moans and groans and heavy coughs. He noticed Lisa and said, "Honey, I really think I got some bad food earlier today. I probably won't go to church tomorrow. I need to get some rest."

She paused and then approached the bookshelf next to the dresser opposite the bed. She pulled some papers out of an envelope and started to read:

Mitral valve stenosis—Mild problems can suddenly worsen. Watch if the following symptoms worsen:
- Shortness of breath, especially with exertion
- Fatigue, especially during increased physical activity
- Heart palpitations
- Dizziness or fainting

- Heavy coughing
- Chest discomfort
- Nausea

"Joel!" Lisa said very forcefully. "We are going to the ER. I'm grabbing some things, and Tracy is coming over for the girls." She looked at him and he was just propped up by a pillow, holding his stomach trying to get more comfortable, but nothing was working.

His eyes locked with hers and he said, "Okay. I'm ready."

Chapter 20:
I'LL JUST CRASH HERE

(Joel—after high school: 2002)

THE CAR DOOR OPENED, and Lisa let Joel out at the emergency room doors, where he stumbled up to the check-in desk. A nurse began to ask him all the standard questions, as everything was sounding more and more garbled. After parking, Lisa rushed in the doors and helped to answer the nurse's questions. She told the nurse that it was probably heart valve related. The nurse said, "You said he is thirty-two years old?"

"Yes," Lisa replied.

"Oh, honey, he is much too young for heart trouble. Just go over and sit in the waiting room and we'll call him when we have a room."

Lisa looked at her in unbelief, but didn't say another word. She took Joel to a quiet spot in the waiting room. Nearly an hour went by, and Joel was sinking lower and lower in his chair without a sign that anyone would be checking on him soon. He told Lisa he was going to use the restroom. On his way back, Lisa noticed how agitated and frustrated he was. Joel collapsed in a chair next to Lisa and gasped, "I can't go to the bathroom. I haven't been able to pee for over a day. There is so much pressure on my bladder. I don't know what to do."

That was all Lisa needed to hear. She marched up to the desk and told the nurse what Joel just told her. That seemed to get some people moving a little faster. Joel was led to an ER exam room, where the waiting game continued. The initial nurse looked at his chart and said to Lisa, "Uncomfortable in the belly, thirty-two. Probably needs a laxative."

Lisa couldn't hold back anymore. Just as she went into full protective mode for the life of her spouse, Joel passed out on the table. He came to as blood was being drawn and a pill was being placed under his tongue. "Mrs. Brunner," the nurse said, "his enzymes are elevated. There is something going on with the heart. We are admitting him overnight and will get a heart catheterization in the morning."

Feeling so much better for his care, Lisa thanked the nurse and ER doctor, then she squeezed Joel's hand as they waited for their room. Lisa looked at Joel with wide eyes and asked, "Now do you believe me that this isn't food poisoning?"

Reluctantly, Joel answered, "Yes, okay. You're right."

During the night, Joel was given IVs and was monitored, but in the light of day, it was clear that his condition had worsened. Visible purple splotches were showing up on his kneecaps and all over his back. He was rushed to the heart catheterization lab. Before they could start, Joel crashed on the cart.

The doctor pulled Lisa aside and asked her to review everything that was going on with Joel. When she mentioned that he has not been able to urinate, they rushed him behind a curtain and started a urinary catheter on him. A flurry of activity was happening all around Joel, which sounded and looked very scary to Lisa.

Joel was taken up to a cardiac ICU room to be monitored and stabilized. In the meantime, Lisa decided she needed the help

Chapter 20: I'll Just Crash Here

of their church. She made a call to Diane, the secretary, asking her to call Joel's mom and dad and tell them they should come as quickly as they could. For the next few hours, Lisa stayed by Joel's side as the kids were being cared for by Kevin and Tracy.

The bloodwork tests came back, showing that all of Joel's organs were losing function. It was decided to conduct a Swan-Ganz catheterization. This procedure would thread a sensitive wire through an artery in the neck and over to the inner heart, then down and around the chambers to have continuous cardiac output monitoring along with temperature and pulmonary artery pressures. Joel was in a very critical state. He was non-responsive, lying in the critical-care cardiac ICU with one dedicated nurse who only had him as a patient.

Joel's parents made it to the hospital later that afternoon. They found Lisa at his bedside. When she saw them, Lisa got up and went out into the hallway to exchange a hug with them. She told them that only one person was allowed in at a time. There was a family waiting room around the corner where they could talk further, but they needed to take turns and visit him. After his mom and dad took a turn standing next to him and spending time in prayer asking God for his healing touch, they waited to see if this young man's organs would respond and begin to stabilize.

The first signs emerged as Joel started waking up and began thrashing back and forth. He quickly asked for water, but the nurse had strict orders that no water could be given. They did not want to activate any of the digestive organs during this recovery period. Joel slipped in and out of consciousness, always thrashing his way out of a place that he did not want to stay. Each time he woke up, he begged for water.

Afraid to swallow, he was convinced his tongue would choke him; but the involuntary swallowing response would happen, and like a rusty gate needing oil, or water in this case, the epiglottis (the flap) for the airway opened in time for him to take his next breath. All he wanted, but couldn't have, was water, that basic necessity of life. When some of the numbers began to show positive results, relief was finally granted; his nurse soaked a small sponge on a stick and let Joel suck it dry.

Joel continued to improve, and by the fourth day he was coherent enough to hear from Lisa, his saving angel, about some of the details of his trauma. She only told Joel that there were a lot of people on his trauma team making sure he got stabilized, and a lot of people on his prayer team were asking for God's healing touch.

A couple more days passed by, and Joel was transferred from a critical-care ICU room to a step-down ICU room. During that time, he slowly started to feel more alert and was able to process what was being done and said about him.

One evening after Lisa got the kids settled for the evening with the neighbors, she arrived and greeted Joel with a calming smile and gentle kiss. For the first time since his hospital admittance, Joel showed interest in the outside world. He asked, "How are the girls?"

Lisa said, "They are worried about Daddy, but they know his heart needs fixed."

"Speaking of getting my heart fixed," Joel said, "what are the doctors telling you?"

"Well, mister," she said as she sat on the edge of the bed, "all of your organs were in full shut-down mode and they had to get all that stabilized, which they feel is well underway. The next thing is to do a heart catheterization, which will determine two things. It will check for damage and will also see everything the surgeon will need to see for the heart-valve surgery. After you get the heart cath, we will have more information and a better idea of the timing of what's needed. Right now, the best thing we can do is pray, which is what I want to do now with you."

"That's fine," Joel agreed. "Go ahead and pray."

"Lord Jesus, thank you for keeping this man around. I need

Chapter 20: I'll Just Crash Here

him, and his girls need him. The doctors have done some amazing things to care for him, and it was all guided by you. Thank you. I ask that you continue to hold his heart in your hands and allow us to be able to have the best outcome to restore Joel's health so he can continue to be the loving provider you made him to be. You are our source of healing and strength. It's in your name I pray. Amen."

"Amen," Joel repeated.

The next day, Joel was wheeled down to the heart catheterization surgical room. He was placed under a big machine with lights and screens everywhere. All of a sudden, a man's voice boomed out over all the other voices, barking out orders to turn on his stereo. The Motown song from the Isley Brothers, "This Old Heart of Mine," started playing. He began to feed the cath up through the artery at Joel's groin and inner thigh.

Joel was lying there enjoying the inner workings of a surgical unit. It almost felt like an episode of ER, as the doctors and nurses were talking about everything else around him except his procedure. Joel picked up on conversations about a nurse's boyfriend looking for another job and another nurse whose three dogs kept her up all night. All along, the doctor in charge was singing the lyrics real softly as he was getting the pictures the other specialists needed.

Then out of nowhere, in mid-lyric, the doctor said "Blast it!" Joel just stayed there as still as possible, not knowing if he did something wrong. The doctor repeated, "Blast it!" and then said, "I can't go any further. That valve is severely damaged, and I don't want to risk anything more for this young man. I got what I could." The surgical cath team backed everything out and finished the procedure. Joel was taken back to his ICU room, where he fell asleep.

He was awakened by Lisa's animated voice and a team of doctors who were standing outside his room. Joel watched her throw her hands around like she received the worst news ever.

Then he realized they were talking about him. He felt a little smile come to his face, followed by a peace. Soon everyone approached the foot of Joel's bed. Joel said, "Wow! A real medical huddle. I have only seen those on TV."

Lisa said, "Well, guess what's next for you, mister?"

"A marathon?" Joel quipped, with another smile.

"No. A helicopter ride to Cleveland," she said.

The doctors explained to Joel that the Cleveland Clinic would give him the best chance to have a successful outcome with his heart valve replacement, and if something didn't work out right, they were LVAD (left-ventricular assist device) and heart transplant capable.

It was only a couple hours later when Joel gave his mom, dad, and Lisa each a kiss; then right before he boarded the helicopter he said, "Hey guys, I'll race you to Cleveland!" They smiled back as the flight crew finished loading him in and shut the door.

Joel sat up on the exam table. Dr. Schory came in all smiles and said, "We're halfway through the season, and my Yankees look pretty good, don't they? Is Cleveland going to be good enough to overtake them?"

Joel laughed and replied, "Well, I hope so, but I do know that Cleveland has a very good surgeon to replace heart valves."

They both laughed, and the doctor continued to look at his chart. Dr. Schory then said, "Four months post-op, and everything looks really good with your cardiac rehab. Let me look at that zipper down your chest. Okay. Good. It's healing nicely. Any questions for me?"

"As a matter of fact, just one," Joel said. "Can I go to my fifteen-year high-school reunion later in the fall? I have quite a tale to tell everyone."

Chapter 20: I'll Just Crash Here

Dr. Schory responded with a smile, "Yes, but don't have too much fun."

Then Joel said, "I promise."

Lisa remembered that her great grandmother's ninetieth birthday party was in Findlay, Ohio, on the same day as Joel's class reunion. Just like the doctor, she felt very comfortable letting Joel make the trip back by himself. She also knew that he would be staying with his parents, and that made her feel at peace.

Chapter 21:

LIFE JUST GOT BIGGER

(Colleen—after high school: 1987-1988)

"HONEY," A SWEET VOICE from the other room called, "are you sure you're okay with not going to the reunion?"

"Yes, dear, I am," said a deep voice from the kitchen. "I will be fine taking care of the two toddlers that are sharing chicken pox. We're certainly not leaving them with a teenage boy."

"Yeah. That wouldn't be very good parenting of us, and it would definitely be torture for him. He's always outside doing something and never wants to be inside with his little brother and sister."

"Sick toddlers. I don't blame him a bit." They both laughed.

A stunningly beautiful woman rounded the corner from the bedroom into the kitchen and asked, "How do I look?"

Then the little girl said, "Mommy, you look like a princess."

"Thank you, honey," she replied, "but Mommy was really going for a super model in her twenties."

Her husband smirked and said, "Collie, you look great, but not that great." She hauled off and smacked him. "I mean when you were in your twenties . . ." She smacked him again. "I mean . . ."

Colleen laughed and said, "Mister, you better quit, or I'll stay the night and you can deal with these two for another day."

"Okay, okay. You win," he said.

Colleen gave him a look, a smile, and a kiss. "Don't wait up," she said, and then laughed as she made her way down the sidewalk to the car. As she left the house and drove down the long driveway, she knew she had about an hour drive before she was back in Alliance. It gave her time to replay these last fifteen years like a movie in her mind. Looking into the rearview mirror, she noticed her perfectly applied makeup and remembered that life was far from perfect, starting when she got to the University of Cincinnati. Taking in a long deep breath, her movie began to play.

With Ryan's tragedy still on her mind, Colleen left for Cincinnati with a sad heart. She was ready for new places, new people, and new challenges. College was amazing. Colleen excelled in all of her classes. She knew she could not afford to slip up, because the program was highly competitive and prestigious. It was the Thursday night at the start of fall break early in October when she finally began to process the emotion of everything that had happened over the last two months. She began to wonder. She wondered about a possibility that she tried to push away. Was she pregnant?

She lay awake all night asking God to please allow her to have a chance at a life that was coming true. She must have fallen asleep right before dawn, because she was startled awake by her neighbor's dorm door. She quickly put on sweatpants, threw a long winter coat over her pajama top, and headed out on a trek to the corner drugstore.

Chapter 21: Life Just Got Bigger

She went there for one thing, got it, and came back to the dorm and went straight into the bathroom. She really had to pee! Colleen didn't even have to wait the recommended three minutes to find out. As she was washing her hands at the sink, a big bright plus sign was staring back at her. She was pregnant.

Colleen knew she had only herself to blame. She might have been several hours from home, but all she wanted right now was to be back in her bedroom on her bed sketching her castles and kingdoms. Since that wasn't going to happen, she decided the next best thing was to call her mom to talk.

Back in Alliance, the phone rang. Colleen's mom answered, "Hello."

"Hi, Mom," Colleen said.

"What's wrong?" her mom immediately blurted out.

Colleen began to cry.

"What is wrong, Colleen?"

"I need you to come down," Colleen answered.

"Are you homesick?" her mom asked.

"No," she said as she cried some more. After she settled down a bit, she cried out, "I'm pregnant!"

There was silence on the other end of the phone. Finally, Colleen's mom said, "Are you kidding me? I can't believe you. I really can't believe you!"

More tears and sounds of wailing came out of the phone.

Her mom breathed audibly and loudly and said, "I'm coming down to see you. I'll be there by lunchtime." With Colleen still whimpering in the background, Colleen's mom said, "Honey, get your rest. I'll see you in three, maybe four hours."

"Okay, Mom. I love you."

"I love you, too."

Colleen's mom immediately placed a call to her husband. He was in the main office and not on the road for sales calls. She told him the devastating news and informed him that she was going down to see Colleen. Colleen's dad said, "Not without me, you're not. I'm taking the rest of the day off. I can't believe what you're telling me. Why would she let something like this happen?"

"Honey, it did. Let's go see Colleen and get more answers."

By the time he got back to the house, his wife was ready for the long trip to Cincinnati. Mr. Newcome fidgeted and pounded the steering wheel the whole way down there. When they got to UC, they saw Colleen waiting for them outside the dorm. As soon as the car stopped, her mom ran over to her and just held her as she began to cry and shake. Her dad was a lot slower to come to console her, and he did so only with a hug. That comforted Colleen, because she knew how much this devastated and disappointed him. They decided to get a quick lunch and take it to a private place near campus, to a park overlooking the Ohio River.

As they ate, Colleen's dad couldn't help himself. He said, "Colleen, I thought you came down here to study and to become what you always wanted to be."

Colleen burst into tears as her mom started rubbing her back and giving her husband a dirty look. Again, Mr. Newcome couldn't control himself, and in a very sarcastic tone said, "Please tell me about the man of your dreams who swept you off your feet and you had sex with."

Mrs. Newcome abruptly said, "Now that is enough! That is not helping now."

Mr. Newcome responded, "Well? I'm waiting. Who is the father?"

Colleen sat with her arms around her knees and her head tucked down, as her mom was covering her like a blanket and rubbing her back. They could still hear the sobbing as the two were exchanging nonverbal messages.

Then Mr. Newcome said a little more calmly, "Colleen, who is the father?"

Chapter 21: Life Just Got Bigger

Colleen didn't look up, but only said quietly, "Don't make me say it."

"Don't make me say it!" her dad repeated and felt the rage beginning again. "You better get used to saying it!"

She unraveled and screamed out, "The father is Ryan Huff!" and now began crying hysterically.

Her mom was trying to comfort her even more by holding her tighter and rocking her like she used to do not so many years ago. Again, Mr. and Mrs. Newcome only exchanged glances of astonishment and stayed quiet. Then as Colleen calmed down she said, "I am so sorry for disappointing you guys with this news. I wasn't thinking at the end of the night of the Three-Month Reunion. It all happened so fast and emotions got the best of me. I'm sorry. I understand if you hate me and make me deal with this myself, but I'm scared."

Colleen's dad bent down, put his hand under her chin, and pulled it up until their eyes met. "Collie, your mom and I love you so much and only want the best for you. This isn't what we had hoped for you, but it is a part of a new life that you now have. I have my feelings about what should be done next, but I want to hear your heart, your thoughts."

"Mom, Dad, I know you probably want me to give up the baby for adoption, and I definitely thought about it. But something deep down inside is telling me I need to have this baby and keep it. It will be extremely difficult, and I will be giving up a lot to be an unmarried mother, but I just know this is the best thing."

Mr. Newcome said, "You're right. That is the option I think is best for you, but I am going to leave and let you and your mother talk some more. I'll be waiting in the car." He gave her a kiss on the head and left.

Colleen's mom looked at her and said, "Honey, I love you. We love you. The one thing I do know is that we need to check on the baby you have growing inside you. We are going to find out where a crisis pregnancy center is and get you a check-up. Okay?"

"Okay, Mom," Colleen answered. She was very glad that her mom and dad had come down. She already felt calmer about everything. She hadn't been as ready to figure things out herself as she had thought. Hand in hand, they walked back to the car. Out of the corner of Mr. Newcome's eye, he saw them approaching and quickly stopped jotting notes on a piece of paper. He quickly folded his note and stuffed it into his jacket.

He then said, "What's the plan?"

Mrs. Newcome said, "We're going back to the dorm to look up the services of a local crisis pregnancy center for her. I want to know that my baby and her baby are healthy for this pregnancy." They drove back to campus, and with the help of the Yellow Pages, they found out where they needed to go. It was fairly close by and did not take long at all to get there. Mr. Newcome dropped them off and drove away.

Walking into the crisis pregnancy center, they were greeted by a large bulletin board with baby pictures plastered all over it. Colleen was drawn to it as she saw all the precious little ones tacked up. There were newborns all swaddled up and babies posing for their one-year pictures. They were all so beautiful and innocent. A lady hung up the phone and greeted them. "Hi. Can I help you?"

Colleen said, "I just learned that I am pregnant, about eight or nine weeks along. This is my mom, and also my dad knows about it. I know what I want to do, but my mom wanted me to come and get checked out."

The lady said, "Please come with me to one of our private meeting rooms." As they sat down she asked, "So, what is it that you plan to do?"

Colleen took a deep breath and said, "I am going to keep the baby."

Chapter 21: Life Just Got Bigger

The lady smiled and said, "Thank you for choosing life for your baby. Do you realize that your precious one has a heartbeat right now? We don't have the instruments to pick it up here, but that little one is growing each and every day. Right now, all of its organs and muscles are beginning to function. In the baby's brain, nerve cells are branching out and making connections. Your baby's hands are bending at the wrists. Fingers and toes are getting nails and the eyelids are almost complete, as are the taste buds on the tongue. Little earlobes are beginning to form. Within the next week there will be teeth, an outline of the spine, and even peach-fuzz hair starting, besides the changes that you should be noticing."

Colleen quickly said, "Like my bras not fitting anymore!"

The lady and Mrs. Newcome began to laugh, and the lady said, "Yes, for sure. You are going to start to get bigger in all the baby-carrying places: breast, belly, and hips." The lady asked Colleen, "Do you feel like you have any issues with bleeding or unusual cramping?"

"No," Colleen said. "Just a little morning sickness, but that's about it."

"Good. I'm going to send you home with some information about nutrition and other things that will help you care for yourself and your baby until your obstetrician wants to see you for your first visit and ultrasound. I'm so glad to have met you, and I'm so glad you have the support of your family."

Colleen looked at her mom and said, "Me, too."

They walked out to the waiting room to see Mr. Newcome. He stood up and met Colleen with a smile and a comforting hug. She said, "Daddy, my baby has a little heartbeat and fingers and toes."

Mr. Newcome asked, "Is everyone healthy?"

"Everything seems normal, and normal is good!" replied Mrs. Newcome.

"Great!" he said, as he gave Colleen another hug. Then he asked, "Is anyone hungry?"

Mrs. Newcome answered sarcastically, "Ah, honey, there is a pregnant lady here; of course she's hungry." Colleen laughed and was starting to feel a little better about everything.

"Good," he said. "I want to run a plan by you two before moving forward."

As soon as Colleen heard those words, she felt unsettled, but she knew that her dad had her best interests at heart, and she wanted to listen.

Then he said, "Let's wait until we get somewhere to eat." Colleen and her mom looked at each other with wide eyes and puzzled looks.

Mr. Newcome pulled into a local pizzeria and said, "Yes. This is the best pizza around." They found a corner booth in which to sit. After placing their order, Mr. Newcome pulled out a very harshly folded piece of paper, smoothed it out, and said, "Okay, Collie. If you don't want to go through with the option of adoption, then you are going to follow through with another grown up response, and that is preparing to be a single parent, working, and going to school. It will be the hardest thing you will ever do, but it will be the best thing you can do. You will finish up your semester here and leave in good standing. You will then continue your college career at Mansfield Technical Institute and get your degree in a drafting field. From there, you will be very prepared for the workforce and be one of the best to ever come out of there."

He paused for a minute and winked. He then said, "I have already talked to your Aunt Margie and Uncle Bill, who live very close to Mansfield. They understand the situation and are more than willing to help you out. Uncle Bill will be putting together a list of people you can talk to for a job when you come back in December. I think it's best if we don't burden the Huffs during their extreme grief right now. Let's let that baby grow inside

Chapter 21: Life Just Got Bigger

you. I really think we will know when the time is right, and we will be ready to share with them then. Do you understand and agree with the plan?"

Colleen leaned over and gave her dad a hug and said, "Thanks for standing by me and helping me figure this out." She dropped her head down very reflectively as her mom came alongside to embrace her as well.

Suddenly, Colleen looked at her mom and dad and said, "Really? From UC to MTI? Wow! This is a crazy life lesson. You know what they say about MTI."

Her dad laughed and said, "Yeah. It's for those in Ohio who can't spell MIT!" They all laughed and finished their supper.

Colleen got through the rest of 1987 in Cincinnati with only a little morning sickness. She completed her college semester and transferred to MTI in Mansfield. She moved in with her aunt and uncle, whose two kids were already out of the house. Her aunt really became a second mom to her as her belly grew. The classes at MTI were easier and did not require as much time as UC's workload.

Colleen was able to land a job at the local Builder's Square. She worked at the Contractor Project Desk and helped wherever else they needed her. She mostly did the ordering of the building materials after the design was finalized, but occasionally the boss would let her help propose ideas and designs or even do some easy estimating jobs. She loved her job and felt very thankful for those who were helping make this all work out. She worked with all guys, and they always made her feel like she was their little sister or daughter. It was a comforting and secure feeling, but right around the corner it would be time for her little project in her tummy to make an appearance and change her world.

As spring showed up in central Ohio, classes were getting more involved and work at the project desk was very busy. Colleen could always keep up with the hurried nature of contractors, but with her getting so big with the baby on board, she was strutting more of a waddle than a racer's walk. She just hoped none of the guys would put a "wide load" sign on her as a prank.

Finals were the first week of May, which hit at week thirty-nine of the pregnancy. She went to see the OB during her lunch hour once a week during the month of April. Also once a week, Aunt Margie attended her childbirth/Lamaze class with her. Aunt Margie rounded up some additional help from members of their church who would be ready to help after the blessed event. Colleen had been attending church with them since she moved in. Aunt Margie knew she would eventually need some babysitting help, and so was grateful that the help was all lined up.

The week of finals came, and Colleen was getting through each one. She was extremely uncomfortable and was definitely ready for the birth. She was also ready for school to be done until the fall. She was looking forward to this new challenging chapter of motherhood, and she continued to have peace about it.

After her last final, in her CAD electronic drafting class, she began to feel more pressure and became even more uncomfortable. She was only a few minutes from the OB office, so she drove herself there. Waddling into the office, Colleen said, "I'm not sure, but I think I might be starting to have my baby."

The nurse looked at her and then pushed a button that blinked everywhere in the back offices. Doctors, nurses, and technicians all rushed to the waiting room and helped her to one of the exam rooms. A doctor examined Colleen and said, "Well, you are four centimeters and effaced to 50 percent. You are getting a ride to the hospital and are going to have a baby tonight." He snapped his gloves off and went back to his other patient.

Colleen said, "May I please call my aunt before I go?"

"Yes, sweetie," one of the office workers said. "Just see me on your way out. We'll get hold of her."

After things calmed down, she called her aunt. "Aunt Margie,

Chapter 21: Life Just Got Bigger

I am at the doctor's office. They tell me I'll be having my baby tonight. Can you please call my mom and dad and tell them?"

"Yes, Collie, I sure will," she said. "I'll bring everything you packed up and bring it to you after I talk to them. I'll see you in a little while. I love you."

"I love you, too. Thanks," Colleen replied.

Colleen was taken to the hospital and was immediately put into a birthing room. The nurse said, "Honey, it could be a while, so get comfortable." Colleen was really hoping that it would be several hours. She wanted time to be with her mom and aunt.

Aunt Margie came into the room with an armful of labor and delivery aides to make the experience as relaxing as possible. She said in a giddy, almost song-like way, "Our Collie is having a baby; our Collie is having a baby."

Colleen said, "Aunt Margie, please stop. You are going to make me laugh and have this baby before my mother gets here."

"Oh, sorry, honey. I guess I'm a super-excited coach! I promise I'll turn it down and start getting you relaxed. Look, here is your cassette tape of Kenny G's greatest hits. I have a lilac for you and I also brought vanilla air freshener. And finally, here is your focal-point picture—the Eiffel Tower in the springtime. I think you're ready.

"Uh, no," Colleen said.

"No?" her aunt repeated, confused.

Just then her first contraction hit, and she screamed, "My mommy!"

Chapter 22:

FALLING IN LOVE TWICE

(Colleen—after high school: 1988-1990)

THE BABY DECIDED TO hold off, allowing Mrs. Newcome a chance to arrive in time. Once there, Colleen squeezed her mom's hand and pleaded, "I need the epidural!"

Colleen's mom said, "Okay, honey. I'll talk to someone." Moments later a nurse cleared the room out and the shot was given. Colleen was able to regain a little more focus. When the nurse walked back into the room to check on her, she took one look at the monitors for Colleen and the baby and suddenly ran out. Colleen looked to her mom and aunt for answers, but all they could do was squeeze her hand. Aunt Margie said a quick prayer out loud. As she said "Amen," the OB ran into the room glancing at the monitor and saying very directly to Colleen, "It's time to have this baby. Now *pushhhhh*. Again. *Pushhhhhhhhhh*."

Sweat began to pour off her forehead and she felt an intense headache as blood vessels popped in her eyes and all over her face. The doctor asked for the baby forceps, and when he asked Colleen to give him one more "*Pushhhhhhhhhh*," he put the baby's head in the instrument, and with his gifted hands he delivered a baby before its heart rate would go any lower. The doctor said, "It's a boy. Come on, fella; let me hear you cry." When the baby didn't make a sound, the doctor handed the baby to the nurse, who then rushed out of the room.

Exhausted and now concerned, Colleen exclaimed, "My baby! My baby! Where are they taking him?" The doctor told the three astonished women that they were going to care for the baby where they could keep him warm and work to get some fluid out that the baby swallowed. They had to get him breathing properly.

The women remained calm, mainly because the doctor seemed calm; but when ten minutes turned into thirty minutes, Colleen let out a cry again, "Where's my baby?" The nurse came running in and told her that the baby had been crying for a little while now. They were finishing cleaning him up and she would get to see him soon. A few minutes later, a nurse brought a tightly wrapped baby wailing away at the top of his lungs and handed him to Colleen.

Colleen's mom leaned into the bed and kissed Colleen's forehead and said with a comforting voice, "Collie, he's beautiful."

"He sure is, Mom, and I love him so much already. Thank you both for being here with me."

Aunt Margie quickly asked, "What's his name?"

Without hesitation, Colleen said, "Ryan James. We'll call him RJ."

"Oh, that's very sweet," Aunt Margie said. "Your dad will be thrilled that you used his first name as the baby's middle name."

Colleen's mom began to cry again, but stopped long enough to say, "Ryan James. How perfect."

Then Aunt Margie said, "Come on, ladies. Let's unwrap this bundle of cuteness and count fingers and toes."

The next couple of days passed quickly. When it was time to go home, Colleen was apprehensive to leave the security of

Chapter 22: Falling in Love Twice

the hospital and go back to her aunt and uncle's house. Even though she knew she had their help and support anytime, adding this little one into her life made her spend more time in prayer. This was not just prayer in which she would mention a laundry list of "Please" and "Thank you," but now she was having real conversations with God and was listening for his voice to touch her spirit.

Colleen loved the fact that she wasn't taking classes at MTI during the summer session, and for a full six weeks she stayed home to bond with RJ and learn how to best care for him. When that time was up, she added work back into her life by going back to Builder's Square. Everyone was happy to see her come back, and she picked up right where she left off. Most days she stayed very busy, and her shift would go by quickly, allowing her to keep her mind off how much she missed RJ. She knew her aunt or other friends from the church were giving him the best care and attention that they could, but it was still a pull on her heart. Whenever she got sad, she would start a conversation with the Lord, and his peace would always comfort her.

The summer flew by for Colleen. It was time to add college back into her life. She now counted on her aunt and others more than ever. She hoped that she could repay them some day, but for now she had to accept their generosity with thankfulness.

Even though Colleen's college program was a two-year associate degree in mechanical drafting, she had to back off with her schooling in order to work the necessary hours to provide for RJ and to give her aunt and uncle a little money for room and board. Going the extra year didn't bother Colleen a bit, because she found Mansfield to be a place where she could see herself staying. She was making a lot of new friends from work, school, and church.

It was early December 1988, when a group from school wanted to celebrate the end of another semester by going to see the new comedy movie, Twins. They asked Colleen to go, but when she heard they were going to see Twins, it freaked her out a little. She initially said no, telling them that she didn't want to miss any more time away from RJ than for school or work. Then one of her closest friends, Molly, said, "I thought you said your baby is never fussy at night."

Colleen replied, "He never is. He goes right to sleep, and I am able to do my homework with no problem."

"Well then," said Molly, "bring him with you. We can sit in the back where it's not too loud, and it will give me a chance to hold and cuddle him."

Colleen took a deep breath. She knew she had to take a step out socially sometime, and she decided tonight would be a good night. So, she changed her mind and said, "How can I say no when you have everything figured out? But, I don't care that this is a comedy. I'm still bringing some tissues."

They decided to go to the 7:35 p.m. show. The group showed up and found their seats toward the back, but Molly, Colleen, and baby RJ claimed the back row. RJ was already sucking on a pacifier and his eyes were half-closed. The theater darkened, and Molly reached over to scoop up the baby. For the next two hours Colleen laughed and even cried, and she had a wonderful time out with her friends.

Immediately after the movie was over, Colleen took over holding the sleeping prince. She told the group that she couldn't go out for any after-movie munchies. She needed to get back to put both RJ and herself to bed. She thanked Molly for insisting that she go to the movie and also for holding RJ. They said goodbye as she was strapping RJ into the baby's car-seat carrier and checking her own seat to make sure she didn't leave anything behind.

Nearly the last one out of the theater, she walked down a long dark hallway to where it met the lobby. There the crowd was in a bulging line ready to storm the theater for the best seats for the 10:05 show.

Chapter 22: Falling in Love Twice

As she was in her own world leaving and thinking about how ironic it was for her to see the movie Twins, she heard a familiar voice call her name, and she saw a flash of someone who darted out of the corralled line in front of her. "Colleen!"

She quickly squeezed the baby carrier and looked up to focus her eyes on Scott Huff. She quickly said, "Scott!" and then they froze in each other's gaze.

They began talking back and forth about where each was going to school, and then Scott asked, "And who is this sleeping cutie?" Colleen shuffled to the opposite wall and put the car seat down on a bench under a big poster of the movie *Big*.

"She then answered, "This is RJ."

"RJ," Scott repeated. "What a cool name, I mean initials, I mean I don't know, but it's cool," and then they both laughed. Blown away by running into Colleen and meeting her baby, he started firing so many more questions at her to the point that she said, "Scott, you need to get going. Your movie?"

He quickly replied, "Uh, no. Not again. I've been thinking about you a lot lately and was going to stop by your mom and dad's during this Christmas break to track you down."

Colleen interrupted, "What? Why?"

Scott continued, "I have always, always . . . I wish I had enough nerve to ask you out back in high school. It's just my loss. You have started a family and have a beautiful son."

Colleen was really conflicted about her feelings. She said, "Scott, how can I get hold of you? I want to talk more."

He said, "No, I don't need to see that movie. I need to see and talk to you some more. Please, let's go somewhere. You can bring me back when the movie is over." Scott introduced his friends to Colleen and told them the plan. By 10:30, the baby was laid down in his crib fast asleep after sleeping through his first movie.

Colleen brought Scott into the family room to say hi and to introduce him to her aunt and uncle. It didn't take long for

285

Aunt Margie to get the hint that Colleen needed to talk to Scott about the past. Her aunt closed the recliner and said to her husband, "Come on, dear. You have been falling asleep most of the program. Let's call it a night."

As she gave Colleen a hug, Colleen whispered that she would need to take Scott back to the theater, so she would like her to just keep an ear on her room." Aunt Margie nodded and squeezed her hand. That gave her a quick shot of confidence that she could tell him everything.

Sitting on the couch together, she clicked off her uncle's prized possession—his new big-screen TV that took up over a third of the room. Scott could sense he was in for the story of his life, so he quickly said, "Colleen, before you tell me about the last sixteen months, I want to say again that I care about you a lot, and I meant it when I told you that I was going to track you down over Christmas."

Colleen's heart was touched. With a cautious smile she began by saying, "RJ stands for Ryan James." Immediately Scott's eyes got huge, but his face looked even more puzzled than before. Colleen continued, "Your brother Ryan . . ."

Before she could finish that sentence, Scott pulled her up from the couch and off the ground for a twirling hug. "You and Ryan had a baby?"

Colleen just looked at him and smiled. Scott quickly sent her around for another couple spins and said, "This is the best day of my life. You are the best thing . . ." Scott stopped mid-sentence and looked at Colleen. Her eyes and face had a look of relief and love in return. Scott pulled her close and kissed her lightly on the lips and said, "You are the best thing I lost in high school."

She relaxed in his embrace and they began to share a long passionate kiss. Then with a deep breath Colleen said to Scott, "High school is such an awkward time, but I wish you would have asked me out, too. I would have said yes." They talked and

Chapter 22: Falling in Love Twice

kidded around so much that they didn't even notice what time it was until the grandfather clock chimed once. Colleen knew that it was 11:30 and time to take Scott back to the movie theater.

As Colleen dropped Scott off, he said, "I am so glad I listened to that voice tonight that told me to go to the movies."

She smiled and replied, "Me, too."

They shared another kiss before he ran off to find his friends. He suddenly stopped and yelled to her, "Don't worry. I'm still going to track you down at Christmas."

Colleen yelled back, "You better!"

Then Scott said, "I need to take you back to my house. What a Christmas gift you will be giving my mom and dad!"

Colleen smiled and waved, but didn't want to think about breaking any more news. She was exhausted and had to be at work at 8:00 a.m.

Scott went home to Alliance while ATI was on winter break. He eagerly looked forward to Christmas Eve, when he would see Colleen next. At that time, they would be sharing the news with his parents. While on break, Scott was able to work at the feed mill to earn some extra money and to pass the time away.

It was finally mid-morning on Christmas Eve, and Scott could not wait any longer. He drove past Colleen's parent's house and saw Colleen's car in the driveway. He parked and walked up to the door. After ringing the doorbell, he stepped back off the stoop and took a deep breath. Mrs. Newcome opened the door with a big smile and said, "Hi, Scott. Please come in."

"Thank you, Mrs. Newcome, and Merry Christmas," Scott said. "I saw Colleen's car and . . ." Before he could finish his sentence, Scott heard the sound of someone running down the stairs. He looked over just in time to catch Colleen in his arms for a spinning hug.

Mrs. Newcome burst out laughing and said to Colleen, "Don't put our guest in the hospital on Christmas Eve."

As everyone was laughing, Mr. Newcome came up from the basement smiling and holding a coffee cup. He asked, "What's all the racket up here? Don't we still have a baby sleeping?"

"Daddy," Colleen said, "it's fine. Scott popped in to say hi."

Mr. Newcome said to Scott, "Well, I heard the story of how you two ran into each other at the theater."

Scott replied, "Yes, sir. Very crazy. It was the best day of my life."

Mrs. Newcome invited Scott into the kitchen for some coffee cake. Mr. and Mrs. Newcome talked some more with Scott and Colleen and immediately got the sense that both were in the right place to continue with their studies and dating arrangement from Mansfield and Wooster when schedules allowed. Colleen had another year and a half to go in the drafting program, and Scott had one more semester before completing his associate degree in soil and water management, but knew he wanted to continue on for a bachelor's degree somewhere. Mr. and Mrs. Newcome were very thankful to see their daughter so happy about Scott coming into her life.

As the morning turned to the noon hour, Scott asked Colleen if she was ready to come over to his house with the baby for lunch. With a deep audible breath, she said, "Yes." Scott asked to use their phone to call home.

Mrs. Huff answered the phone, "Hello?"

"Hi, Mom," Scott replied. "I wanted to tell you that I'm bringing someone over for lunch. Is that okay?"

"Sure. I'm just getting stuff out to make sandwiches."

"Okay. I'll be over in ten minutes," Scott said with glee.

Mrs. Newcome and Colleen bundled RJ up and put him in the car-seat carrier. They said their goodbyes and drove down the road. They got to the Huff's driveway, and Scott leaned over to Colleen and gave her a kiss. He then said, "This will be the best Christmas gift ever for them."

Chapter 22: Falling in Love Twice

Colleen answered intrepidly, "I sure hope so."

Scott gave her a reassured look and said, "I know so. Come on. Let's show RJ his other grandma and grandpa."

They smiled and kissed again.

Colleen carried the car seat in one hand, while Scott held her other hand as they walked through the open garage door to enter the house.

Mr. and Mrs. Huff were waiting at the small lunch table with two more places set. Mrs. Huff noticed that the girl in front of her had a baby's car-seat carrier, and she jumped up out of her seat. On her way to see Scott, she recognized Colleen and said, "Colleen! What are you doing? Where have you been? I can't believe it! You look so grown up to me! A baby?"

Scott and Colleen laughed as Colleen put the carrier down and started to unzip and unbuckle the baby. Colleen said, "I have been away studying at MTI and working in Mansfield. I ran into Scott a few weeks ago, and I introduced him to this little guy." As she finished saying that, she lifted him out and his little sleeping eyes opened.

Mrs. Huff, who was immediately ready to take the baby out of Colleen's hands, asked, "Who is this?"

Colleen said, "RJ."

Scott, full of emotion, could not contain himself any longer; he blurted out, "Ryan James!"

The Huffs looked at each other in bewilderment. Colleen then asked, "Can we all sit down?" Colleen explained everything that happened on that night, before the tragedy with Ryan. She went into the details of the discovery when she was at UC and how the decision was made for her to transfer to MTI and live with her aunt and uncle until she had the baby. She went on to say, "Here at Christmas is when I was going to share everything about the baby with you, but then I ran into Scott, and other things began to happen, too."

Mr. Huff said, "Oh, really?"

"Yes, Mom and Dad," Scott replied. "Colleen and I want to continue our schooling, but being only about thirty minutes apart, we can keep dating, too. I told her how I feel about her now, and that I honestly had feelings for her in high school but was too scared to tell her."

Still in a state of shock, Mrs. Huff spoke up and said, "Colleen and Scott, what you both told us is so beautiful. I'm proud of you, Colleen, for being so brave as to face being a single teenage mother. And Scott, I'm real proud of you for following your heart. I really hope the best for you guys. You make such a cute couple."

Mr. Huff said, "Cool it, Grandma! Let the kids figure it out. What I want to say is how proud I am of you, Scott. I know things have been difficult for you growing up, but I am so glad you have turned out the way you did, in spite of me." Mr. Huff looked away.

"Dad," Scott said quickly, "I had other interests than you and the twins had, but you did the best you could. I love you and Mom." He went to his dad and they shared a hug.

Mrs. Huff then said, "Grandma is ready to hold RJ!" Colleen transferred the little one into her arms as she said, "You guys eat. I need to kiss this baby all up." She then whispered in RJ's ear, "You're Grandma's very sweet boy. I love you."

Once they were finished with lunch, the baby took his bottle and then fell asleep in Mrs. Huff's arms. They laid him down in his carrier where he continued his afternoon nap. Mr. Huff said, "With all this excitement, I'm ready for my nap, too."

Colleen spoke up before he had a chance to leave and said, "Yes, I need to get back home, but I was wondering if you guys would like to meet me, RJ, and my parents at the Christmas Eve service tonight at 7:00 p.m.

Mrs. Huff quickly answered for everyone, "Yes, of course. We'll be there. It will be good to see Pastor Russell."

Chapter 22: Falling in Love Twice

Mr. Huff nodded in agreement and gave Colleen a hug before he headed down the hallway. Scott took Colleen back to her house, and they hung out a little more before he went back to get ready for the Christmas Eve service.

The Newcomes got to church first and quickly updated Pastor Russell on the latest surprise—Scott Huff—who had come into Colleen's life. They went into the sanctuary to save three more seats beside them. The Huffs arrived just as the music for "Joy to the World" started playing. They saw the Newcomes halfway down, waving them on down. Mr. and Mrs. Huff quickly entered the row and gave the Newcomes a happy embrace. Scott and Colleen did the same.

Exactly two years later, Alliance had the most anticipated wedding ever. On December 24, 1990, Scott and Colleen were married with family and friends in attendance. Some of the friends included Colleen's close high-school band friends and some of her friends from Mansfield from school and work who could make it. Scott made sure Joel, Mandy, and Beth were given invitations because of what they shared on that tragic night together. He also included several of his friends from ATI in Wooster. The one person who couldn't make it was Shon, who was on a secret mission with the Navy Seals.

The wedding was beautiful and perfect. The flower girls were a couple girls whom Colleen used to babysit, and the ring bearer was none other than RJ, who was officially adopted by Scott a week later.

As Colleen pulled into the banquet-hall parking lot, she had to put her movie on pause for now.

Part Three:

SEPTEMBER 2002 — THE
FIFTEEN-YEAR
REUNION

Chapter 23:

LET'S GO

(Everyone)

JOEL ARRIVED AT THE hall to see Mandy, Beth, and Colleen already sitting at a round banquet table in the middle of the dining area, talking and laughing. He walked over to them, and they noticed that he didn't have Lisa on his arm. Beth quickly said, "You better not have pulled one of your epic pranks and made Lisa mad enough to walk out on you." All of the girls at the table cracked up.

"No," Joel said. "I for sure wouldn't do that now. She saved my life a few months ago." Again all the girls cracked up and told Joel to have a seat with them. He just looked at them like he couldn't believe they wouldn't ask him any follow-up questions. He dropped his program on the table and said to the girls in an irritated manner, "I'm going to mingle before I sit down."

Joel enjoyed reconnecting with everyone he ran into. Each person told him about some of the highlights of their families and careers. Joel reciprocated eagerly with highlights from his family, career, and then the dramatic tale about being on death's doorstep. Just like with the girls, each person laughed and changed the subject as soon as he mentioned his life-threatening scare. Dejected, Joel returned to the table just in time for everyone to notice Shon walking in the door.

A cheer went up for Shon and he smiled and raised his hand to acknowledge it. Then one of the class alums took the microphone and announced, "Three cheers for our Gulf War hero, Shon Huff: Hip hip hooray! Hip hip hooray! Hip hip hooray!"

Then someone else yelled, "Speech. Speech," as the entire group began clapping and whistling to encourage him. Shon finally gave in and walked up to the microphone. When the applause died down, Shon said, "Thank you very much, everyone, for your kindness. There are a lot of people who deserve credit for their bravery during Desert Storm. I was honored to have been part of it, but I don't want to fail to say something publicly tonight."

Shon purposely paused and scanned the crowd of his old classmates. He then swung his head around and fixed his gaze on Joel, saying, "Joel Brunner, we're all glad you survived your heart-valve trauma and surgery!" The room erupted in laughter and applause. Shon then said, "We got you, buddy. We totally got you. The prank is on you!"

Joel covered up his red face with his hands and then dropped his head on the table. His fist began beating the table. Everyone continued to applaud as Joel picked his head off the table and looked around with a smirk, still shaking in unbelief.

Shon approached the table, kissed Colleen on the head, and said, "Hi, sis. I see Scott knew what was best—letting Momma out for a little fun!" He continued around the table, giving Mandy and Beth friendly kisses on the cheek before taking his seat next to Joel. Joel tried to give him a friendly push, but the rock-hard Navy Seal didn't budge.

The reunion organizer scrambled up to Joel and said, "Would you mind saying grace for us?"

Chapter 23: Let's Go

Joel said, "Sure," and went to the microphone. "Dear Lord, thank you for the blessing of life and friendships. We ask your blessing on this food we are about to eat. May we get our strength from it and from you. I pray in your Son's name. Amen."

Joel sat back down next to Mandy as the food was being brought out. There were still three open seats at their table, but Shon was guarding the one next to him. There was no doubt who was occupying that seat tonight. As each course was being consumed, more conversation and stories were being offered. As everyone was sipping coffee, Joel said, "You know, I should write a book about some of our past."

Mandy quickly said with a giggle, "I definitely thought about that for Beth!"

Beth responded, "Me? What?"

Shon then added, "Well, I've actually started something for my chapters. The 90s were some crazy scary times for this Seal. I give God all the credit for keeping me around." Everyone at the table nodded their heads in agreement.

Then Joel said, "And the title can be A Perfect Alliance."

As they were pondering their contributions, Joel said, "How about we talk more about our book at the thirty-year class reunion, when things slow down a little." Everyone came back to their senses, nodded their heads, and agreed.

Seconds later, the loudspeakers started to blast the opening keyboard riff to the Huey Lewis and the News' song "The Power of Love." Once the music started, the conversations died down. One had to scream to answer anyone's question, and even then no one was sure if they were answering the question asked. It turned into People Watching 101 as classmates in their thirties were dancing like they were sixteen and seventeen again. It wasn't a good look for the many who were out of shape and struggling with stamina, and for those who were in decent shape, they seemed to struggle with rhythm. Let's just say that those watching had just as good of a time as those "dancing."

When Shon couldn't take it anymore, he yelled to those at his table, "Let's go outside!" The group of friends followed Shon out of the hall. Around back they found a gazebo that no one was using.

Joel said, "That's more like it. I wasn't sure if my new heart valve was quite ready to rock and roll yet." As the conversations were turning toward more serious things, Beth said, "I am so glad Jesus had patience with me and had a plan for my life; just like Shon said about turning to him during those crazy times."

Then Mandy responded, "During every time."

The entire group verbally agreed and thoughtfully nodded.

All of sudden Joel got an amazed look on his face and said, "I know we were all baptized as kids, but back in college I was baptized at a lake on a retreat, and it meant so much to me."

Then Beth said, "Guys, my dad would totally be up for that!"

Mandy added, "I can fit all of us in my Grand Caravan."

Shon then said in his best deep military voice, "Alliance Lake, here we come!"

The five friends piled into the van and made their way to Beth's old house. On the way to the house, Beth called her dad to tell him what they wanted to do. Excited about what Beth was describing, he said, "I'll grab some T-shirts, trunks, and towels."

"Thanks, Daddy. See you in a few minutes."

Pastor Russell was ready and waiting outside when the van pulled into the driveway. "Hello, kids," he said, as he got in and buckled the seat belt.

"Daddy, we're not six anymore running around the church."

"Well, that may be true, but all of you are kids to me, forever. Just wait. You'll see."

Beth rolled her eyes and said, "Okay, Daddy."

Shon interrupted the sarcasm from Beth and said, "Mandy, are you okay driving in this fog?"

"Yep. So far," she said with a cautious chuckle. "I'm taking it slow."

Chapter 23: Let's Go

Traveling up and over one small hill and back down into the valley floor, the van would pierce in and out of the fog layer that was settling in for the night. A few more twists and turns in the road, and it was time to drive on the gravel for the final couple of miles. Mandy pulled off and parked at the first cove and said, "I don't want to drive any further in this soup." Pointing her headlights toward the water next to a small boat launch, she said, "This will work."

Shon jumped out and said, "Water! I love the water! I'm a Seal! Let's do this!" The rest of the group wanted to be baptized, but they knew that the water was going to be shockingly chilly.

Everyone took turns grabbing a T-shirt, trunks, or both, and slipped them on. As Joel was wading out into the water, he said, "Hey, let's stay together. It's still really foggy out here." Even though Joel already had his believer's baptism experience, he wanted to join the moment and help out.

Once in the water, Mandy, Beth, and Colleen started to scream and gasp for their breath as the cold water knocked it out of them again and again. They quickly huddled together with Shon and formed a small circle facing each other, with Joel and Pastor Russell in the middle. The van's headlights still showed how much fog had settled on the lake. Pastor said, "You know, you four are just a little older than Jesus when he obeyed the Father and was baptized by John in the waters of the Jordan. Tonight, I have the privilege of baptizing you four again, but in the same manner. Before I do, I want to ask you the most important question ever. Do you believe that Jesus is the Christ, the Son of the living God?"

In unison they said, "I do."

Then Pastor Russell waded to the outside of the circle and took Mandy's hands. He covered her mouth with one hand and supported her back with the other. He then said, "Mandy, upon your confession of faith here to us tonight, I now baptize you in the name of the Father, the Son, and the Holy Spirit. Amen."

As she was dipped back, she felt her legs leave solid footing. She began to kick and throw her arms everywhere. By the time Pastor Russell and Joel helped her up out of the water, she was gasping for a breath. Everyone began laughing and cheering. Even Shon started pounding the water with excitement.

Pastor Russell patted Mandy on the back and said, "I know it's strange to have someone dunk you without your control, but that's the picture God wants for us—giving God control of our spiritual death and burial of self, and our resurrection to a new life." Next he baptized Shon and then Colleen. After each one was finished, there was more cheering and smacking the water. Lastly, he faced his daughter, and they both began to cry. She said, "Daddy, I love you, and I love Jesus, too."

Pastor Russell said, "And you have made us both very, very happy." He held Beth's hands and back, and said, "Beth, upon your confession of faith here to us tonight, I now baptize you in the name of the Father, the Son, and the Holy Spirit. Amen."

With the final baptism, Beth came out of the water, and the fog that had been hovering near the water briefly parted as the entire group was embracing in one big circle. Of course, Joel had to jump on Shon, causing everyone to lose their balance, causing more flailing arms and more water splashing. Shon then grabbed Joel and gave him a toss over his shoulder. Everyone regained their footing and began the hugging circle once again as the fog on Alliance Lake settled back down. Afterwards everyone piled back into the van and drove away with the muted red tail lights piercing through the fog.

Epilogue

COLLEEN GOT HOME EXCITED to tell Scott everything that happened at the reunion, and especially what happened at Alliance Lake. As she was describing it, his imagination was painting a vivid picture with every detail in high definition. Then Scott said, "Collie, these last twenty-four hours have been a little busy and stressful with the sick kids. Can I go for my run around Mohican Lake?"

"Yeah, go ahead. Don't worry, I won't pull your Father-of-the-Year nomination."

Scott, who was already putting on his second shoe, said, "Good. Thanks!" and out the door he ran.

In the middle of his run, he suddenly stopped, put his hands on his hips, and said out loud, "A Perfect Alliance. Well, I have done a few pretty interesting things since high school that only a few people in the world get to do. I hope those popular kids give me at least one chapter." After he chuckled and wiped the sweat off his forehead, he continued his run to complete his circle the rest of the way around the lake. At the end of the run, he stopped to catch his breath at his usual place, a cove overlooking the water and the surroundings. He noticed it was that perfect time of day when the colors were so vibrant. As he surveyed everything, he said out loud, "God is so perfect. His sights and His sounds; I just need to be still."

THE END

Thank you, Lord Jesus, for your wonderful calming voice, when we are willing to be still.